Bernard Manin's challenging book defines the key features of modern democratic institutions. For us representative government has come to seem inseparable from democracy. But its modern history begins, as Professor Manin shows, as a consciously chosen alternative to popular self-rule. In the debates which led up to the new constitution of the United States, for the first time, a new form of republic was imagined and elaborated, in deliberate contrast to the experiences of ancient republics from Athens to Renaissance Italy. The balance between aristocratic and democratic components within this novel state form was not, as has been widely supposed, a consequence of a deliberate mystification of its real workings; it was a rationally planned aspect of its basic structure. With its blend of historical and theoretical analysis, Professor Manin's book captures with quite new clarity and precision both the distinctiveness and the fundamental.

The principles of representative government

The principles
of representative government

BERNARD MANIN

New York University and CNRS, Paris

CAMBRIDGE
UNIVERSITY PRESS

Published by the Press Syndicate of the University of Cambridge
The Pitt Building, Trumpington Street, Cambridge CB2 1RP
40 West 20th Street, New York, NY 10011–4211, USA
10 Stamford Road, Oakleigh, Melbourne 3166, Australia

First published 1997

A catalogue record for this book is available from the British Library

Library of Congress cataloguing in publication data
Manin, Bernard.
[Principe de gouvernement représentatif. English]
The principles of representative government / Bernard Manin.
p.   cm. – (Themes in the social sciences)
Includes index.
ISBN 0 521 45258 9 (hardback). – ISBN 0 521 45891 9 (pbk.)
1. Representative government and representation.
I. Title.   II. Series.
JF1051.M2513   1997
324.6'3 – dc20   96–19710   CIP

ISBN 0 521 45258 9 hardback
ISBN 0 521 45891 9 paperback

Transferred to digital printing 2002

CE

Contents

Contents

Acknowledgments

The present volume is the English edition of a work that I first wrote in French (*Principes du gouvernement représentatif*, Paris: Calmann-Lévy, 1995). Although it is substantially the same work, preparing the English edition led me to modify a number of formulations in the original. I wish to express my gratitude to J. A. Underwood, without whose expert help turning the French into English would not have been possible. Thanks are due also to Paul Bullen who provided very precious further assistance in finalizing the English version.

I am most grateful to John Dunn for his invitation to publish the essay out of which this book has grown. The ideas expressed here owe a great deal to discussions with Pasquale Pasquino and Adam Przeworski; I am indebted beyond estimation to each of them. I have been fortunate to receive the detailed comments and criticisms of Jon Elster, who read the original French. In preparing the English version I tried to meet the objections he raised. I owe a more general debt to Albert Hirschman whose encouragement and conversation have stimulated my work over the years. I am also thankful to James Fearon, Russell Hardin, and Susan Stokes for their helpful comments on parts of the draft; to Robert Barros and Brian M. Downing for their assistance in putting the finishing touches to the manuscript.

I wish to record my debt to Philippe Breton, Elie Cohen, Jean-Louis Missika, Elisabeth Sahuc, and Bernard Sève. Without their sustaining friendship, encouragements and suggestions, I would never have finished this book.

Introduction

Contemporary democratic governments have evolved from a political system that was conceived by its founders as opposed to democracy. Current usage distinguishes between "representative" and "direct" democracy, making them varieties of one type of government. However, what today we call representative democracy has its origins in a system of institutions (established in the wake of the English, American, and French revolutions) that was in no way initially perceived as a form of democracy or of government by the people.

Rousseau condemned political representation in peremptory terms that have remained famous. He portrayed the English government of the eighteenth century as a form of slavery punctuated by moments of liberty. Rousseau saw an immense gulf between a free people making its own laws and a people electing representatives to make laws for it. However, we must remember that the adherents of representation, even if they made the opposite choice from Rousseau, saw a fundamental difference between democracy and the system they defended, a system they called "representative" or "republican." Thus, two men who played a crucial role in establishing modern political representation, Madison and Siéyès, contrasted representative government and democracy in similar terms. This similarity is striking because, in other respects, deep differences separated the chief architect of the American Constitution from the author of *Qu'est-ce que le Tiers-Etat?* in their education, in the political contexts in which they spoke and acted, and even in their constitutional thinking.

1

Madison often contrasted the "democracy" of the city-states of Antiquity, where "a small number of citizens ... assemble and administer the government in person," with the modern republic based on representation.[1] In fact, he expressed the contrast in particularly radical terms. Representation, he pointed out, was not wholly unknown in the republics of Antiquity. In those republics the assembled citizens did not exercise all the functions of government. Certain tasks, particularly of an executive nature, were delegated to magistrates. Alongside those magistrates, however, the popular assembly constituted an organ of government. The real difference between ancient democracies and modern republics lies, according to Madison, in *"the total exclusion of the people in their collective capacity from any share in the latter, and not in the total exclusion of the representatives of the people from the administration of the former."*[2]

Madison did not see representation as an approximation of government by the people made technically necessary by the physical impossibility of gathering together the citizens of large states. On the contrary, he saw it as an essentially different and superior political system. The effect of representation, he observed, is "to refine and enlarge the public views by passing them through the medium of a chosen body of citizens, whose wisdom may best discern the true interest of their country and whose patriotism and love of justice will be least likely to sacrifice it to temporary or partial considerations."[3] "Under such a regulation," he went on, "it may well happen that the public voice, pronounced by the representatives of the people, will be more consonant to the public good than if pronounced by the people themselves, convened for the purpose."[4]

Siéyès, for his part, persistently stressed the "huge difference" between democracy, in which the citizens make the laws themselves, and the representative system of government, in which they

---

[1] Madison, "Federalist 10," in A. Hamilton, J. Madison, and J. Jay, *The Federalist Papers* [1787], ed. C. Rossiter (New York: Penguin, 1961), p. 81.

[2] Madison, "Federalist 63," in *The Federalist Papers*, p. 387; Madison's emphasis.

[3] Madison, "Federalist 10," in *The Federalist Papers*, p. 82. Note the dual meaning of the phrase "a chosen body of citizens." The representatives form a chosen body in the sense that they are elected but also in the sense that they are distinguished and eminent individuals.

[4] *Ibid.*

2

entrust the exercise of their power to elected representatives.[5] For Siéyès, however, the superiority of the representative system lay not so much in the fact that it produced less partial and less passionate decisions as in the fact that it constituted the form of government most appropriate to the condition of modern "commercial societies," in which individuals were chiefly occupied in economic production and exchange. In such societies, Siéyès noted, citizens no longer enjoy the leisure required to attend constantly to public affairs and must therefore use election to entrust government to people who are able to devote all their time to the task. Siéyès mainly saw representation as the application to the political domain of the division of labor, a principle that, in his view, constituted a key factor in social progress. "The common interest," he wrote, "the improvement of the state of society itself cries out for us to make Government a *special profession*."[6] For Siéyès, then, as for Madison, representative government was not one kind of democracy; it was an essentially different and furthermore preferable form of government.

At this point we need to remind ourselves that certain institutional choices made by the founders of representative government have virtually never been questioned. Representative government has certainly seen changes over the past two hundred years: the gradual extension of voting rights and the establishment of universal suffrage being the most obvious among them.[7] But on the other hand several arrangements have remained the same, such as those governing the way representatives are selected and public

---

5   *Dire de l'Abbé Siéyès sur la question du veto royal* [7 September 1789] (Versailles: Baudoin, Imprimeur de l'Assemblée Nationale, 1789) p. 12; see also Siéyès, *Quelques idées de constitution applicables à la ville de Paris* [July 1789] (Versailles: Baudoin, Imprimeur de l'Assemblée Nationale, 1789), pp. 3–4.

6   Siéyès, *Observations sur le rapport du comité de constitution concernant la nouvelle organisation de la France* [October 1789] (Versailles: Baudoin, Imprimeur de l'Assemblée Nationale, 1789) p. 35. On the link between the advocacy of representation and that of division of labor and modern "commercial society," see Pasquale Pasquino, "Emmanuel Siéyès, Benjamin Constant et le 'Gouvernement des Modernes'," in *Revue Française de Science Politique*, Vol. 37, 2, April 1987, pp. 214–28.

7   A detailed and penetrating analysis of this change and in particular of its symbolic significance in France is given in Pierre Rosanvallon, *Le sacre du citoyen. Histoire du suffrage universel en France* (Paris: Gallimard, 1992).

3

decisions made. They are still in force in the systems referred to as representative democracies today.

The primary goal of this book is to identify and study those constant elements. I shall call them principles of representative government. By principles I do not mean abstract, timeless ideas or ideals, but concrete institutional arrangements that were invented at a particular point in history and that, since that point, have been observable as simultaneously present in all governments described as representative. In some countries, such as Britain and the United States, these arrangements have remained in place ever since their first appearance. In others, such as France, they have occasionally been abolished, but then were revoked all of a piece and the form of government changed completely; in other words, the regime ceased, during certain periods, to be representative. Finally, in many countries none of these arrangements was ever put in place. Thus, what was invented in the seventeenth and eighteenth centuries, and has not seriously been challenged since, was a particular combination of these institutional arrangements. The combination may or may not be present in a country at any given time, but where it is found, it is found *en bloc*.

In the late eighteenth century, then, a government organized along representative lines was seen as differing radically from democracy, whereas today it passes for a form thereof. An institutional system capable of sustaining such divergent interpretations must have an enigmatic quality about it. One might, of course, point out that the meaning of the word "democracy" has evolved since the rise of representative government.[8] Undoubtedly it has, but that does not get rid of the difficulty. In fact, the meaning of the word has not changed entirely; what it meant then and what it means now overlap to some extent. Traditionally employed to describe the Athenian regime, it is still in use today to denote the same historical object. Beyond this concrete common referent, the modern meaning and the eighteenth-century meaning also share the notions of political equality among citizens and the power of the people. Today those notions form elements of the democratic idea, and so

---

[8] On this point, see Pierre Rosanvallon, "L'histoire du mot démocratie à l'époque moderne," and John Dunn, "Démocratie: l'état des lieux," in *La Pensée politique, Situations de la démocratie* (Paris: Seuil-Gallimard, 1993).

they did then. More precisely, then, the problem appears to lie in discerning how the principles of representative government relate to these elements of the democratic idea.

But genealogy is not the only reason for looking into the relationship between representative institutions and democracy. Modern usage, which classifies representative democracy as one type of democracy, when looked at more closely reveals large areas of uncertainty regarding what constitutes the specific nature of this type. In drawing a distinction between representative and direct democracy, we implicitly define the former as the indirect form of government by the people, and make the presence of persons acting on behalf of the people the criterion separating the two varieties of democracy. However, the notions of direct and indirect government draw only an imprecise dividing line. In fact, as Madison observed, it is clear that, in the so-called "direct democracies" of the ancient world – Athens, in particular – the popular assembly was not the seat of all power. Certain important functions were performed by other institutions. Does that mean that, like Madison, we should regard Athenian democracy as having included a representative component, or ought our conclusion to be that the functions of organs other than the assembly were nevertheless "directly" exercised by the people? If the latter, what exactly do we mean by "directly"?

Furthermore, when we say that in representative government the people govern themselves *indirectly* or *through* their representatives, we are in fact using somewhat muddled notions. In everyday parlance, doing something indirectly or through someone else may refer to very different situations. For example, when a messenger carries a message from one person to another, we would say that the two persons communicate indirectly or through the messenger. On the other hand, if a customer deposits funds in a savings account, charging the bank with the task of investing his capital, we would also say that the customer, as owner of the funds, lends indirectly or through the bank to the companies or institutions that are borrowing on the market. There is obviously, however, a major difference between the two situations and the relationships they engender. The messenger has no control over either the contents or the destination of the message he bears. The banker, by contrast, has the task of choosing what in his judgment is the best investment possible, and the customer controls only the return on his capital. Which of these two types of indirectness – or indeed what other type – best represents the role of political representatives and the power the people have over them? The modern view of representative democracy as indirect government by the people tells us nothing here. In reality, the information provided by the usual distinction between direct and representative democracy is meager.

The uncertainty and poverty of our modern terminology, like the contrast that it presents with the perception of the eighteenth century, show that we do not know either what makes representative government resemble democracy or what distinguishes it therefrom. Representative institutions may be more enigmatic than their place in our familiar environment would lead us to believe. This book does not aspire to discern the ultimate essence or significance of political representation; it merely sets out to shed light on the unobvious properties and effects of a set of institutions invented two centuries ago.[9] In general, we refer to governments in which those institutions are present as "representative." In the final analysis, though, it is not the term "representation" that is important here. It will simply be a question of analysing the elements and consequences of the combination of arrangements, whatever name we give it.

Four principles have invariably been observed in representative regimes, ever since this form of government was invented:

1   Those who govern are appointed by election at regular intervals.
2   The decision-making of those who govern retains a degree of independence from the wishes of the electorate.
3   Those who are governed may give expression to their opinions and political wishes without these being subject to the control of those who govern.
4   Public decisions undergo the trial of debate.

The central institution of representative government is election,

---

[9]   In this the present work differs from two books that particularly stand out among the many studies of representation: G. Leibholz, *Das Wesen der Repräsentation* [1929] (Berlin: Walter de Gruyter, 1966) and H. Pitkin, *The Concept of Representation* (Berkeley: University of California Press, 1967).

and a large part of this book will be devoted to it. We shall also be analysing the principles that shape the policies pursued by those who govern and the content of public decisions. A final chapter will look at the different forms assumed by the principles of representative government from the time of its invention to the present day.

I

Direct democracy and representation: selection of officials in Athens

Representative government gives no institutional role to the assembled people. That is what most obviously distinguishes it from
the democracy of the ancient city-states. However, an analysis of the
Athenian regime, the best-known example of classical democracy,
shows that a further feature (one less often commented on) also
separates representative democracy from so-called direct democracy. In the Athenian democracy, many important powers were not
in the hands of the assembled people. Certain functions were
performed by elected magistrates. But what is particularly remarkable is that most of the tasks not done by the Assembly were
entrusted to citizens selected by a drawing of lots. By contrast, none
of the representative governments set up in the last two centuries
has ever used lot to assign even one modicum of political power,
whether sovereign or executive, central or local. Representation has
only been associated with the system of election, sometimes in
combination with heredity (as in constitutional monarchies), but
never with lot. So consistent and universal a phenomenon ought to
invite attention and indeed scrutiny.

It cannot be accounted for, as can the absence of the popular
assembly, by material constraints alone. To explain why representative governments grant no role to the assembly of citizens, authors
usually talk about the size of modern states. It is simply not possible,
in political entities so much larger and more populous than the city-
states of Antiquity, to bring all the citizens together in one place to
deliberate and make decisions as a body. Inevitably, therefore, the
function of government is performed by a number of individuals

smaller than the totality of citizens. As we have seen, the practical impossibility of gathering the whole people together was not the prime consideration motivating such founders of representative institutions as Madison or Siéyès. The fact remains that the sheer size of modern states had the effect of making it materially impracticable for the assembled people to play a part in government. Moreover, this is likely to have counted for something in the establishment of purely representative systems. On the other hand, it cannot have been the size of modern states that prompted the rejection of the lot system. Even in large, densely populated states it is technically feasible to use lot to select a small number of individuals from a bigger body. Whatever the size of that body, lot will always make it possible to extract therefrom as small a group of individuals as is required. As a method of selection, it is not impracticable; in fact, the judicial system still makes regular use of it today in constituting juries. So this exclusive recourse to election rather than lot cannot stem from purely practical constraints.

The political use of lot is virtually never thought about today.[1] For a long time lot has had no place in the political culture of modern societies, and today we tend to regard it as a somewhat bizarre custom. We know, of course, that it was used in ancient Athens, and this fact is occasionally remarked upon, though chiefly in tones of amazement. In fact, that the Athenians could have adopted such a procedure seems to be the major puzzle. However, we may benefit from an inversion of the usual point of view whereby the culture of the present constitutes the center of the world. It might be better to ask: "Why do not we practice lot, and nonetheless call ourselves democrats?"

It might, of course, be objected that there is not a great deal to be learned from such a question and that the answer is obvious. Lot, it can be argued, selects anyone, no matter whom, including those with no particular aptitude for governing. It is therefore a manifestly

---

[1] Recently, a few works have helped revive interest in the political use of lot. See in particular Jon Elster, *Solomonic Judgements: Studies in the Limitations of Rationality* (Cambridge: Cambridge University Press, 1989), pp. 78–92. It has also been suggested that a citizen selected at random might elect the candidate of his choice to represent a constituency (see A. Amar, "Choosing representatives by lottery voting," in *Yale Law Journal*, Vol. 93, 1984). However, this suggestion gives lot only a limited role: it is used to select a voter, not a representative.

defective method of selection, and its disappearance requires no further explanation. This is an argument, however, in which the obviousness of the premise ought to cast doubt on the soundness of the conclusion. The Athenians, not generally regarded as unsophisticated in political matters, must have been aware that lot appointed people indiscriminately, yet they continued to use the system for two hundred years. The fact that selection by lot risks elevating unqualified citizens to public office is not a modern discovery. Incompetence in office was as much a danger in Athens as it is in present-day polities. Moreover, if Xenophon is to be believed, Socrates himself ridiculed the appointment of magistrates by lot on the grounds that no one chose ships' pilots, architects, or flute-players by this method.[2] That means, however, that the question we should be asking is whether the Athenian democrats really did have no answer when faced with this objection. Possibly they saw advantages in lot that, all things considered, they felt outweighed this major disadvantage. Possibly, too, they had found a way of guarding against the risk of incompetence through supplementary institutional arrangements. Concerning lot, it is by no means clear that the danger of incompetence is the last word. We cannot pronounce this selection method defective and destined to disappear before we have carefully analysed how it was used in Athens and how democrats justified it.

In any case, whatever the reason lot disappeared, the crucial fact remains that Athenian democracy employed it to fill certain posts, whereas representative regimes give it no place whatsoever. The difference can hardly be without consequence on the exercise of power, the way it is distributed, and the characteristics of those who govern. The problem is identifying the consequences with any precision. So if we wish to throw light on one of the major differences between representative government and "direct" democracy, we need to compare the effects of election with those of lot.

Analyses of representative government typically contrast election with heredity. In part, such a viewpoint is justified: elected governments directly replaced hereditary governments, and there is no doubt that, in making election the chief basis of political legitimacy,

---

[2] Xenophon, *Memorabilia*, I, 2, 9.

the founders of our modern representative republics were above all rejecting the hereditary principle. Modern representative systems are certainly characterized by the fact that in them power is not inherited (not in essence, anyway). But what also distinguishes them, even if it receives less attention, is the complete absence of the use of lot in the assignment of political functions exercised by a restricted number of citizens. The contrast between election and lot might reveal an aspect of representative government that remains hidden so long as the hereditary system constitutes the sole point of contrast.

A study of the use of lot in Athens is in order, not only because lot is one of the distinguishing features of "direct" democracy, but also because the Athenians employed it side by side with election, which makes their institutions particularly well suited for a comparison of the two methods. Moreover, the recent publication of a superb study of Athenian democracy, remarkable in both its breadth and precision, has thrown fresh light on these points.[3]

The Athenian democracy entrusted to citizens drawn by lot most of the functions not performed by the Popular Assembly (*ekklēsia*).[4] This principle applied mainly to the magistracies (*archai*). Of the approximately 700 magistrate posts that made up the Athenian

---

[3] I refer to M. H. Hansen, *The Athenian Democracy in the Age of Demosthenes* (Oxford: Basil Blackwell, 1991). This is a condensed version, translated into English, of the very much larger work that Hansen originally published in Danish (*Det Athenske Demokrati i 4 årh. f. Kr.*, 6 vols., Copenhagen, 1977–81). Hansen deals primarily with the Athenian institutions of the fourth century BC (from the second restoration of democracy in 403–402 to its final collapse in 322). Indeed, he points out that the sources are very much more plentiful and detailed for this period than for the fifth century, and he stresses that we do not really know much about how the Athenian democracy functioned in the age of Pericles. The institutional histories that focus on the fifth century (on the grounds that it was then that Athens reached the zenith of its power and artistic brilliance), as well as those that deal with the period from the reform of Ephialtes (462) to the final disappearance of democracy (322) as a single entity, are thus obliged to extrapolate on the basis of data that actually relate to the fourth century. Through his choice of period, Hansen avoids such extrapolation, which he regards as unjustified (*The Athenian Democracy*, pp. 19–23). This does not prevent him, however, from touching on certain features of the institutions of the fifth century.

[4] On lot and election in Athens, see also, in addition to Hansen's book: James Wycliffe Headlam, *Election by Lot at Athens* [1891] (Cambridge: Cambridge University Press, 1933); E.S. Staveley, *Greek and Roman Voting* (Ithaca, NY: Cornell University Press, 1972); Moses I. Finley, *Democracy Ancient and Modern* (New Brunswick, NJ: Rutgers University Press, 1973), and *Politics in the Ancient World* (Cambridge: Cambridge University Press, 1983).

administration, some 600 were filled by lot.[5] The magistracies assigned by lot (*klēros*) were usually collegial.[6] The term of office was one year. A citizen was not permitted to hold a given magistracy more than once, and while he might be appointed to a number of different magistracies during his lifetime, the timetable for rendering account (no one might accede to a fresh post before having rendered account for the previous one) meant that a person could not in practice serve as a magistrate two consecutive years. All citizens thirty years of age or older (about 20,000 persons in the fourth century) who were not under penalty of *atimia* (deprivation of civil rights) might accede to these magistracies.[7] Those whose names had been drawn by lot had to undergo examination (*dokimasia*) before they could take up office. This test examined whether they were legally qualified to be magistrates; it also checked whether their conduct towards their parents had been satisfactory and whether they had paid their taxes and had performed their military service. The test had a political side to it, too: an individual known for his oligarchical sympathies might be rejected. In no way, however, did *dokimasia* seek to weed out incompetents, and usually it was a mere formality.[8]

Nevertheless, the Athenian system did offer certain safeguards against magistrates whom the people decided were bad or incompetent. In the first place, magistrates were subject to constant monitoring by the Assembly and the courts. Not only did they have to render account (*euthynai*) on leaving office, but during their term of office any citizen could at any time lay a charge against them and demand their suspension. At Principal Assemblies (*ekklēsiai kyriai*)

---

[5] These figures do not include the Council (*boulē*), although it was a board of magistrates. In fact, the powers of the Council were significantly different from those of other magistracies, so it is preferable to consider it separately (see below).

[6] The word *klēros* is a noun, the corresponding verb being *klēroun* (to draw lots). The fact of obtaining a post by lot is indicated by the verb *lanchano*, used in the aorist tense and occasionally qualified by a determiner: *tō kuamō lachein* (to have been appointed by lot using a bean) or, in an earlier period, *palō lachein* (to have been appointed by lot drawn from a helmet).

[7] Fourth-century Athens had around 30,000 citizens who had reached their majority (i.e. were 20 or over). In the fifth century, the number was probably 60,000 (see Hansen, *The Athenian Democracy*, pp. 55, 93, 232, 313). These figures do not, of course, include women, children, metics (aliens with some civic privileges), or slaves. There is a tendency today to exaggerate the smallness of Athens. Granted, the city was not large, compared with modern states, but neither was it a village.

[8] Hansen, *The Athenian Democracy*, pp. 218–20, 239.

voting on the magistrates was a compulsory agenda item. Any citizen might then propose a vote of no confidence against a magistrate (whether appointed by lot or by election). If the magistrate lost the vote, he was immediately suspended and his case was referred to the courts, which then had the responsibility of either acquitting him (whereupon he would resume his functions) or condemning him.[9]

Since these arrangements were common knowledge, every citizen was aware in advance that, if he were to become a magistrate, he would have to render account, face the constant possibility of impeachment, and undergo punishment if the case went against him. But – and this deserves particular attention – only the names of those who wished to be considered were inserted into the lottery machines, the *klēroteria*. Lots were drawn not among all citizens thirty and over, but only among those who had offered themselves as candidates.[10] In other words, when the selection of magistrates by lot is placed in its institutional context it looks far less rudimentary than is commonly supposed today. The combination of the voluntary nature of such service and this advance knowledge of the risks incurred must in fact have led to self-selection among potential magistrates. Those who did not feel up to filling a post successfully could easily avoid being selected; indeed, they had strong incentives to do so. The whole arrangement thus had the effect of giving every citizen who *deemed himself* fit for office an opportunity of acceding to the magistracies. Anyone taking up that opportunity exposed himself to the virtually constant judgment of others, but that judgment took effect only *a posteriori* – after the candidate had begun to act in office. Chance apart, access to office was determined only by the assessment each candidate made of himself and his own abilities. In the case of elective magistracies, on the other hand, it was the judgment of others that opened the way to public office. It follows that such judgment was exercised not only *a posteriori*, as in the case of magistracies assigned by lot, but also *a priori* – that is,

---

[9] The Assembly met ten times a year as *ekklēsia kyria* (once in each prytany, or five-week period), out of a total of forty meetings annually.

[10] Hansen, *The Athenian Democracy*, pp. 97, 230–1, 239. Note that there was even a verb (*klērousthai*) meaning "to present oneself for selection by lot"; see Aristotle, *Constitution of Athens*, IV, 3; VII, 4; XXVII, 4.

before the candidates had had a chance to prove themselves (at least for candidates who had not held office previously).

Like magistracies assigned by lot, elective offices were also constantly monitored by the Assembly. Any citizen aged thirty or over might stand for an elective post. However, there were several differences between elective magistracies and those assigned by lot. In the first place, while the elective offices were annual, like the others, a person might be re-elected to the same office several times in succession; there were no term limits. In the fifth century, Pericles was re-elected general (*stratēgos*) for more than twenty years. The most famous of fourth-century generals, Phocion, held office for forty-five years. Moreover, the Athenians reserved appointment by election for magistracies for which competence was judged vital. These included the generals and top military administrators from the fifth century onwards and the chief financial officials created or reformed in the fourth century (particularly the Treasurer of the Military Fund, the administrators of the Theoric Fund, and the Financial Comptroller).[11] The elective posts were also the most important ones: the conduct of war and the management of finance affected what happened to the city more than any other function. (Athens in fact spent most of the fifth century at war; periods of peace were the exception.) Lastly, it was in the elective offices, rather than among the magistracies filled by lot, that persons of eminence would be found.

In the fifth century, the most influential politicians were elected as generals (Themistocles, Aristides, Cimon, Pericles). The practice was to speak of orators and generals (*rhētores kai stratēgoi*) in the same breath. Although orators were not public officials, it was they who carried most weight in the Assembly. The bracketing together of orators and generals thus suggests that in certain respects they were seen as belonging to the same group, what might today be termed "political leaders." In the fourth century, the link between orators and generals loosened, and orators as a category came to be associated more with the financial magistrates, who were also elected. Also, a social change took place around the time of the

[11] The Theoric Fund was originally set up to distribute payments to citizens enabling them to buy theater tickets for public festivals. In the fourth century, the fund was gradually extended to cover the financing of public works and the navy.

Peloponnesian War: whereas the generals and politicians of influence in the fifth century belonged to the old families of the landed aristocracy (Cimon, for instance, came from the famous Lakiad family, while Pericles was related to the Alcmaionid clan), in the fourth century political leaders tended to be recruited from wealthy families of good standing, whose fortunes were of more recent date and derived from slave-manned workshops.[12] Throughout the history of the Athenian democracy, there was thus a certain correlation between the exercise of political office and membership in political and social elites.

In general, the magistrates (whether elected or selected by lot) did not exercise major political power; they were above all administrators and executives.[13] They prepared the agenda for the Assembly (*probouleuein*), conducted preliminary investigations prior to lawsuits (*anakrinein*), summoned and presided over courts, and carried out the decisions made by the Assembly and the courts (*prostattein, epitattein*). But they did not hold what was regarded as decisive power (*to kyrion einai*): they did not make the crucial political choices. That power belonged to the Assembly and the courts. In this respect, the contrast with modern political representatives is manifest. Moreover, even if in their capacity as chairmen the magistrates drew up the agendas of decision-making bodies, they acted at the request of ordinary citizens and put down for discussion motions that those citizens proposed.

The power to make proposals and take initiative was not the privilege of any office but belonged in principle to any citizen wishing to exercise it. The Athenians had a special expression to denote one who took political initiative. A person who submitted a proposal to the Assembly or initiated proceedings before the courts was called *tōn Athēnaiōn ho boulomenos hois exestin* (any Athenian who wishes from amongst those who may) or *ho boulomenos* (anyone who wishes) for short. The term could be translated as "the first comer," though it had no pejorative connotation in the mouths of democrats. Indeed, *ho boulomenos* was a key figure in the Athenian democracy.[14] He could in fact be anyone, at least in principle, but that was precisely what democrats prided themselves on. "You

[12] Hansen, *The Athenian Democracy*, pp. 39, 268–74. [13] *Ibid.*, pp. 228–9.
[14] *Ibid.*, pp. 266–7.

blame me," Aeschines replied to one of his opponents, "for not always coming before the people; and you imagine that your hearers will fail to detect that your criticism is based on principles foreign to democracy? In oligarchies, it is not anyone who wishes that may speak but only those who have authority [*en men tais oligarchiais ouch ho boulomenos, all'ho dynasteuōn dēmēgorei*]; in democracies, anyone who wishes may speak, whenever he wishes [*en dēmokratiais ho boulomenos kai otan autō dokei*]."[15] Probably it was only a small minority that dared come forward to address the Assembly, with the vast majority confining themselves to listening and voting.[16] In practice, a process of self-selection limited the numbers of those taking initiative. But the principle that anyone wishing to do so was equally able to submit a proposal to his fellow-citizens and, more generally, to address them (*isēgoria*) constituted one of the highest ideals of democracy.[17]

At any rate, the magistrates had no monopoly of political initiative, and their power was, generally speaking, strictly limited. Evidently, then, as Hansen observes, there is an element of deliberate ignorance or even sophistry in the remarks that Xenophon attributes to Socrates. In ridiculing the practice of selecting magistrates by lot on the grounds that no one would choose a ship's pilot, an architect, or a flute-player by that method, Socrates was deliberately missing the crucial point that, in a democracy, magistrates were not supposed to be pilots.[18] That is not the end of the matter, however, because the magistracies, in the strict sense, were not the only offices assigned by lot. Most historical studies choose to discuss the implications of the use of lot in the Athenian democracy only in connection with the appointment of magistrates.[19] However, given that the magistrates wielded only limited power and that the

---

[15] Aeschines, *Against Ctesiphon*, III, 220.

[16] Hansen, *The Athenian Democracy*, pp. 143–5.

[17] Here the distinction between ideal (one might also say ideology) and practice is only a blunt albeit convenient instrument. The process of self-selection that in practice limited the number of speakers actually received explicit recognition, at least in part, in the ideology of the first comer; *ho boulomenos* denoted anyone *wishing to come forward to make a proposal*, not simply anyone.

[18] Hansen, *The Athenian Democracy*, p. 236.

[19] Hansen is no exception here: the main discussion of the relationship between lot and democracy occurs in the chapter about magistrates (see Hansen, *The Athenian Democracy*, pp. 235–7).

responsibilities of those magistracies filled by lot were less than those filled by election, such a choice has the effect of downplaying the importance of lot in Athens. Functions much more important than those of the magistrates were also assigned by lot.

Members of the Council (*boulē*) were appointed by lot for a period of one year, and no citizen could be a member of the Council more than twice in his lifetime. The Council comprised 500 members, who were thirty years or older. Each of the 139 districts of Attica (the demes) was entitled to a certain number of seats in the Council (the number was in proportion to the population of the deme). Each deme nominated more candidates than it had seats to fill (it is not clear whether lot was used at this initial stage of the selection process). Lots were then drawn among the candidates for each deme to obtain the requisite number of councilors. On days when the Council sat, its members were paid by the city. Aristotle regarded payment for such political activities as participation in the Assembly, the courts, and the magistracies as one of the essential principles of democracy. In Athens, that principle also applied to the Council.[20]

Legally, Council membership was a magistracy (*archē*), and like most magistracies was collegial. However, certain features set it apart. In the first place, only the Council could indict its own members: once indicted, a councilor was tried in the courts, but the Council first had to vote on arraigning him before the courts.[21] More important, the *boulē* constituted the most decisive magistracy (*malista kyria*), as Aristotle wrote, because it prepared for the agenda for the Assembly and carried out its decisions.[22] Whereas the

---

[20] Aristotle, *Politics*, VI, 2, 1317b 35–8. The object of such payment was to enable people to take part who would otherwise have been put off political activity by the prospect of losing working time or more generally to attract citizens of modest means. In the fifth century, Athens paid its magistrates, members of the Council, and judges or jurors (citizens who sat in the courts). Judges received three obols (half a drachma) per day they sat. On the other hand, participation in the Assembly was at that time unpaid. In the fourth century, payment of magistrates was probably abolished, but that of councilors and judges was retained, and payment (likewise of three obols) was also introduced for attendance at the Assembly (see Hansen, *The Athenian Democracy*, pp. 240–2). Note, by way of comparison, that at the end of the fifth century the average wage for a day's work stood at one drachma. The allowance for participating in the courts and subsequently in the Assembly was thus equivalent to half a day's pay (see *ibid.*, pp. 150, 188–9).

[21] *Ibid.*, p. 258.   [22] Aristotle, *Politics*, VI, 8, 1322b, 12–17.

activity of the other magistracies was connected with the courts, the Council was linked directly to the *ekklēsia*. The Council deliberated about which proposals were to be considered by the Assembly (*probouleumata*). Some proposals would be formulated in detail; others would be more open, inviting motions from the floor on a particular problem. About half the decrees voted on by the Assembly seem in fact to have been ratifications of precise measures put forward by the Council; the other half stemmed from proposals made directly in the Assembly.[23] The Council had further major responsibilities in the field of external affairs. It received all ambassadors and decided whether or not to bring them before the Assembly, first negotiating with them before submitting the results of such talks to the people in the form of a *probouleuma*. The Council also performed important military functions, being responsible in particular for the navy and for maritime administration. Finally, it had a role of general supervision of public administration, including, very importantly, finance; and in this respect it exercised a degree of control over the other magistrates. Thus the *boulē*, which was appointed by lot, occupied a central position in the government of Athens. Its role may not have been that of a pilot, but neither was it a subordinate one.

However, to assess the full importance of lot in the Athenian democracy we must look at yet another body: the *hēliastai*. Each year, 6,000 persons were chosen by lot from a pool of *volunteers* thirty years or older. The citizens whose names were drawn took the heliastic oath, pledging to vote in accordance with the laws and decrees of the Assembly and the Council, to decide in accordance with their own sense of what is just in cases not covered by law, and to give both defense and prosecution an impartial hearing.[24] From then on, for the space of a year those citizens formed the body of the *hēliastai*. Their being older than the citizens who made up the Assembly, and hence putatively wiser and more experienced, meant that they enjoyed special status.[25] It was from among the *hēliastai* that the members of the people's courts (*dikastēria*) and, in the fourth century, the *nomothetai* were recruited.

---

[23] Hansen, *The Athenian Democracy*, pp. 138–40.   [24] *Ibid.*, p. 182

[25] Citizens had merely to have reached their majority (probably twenty years of age) to take part in the Assembly.

Every day that the courts were in session, any of the *hēliastai* who so desired might present themselves outside the courtroom in the morning. The judges or jurors (*dikastai*) needed for that day were then chosen by lot from among them. Note again the voluntary nature of such participation. Since a number of courts sat simultaneously, another lottery then determined (at least in the fourth century) in which court each judge should sit.[26] A court might comprise 501, 1,001, 1,501, or even more *dikastai*, depending on the seriousness of the matters before it.[27] *Dikastai* received an allowance of three obols per day (which as we have seen was approximately equivalent to half a day's pay). For the most part, it was the poor and the elderly who sat in the courts.[28]

The term "courts" is potentially misleading as regards the nature of the functions thus assigned by lot, and we need to go into more detail here. The fact is, the courts performed important political functions. Disputes between individuals were often settled by arbitration, the courts becoming involved only if one of the parties appealed the decision. Many criminal cases, too, were dealt with outside the people's courts (murders, for example, were judged by the Areopagus). Thus, political trials accounted for most of the activity of the people's courts.[29] Such trials were in no way exceptional. In fact, they were an important element in everyday government.

This was above all the case with the criminal action for illegality (*graphē paranomōn*). Any citizen could bring an action for illegality against a proposal (whether for a law or for a decree) submitted to the Assembly.[30] The charge was against a named person: the individual who had made the offending proposal. Only the initiator was subject to prosecution; a citizen could not be prosecuted for a vote he had cast (which again highlights the special status of the act

[26] Hansen, *The Athenian Democracy*, pp. 181–3.
[27] Note, by way of comparison, that on average around 6,000 persons took part in the Assembly (see *ibid.*, pp. 130–2).
[28] *Ibid.*, pp. 183–6.   [29] *Ibid.*, pp. 178–80.
[30] Actually, it was only in the fifth century that the Assembly voted on both laws (*nomoi*) and decrees (*psēphismata*); in the fourth century, voting on laws was the exclusive province of the nomothetai. In the fifth century, then, the *graphē paranomōn* could target either laws or decrees, while in the fourth century it applied only to decrees, a rather different procedure (the *graphē nomon mē epitēdeion theinai*) being used to challenge laws.

of initiating in the Athenian democracy). More importantly, it should be noted that an action for illegality could still be brought against the proposer of a decree or a law that had already been adopted by the Assembly, even unanimously. When a decree or a law that the Assembly had already passed was challenged as illegal, it was immediately suspended until the courts delivered their verdict. The action for illegality thus had the effect of placing the decisions of the Assembly under the control of the courts: every measure passed by the *ekklēsia* might be re-examined by the courts and possibly overturned, if someone so requested. Furthermore, an action for illegality could be brought not only for technical reasons (for instance, if the proposer had been under penalty of *atimia*), but also for substantive reasons (if the law or decree at issue contravened existing legislation). In the fourth century, substantive reasons included any conflict with the basic democratic principles underlying the laws. This meant that proposals might be challenged purely on the grounds that they were detrimental to the public interest. To that extent, the *graphē paranomōn* quite simply gave the courts political control over the actions of the Assembly.[31] It appears to have been in frequent use: the sources suggest that the courts may have considered as many as one a month.[32]

When a proposal that had already been put to the Assembly was re-examined by the courts through such an action for illegality, the second examination presented certain specific features differentiating it from the first, and accounting for its greater authority. To start with, there were fewer *dikastai* than there were members of the Assembly. They were older, and they had taken an oath. But in addition to this the procedure followed by the courts differed from that of the Assembly. A whole day was set aside for examining a decision that had been challenged as illegal, whereas during an *ekklēsia* session (half a day), it was customary for a number of decisions to be taken. Court procedure was necessarily adversarial, with the person who had proposed the suspect measure being required to defend it and the plaintiff to attack it. Moreover, the two parties had had time to prepare their cases. The Assembly, on the other hand, might make a decision without debate and on the spot,

---

[31] Hansen, *The Athenian Democracy*, pp. 205–8.   [32] *Ibid.*, pp. 153, 209.

provided that no one objected to the proposal concerned. Finally, voting in the Assembly was by show of hands in all but exceptional cases. No precise vote count was taken: with 6,000 people attending, on average, a count would have taken a very long time. In the courts, by contrast, secret ballot was the rule (making nobbling and corruption more difficult there), and votes were counted exactly.[33] So even when they were performing what was properly speaking a political role, the courts constituted an organ that differed substantially from the Assembly in terms of size, composition, and method of operation.

At the end of an action for illegality, if the *dikastai* handed down a verdict in favor of the prosecution, the Assembly's decision was quashed and the assemblyman who had initiated it fined. In some instances the fine was minimal, but it could amount to a substantial sum, making someone a debtor to the city for the rest of his days, thus stripping him of his civil rights (*atimia*). The possibility of incurring this penalty had one important consequence: while, as we have seen, anyone (*ho boulomenos*) could make a proposal in the Assembly, all members were aware that, in doing so, they ran a considerable risk. On the other hand, the system was also designed to discourage frivolous accusations: if an accuser withdrew his complaint before the courts had pronounced on it, he was sentenced to a fine of 1,000 drachmas and banned from ever again bringing an action for illegality. Also, apparently, as with other public accusations (*graphai*), the plaintiff incurred a 1,000 drachma fine and partial *atimia* if his complaint secured fewer than one-fifth of the votes.[34]

The courts also considered denunciations (*eisangeliai*). These were of various kinds. They might be directed either at magistrates accused of maladministration, in which case they were put to the Council before being dealt with by the courts (*eisangeliai eis tēn boulēn*), or at any citizen (including magistrates) for political offenses. In the latter case, the complaint was first laid before the Assembly (*eisangeliai eis ton dēmon*). The notion of political offense

---

[33] Hansen, *The Athenian Democracy*, pp. 147–8, 154–5, 209–12.
[34] To gain some idea of the size of a 1,000 drachma fine, bear in mind that the average wage for a day's work in the late fifth century was one drachma (see n. 20 above).

covered three types of act in the main: treason, corruption (accepting money to give "bad advice to the people of Athens"), and attempted overthrow of the government (i.e. democracy). However, these categories were rather loosely interpreted and in practice permitted a wide range of behavior. The *eisangelia eis ton dēmon* was used mainly against generals. This was the type of legal action used to condemn to death the victors of the naval battle of the Arginoussai (406/5) on the grounds that they had neither picked up survivors nor honored the dead after the victory. Several generals suffered denunciation for having lost a battle or led a fruitless campaign. Such denunciations were frequent: it would appear that one general in five would face an *eisangelia* at some point in his career. Finally, it was the courts that conducted the preliminary examination (*dokimasia*) of magistrates before they took up office and their rendering of accounts (*euthynai*) on leaving it.

The people's courts, whose members were drawn by lot, thus constituted a truly political authority. In the fourth century, a further body appointed by lot was particularly important in the government of Athens, namely the *nomothetai*. When democracy was restored following the oligarchic revolutions of 411 and 404, it was decided that, in the future, the Assembly would no longer pass laws but only decrees, and that legislative decisions would be left to the *nomothetai*. It was then that the distinction between laws (*nomoi*) and decrees (*psēphismata*) was worked out in detail. In the fifth century the two terms had been used more or less interchangeably. After democracy was restored, a law meant a *written* norm (in the fifth century the word *nomos* could refer to a custom), that enjoyed *greater validity than a decree*, and was *equally applicable to all Athenians* (whereas a decree might apply to an individual). These three characteristics were explicitly set out in a law defining laws, adopted in 403/2.[35] Other sources show that at that time a fourth characteristic was added to the definition of a law: *validity for an*

---

[35] The fullest quotation from this law defining laws is found in Andocides's speech *On the Mysteries* (§ 87): "Law: magistrates must under no circumstances use unwritten law. No decree voted on by the Council or the people may have higher validity than a law. No law may be passed that applies only to a single individual. The same law shall apply to all Athenians, unless otherwise decided [by the Assembly] with a quorum of 6000, by secret ballot" (quoted in Hansen, *The Athenian Democracy*, p. 170).

indefinite period, with the term "decree" being reserved for norms of limited duration, which exhaust their content once their purpose has been fulfilled.[36] In 403/2, the existing laws were codified, and henceforth any change in the code of laws had to be decided by the *nomothetai*.

In the fourth century, then, legislative activity assumed the following forms. At the beginning of each year, the code of existing laws was submitted for the approval of the Assembly. If a law currently in force was rejected by the Assembly, anyone might propose a fresh one to take its place. The Assembly then appointed five citizens to defend the existing law, and the two parties argued their respective cases before the *nomothetai*. In addition, at any time throughout the year, a citizen might propose that a particular law be abolished and replaced by another. If he secured the backing of the Assembly, the procedure would then be the same as in the first case. Lastly, six magistrates (the *thesmothetai*) were charged with constantly keeping an eye on the laws. If they found a law invalid, or if two laws seemed to conflict,[37] they brought the case before the Assembly. If that body so decided, the process of revision by the *nomothetai* was then set in motion. In other words, legislative activity invariably took the form of revision, with the Assembly retaining the initiative, but the final decision being taken by the *nomothetai*, following adversarial proceedings. When the Assembly decided that there was occasion for revision, it set up a committee of *nomothetai*, fixing their number in accordance with the importance of the law (501 was the minimum, but the figure was often 1,001, 1,501, or even higher). On the morning of the day set for the review, the requisite number of *nomothetai* was drawn by lot from among the *hēliastai*. It seems that, as with the courts, lots were drawn among those *hēliastai* who had turned up on the day. So in the fourth century, legislative decisions as such were in the hands of an organ distinct from the Assembly and appointed by lot.

Today, when we distinguish between representative and "direct" democracy we usually imagine that in the latter all important political powers were exercised by the assembled people. Closer examination of the institutional system used in ancient Athens

---

[36] *Ibid.*, p. 171.
[37] See, Aischines, *Contra Ctesiphon*, III, 37–40.

shows this image to be false. Even apart from the magistrates, three institutions other than the Assembly, namely the Council, the courts, and the *nomothetai*, exercised a political function of the first importance. The people's courts and the Council merit particular attention. For both institutions played a key part throughout the history of the Athenian democracy. Certain powers of the courts even belonged to what was regarded as decisive power (*kyrion*), notably their ability to overturn decisions of the Assembly.

In his definition of citizenship, Aristotle actually placed participation in the courts on the same level as participation in the Assembly. He made it clear that members of the courts, like members of the Assembly, had "the most decisive power [*kyriōtatoi*]."[38] At the same time, the courts, as we have seen, constituted an organ that was clearly distinct from the Assembly. What is more, in terms of beliefs and perceptions, it was the *ekklēsia* that was regarded as the *dēmos*, not the courts. The latter no doubt acted on the city's behalf (particularly in their political role) and hence on behalf of the Athenian people (*ho dēmos tōn Athēnaiōn*), the city being a democracy. But they were not perceived as the people itself. There appears to be no source in which the term *dēmos* denotes the courts. When the word is applied to a political institution, it never refers to anything other than the Assembly.[39]

As for the Council, despite the fact that it acted on behalf of the city and the Athenian people, it too was never identified with the *dēmos*. A distinction was drawn between decrees enacted by the Council (*boulēs psēphismata*), which did indeed enjoy certain limited

[38] Aristotle, *Politics*, III, 1, 1275a 28. This statement is in fact part of a more complex argument. The concept of the citizen put forward in the *Politics* applies in principle to all regimes, but Artistotle adds that the citizen, as he defines him, "exists primarily under democracy" (*Politics*, III, 1, 1275b 5–6). The citizen is defined by his "participation in the power of judgement and the power of command [*metechein kriseōs kai archēs*]" (*Politics*, III, 1, 1275a 23). According to Aristotle, the power of command belongs to the magistracies as such, which may be held only for a time, but it also belongs to functions that may be performed with no time limit, namely those of assemblyman (*ekklēsiastēs*) and of judge (*dikastēs*). For, he went on, it would be "ridiculous to deny that those who hold the most decisive power [*geloion tous kyriōtatous aposterein archēs*]" (*Politics*, III, 1, 1275a 28–9). At first, Aristotle appears to place the power of the magistrates proper in the same category as that of the Assembly and that of the courts (which radical democrats disputed), but he later reserves the term *kyriōtatos* for members of the Assembly and the courts.

[39] Hansen, *The Athenian Democracy*, pp. 154–5.

powers of its own, and decrees enacted by the Assembly, only the latter being referred to as "decrees of the people" (*dēmou psēphismata*). Moreover, when the Assembly was merely ratifying a detailed proposal put to it by the Council, the decision was prefaced by the words: "It has been decided by the Council and by the people ..." (*edoxē tē boulē kai tō dēmō*). On the other hand, when the decision taken stemmed from a proposal that had originated in the Assembly (the Council having merely placed an item on the agenda by means of an open *probouleuma*), the Assembly's decision began with the words: "It has been decided by the people ..." (*edoxē tō dēmō*).[40] In the Athenian democracy, then, the populace did not itself wield all power; certain important powers and even a portion of the decisive power belonged to institutions that were in fact, and were perceived to be, other than the *dēmos*.

But then what, in that case, does "direct democracy" mean? Anyone insisting that such institutions as the Council and the courts were organs of "direct" government is forced to admit that this directness consisted in the way their members were recruited, which was by lot, rather than from their being identical to or identified with the people.

For a time historians believed that in Athens, the origins and significance of lot were religious. This interpretation was first put forward by N.-D. Fustel de Coulanges and subsequently taken up, with certain variations, by G. Glotz.[41] For Fustel de Coulanges, appointment by lot was a legacy from the archaic period and the priestly quality with which rulers were then endowed. The sacerdotal royalty of the archaic period had been hereditary. When it disappeared, Fustel wrote, "one searched to replace birth with a method of election that the gods should not have to disavow. The Athenians, like many Greek peoples, put their faith in the drawing of lots. However, we must not form a false impression of a process that has been used as a subject of reproach against the Athenian

---

[40] Hansen, *The Athenian Democracy*, pp. 255–6, 139.

[41] Nicolas-Denis Fustel de Coulanges, *La Cité antique* [1864], Book III, ch. 10 (Paris: Flammarion, 1984) pp. 210–13. See also Fustel de Coulanges, "Recherches sur le tirage au sort appliqué à la nomination des archontes athéniens," in *Nouvelle Revue Historique de droit français et étranger*, 1878, 2, pp. 613 ff.; Gustave Glotz, "Sortitio," in C. Daremberg, E. Saglio, and E. Pottier (eds.), *Dictionnaire des antiquités grecques et romaines*, Vol. IV (Paris, 1907), pp. 1401–17; G. Glotz, *La Cité grecque* [1928], II, 5 (Paris: Albin Michel, 1988), pp. 219–24.

democracy." "To the people of antiquity," he went on, "lot was not chance; lot was the revelation of divine will."[42]

For Fustel as for Glotz, the religious interpretation of lot offered a solution to what they both saw as the principal enigma of the process, namely its bizarre, if not absurd, character in the light of modern political thinking. Glotz wrote: "Appointing rulers by lot seems so absurd to us today that we find it difficult to imagine how an intelligent people managed to conceive of and sustain such a system."[43] Neither Fustel nor Glotz could conceive that the Athenians practiced lot for political reasons or, to be more precise, for reasons whose political nature might still be apparent to the modern mind. Since the appointment of magistrates by lot struck them as so alien to the world of politics, they assumed that it must have belonged to a different world, that of religion. They concluded that politics for the Athenians must have been different from politics in the modern age, not merely in content and order of priorities, but also in ontological status. Politics for the Athenians, they surmised, must have been a blend of the here-and-now and the hereafter.[44]

The religious explanation of the Athenian use of lot was certainly based on the interpretation of certain sources. It also rested on an argument by analogy: various cultures have in fact looked on lot as giving signs from the supernatural world. Nevertheless, the theory was challenged in a pioneering work published by J. W. Headlam in 1891,[45] and it no longer enjoys currency among today's specialists.[46] "All in all," Hansen writes, "there is not a single good source that

---

[42] Fustel de Coulanges, *La Cité antique*, pp. 212–13.

[43] Glotz, *La Cité grecque*, p. 223.

[44] The idea that the only way to understand the institutions of antiquity was with reference to their religious origins and dimension runs through the whole of Fustel's book. Note that the author was also pursuing an explicit objective in terms of political pedagogy: in setting out "above all to highlight the fundamental and essential differences that will forever distinguish these ancient peoples from modern societies," he hoped to help discourage imitation of the ancients, which in his eyes was an obstacle to "the progress of modern societies." Echoing Benjamin Constant's famous distinction, Fustel declared: "We have deluded ourselves about liberty among the ancients, and for that reason alone liberty among the moderns has been jeopardized" (*La Cité antique*, Introduction, pp. 1–2).

[45] Headlam, *Election by Lot at Athens*, pp. 78–87.

[46] See Staveley, *Greek and Roman Voting*, pp. 34–6; Finley, *Politics in the Ancient World*, pp. 94–5.

straightforwardly testifies to the selection of magistrates by lot as having a religious character or origin."[47]

On the other hand, countless sources present lot as a typical feature of democracy.[48] What is more, lot is described as *the* democratic selection method, while election is seen as more oligarchic or aristocratic. "What I mean," wrote Aristotle, "is that it is regarded as democratic that magistracies should be assigned by lot, as oligarchic that they should be elective, as democratic that they should not depend on a property qualification, and as oligarchic that they should."[49] The idea of lot being democratic and election oligarchic no doubt strikes us as odd. Aristotle clearly believed otherwise, though, because he brought it into an argument relating to one of the central concepts of the *Politics*, that of the mixed constitution (*memigmenē politeia*).

Aristotle thought that, by synthesizing democratic and oligarchic arrangements, one obtained a better constitution than regimes that were all of a piece. Various combinations of lot, election, and property qualifications allowed just this kind of synthesis. Aristotle even suggests ways of achieving the mixture. One might, for example, decide that magistracies should be elective (rather than assigned by lot) but that everyone, regardless of any property qualification, could vote or stand for election, or both. Another mixture might consist in assigning offices by lot but only within a particular class of citizens defined by a property qualification. Or again, certain posts might be filled by election and others by lot.[50] According to the philosopher, these different combinations produced constitutions that were oligarchic in some respects and democratic in others. For Aristotle, then, election was not incompa-

---

[47] Hansen, *The Athenian Democracy*, p. 51 (for a detailed discussion of the theory advanced by Fustel and Glotz, see *ibid.*, pp. 49–52).

[48] See, for example, Herodotus, *Histories*, III, 80, 27 (the speech of Otanes, a supporter of democracy, in the debate about constitutions); Pseudo-Xenophon, *Constitution of Athens*, I, 2–3; Xenophon, *Memorabilia*, I, 2, 9; Plato, *Republic*, VIII, 561b, 3–5; Plato, *Laws*, VI, 757e 1–758a 2; Isocrates, *Areopagiticus*, VII, 21–2; Aristotle, *Politics*, IV, 15, 1300a 32; VI, 2, 1317b 20–2; Aristotle, *Rhetoric*, I, 8.

[49] Aristotle, *Politics*, IV, 9, 1294b 7–9. On the aristocratic nature of election, see also Isocrates, *Panathenaicus*, XII, 153–4: the ancestral constitution, Isocrates claimed in essence, was superior to the present constitution, since under it magistrates were appointed by election (rather than by lot) and it therefore included an aristocratic element alongside its democratic features.

[50] Aristotle, *Politics*, IV, 9, 1294b 11–14; IV, 15, 1300a 8–1300b 5.

tible with democracy, although taken in isolation it was an oligarchic or aristocratic method, whereas lot was intrinsically democratic.

To understand the link that the Athenians established between lot and democracy, we must first take a look at a key feature of Greek democratic culture: the principle of rotation in office. Democrats not only recognized the existence of a difference of role between the governors and the governed, they also recognized that, for the most part, the two functions could not be exercised by the same individuals at the same time. The cardinal principle of democracy was not that the people must both govern and be governed, but that every citizen must be able to occupy the two positions alternately. Aristotle defined one of the two forms that liberty – "the basic principle of the democratic constitution" – might take as follows: "One of the forms of liberty [*eleutheria*] is to rule and be ruled in turns [*en merei archesthai kai archein*]."[51] In other words, democratic freedom consisted not in obeying only oneself but in obeying today someone in whose place one would be tomorrow.

For Aristotle, this alternation between command and obedience even constituted the virtue or excellence of the citizen.[52] "It would appear," he wrote, "that the excellence of a good citizen is to be capable of commanding well and obeying well [*to dynasthai kai archein kai archesthai kalōs*]."[53] And this dual capacity, so essential to the citizen, was learned through alternating the roles: "It is said, and quite rightly, that no one can command well who has not obeyed well [*ouch estin eu arxai mē archthenta*]."[54] The phrase used by

---

51 Aristotle, *Politics*, VI, 2, 1317a 40–1317b 2. The same idea was expressed by Euripides when he had Theseus say that the fact of taking turns to govern was a fundamental characteristic of the Athenian democracy (*Suppliant Women*, v. 406–8). For Aristotle, the other form of democratic liberty had nothing to do with participating in political power; it was "the fact of living as one likes [*to zēn hōs bouletai tis*]" (*Politics*, VI, 2, 1317b 11–12). The fact that freedom understood as the ability to live as one wishes constituted one of the democratic ideals is also vouched for by Thucydides, both in the famous funeral oration that he has Pericles deliver (*Peloponnesian War*, II, 37) and in the remarks he attributes to Nicias (*ibid.*, VII, 69). This is not the place to discuss Benjamin Constant's distinction between the liberty of the ancients and that of modern man or to enter into the numerous discussions, whether scholarly or ideological, raised by Pericles's funeral oration.

52 The Aristotelian concept of the citizen particularly applied (as Aristotle himself acknowledged) to the citizen of a democracy (see above note 38).

53 Aristotle, *Politics*, III, 1277a 27.

54 *Ibid.*, 1277b 12–13. Aristotle mentions the same idea several times in the *Politics*. In

Aristotle was proverbial. Its origin was attributed to Solon, which gives some indication of its importance in the political culture of Athens. The expression "to command well" should here be understood in its fundamental sense: to exercise the activity of command in conformity with its essence and perfection. Generally speaking, a task may legitimately be entrusted to someone capable of performing it to perfection. Rotation in office thus provided the basic legitimation of command. What gave a right to rule was the fact of having once been in the opposite position.

It has often been pointed out that rotation reflected a view of life according to which political activity and participation in government were among the highest forms of human excellence. But alternating command and obedience was also a device for achieving good government. It aimed to produce political decisions that accorded with a certain type of justice, namely democratic justice. Insofar as those giving orders one day had been obeying them the day before, it was possible for those in power to make allowance, in reaching their decisions, for the views of the people whom those decisions affected. They were able to visualize how their orders

another passage, he explains that alternating command and obedience and having citizens fill the two roles by turns is a just solution (if not in absolute terms the best) when all citizens are equal or deemed to be such, as is the case in democracies (*Politics*, II, 2, 1261a 31–1261b 7). In Book VII, dealing with the unconditionally best constitution, he writes: "Since every political community is made up of rulers and ruled, we must examine whether the rulers and the ruled should change or remain the same for life ... Undoubtedly, were some to differ from others as much as we believe the gods and heroes differ from men, being endowed with great superiority, perceptible first in their bodies and subsequently in their minds, such that the superiority of the rulers over the ruled is clear and unquestionable, obviously it would be better in that case that the same people, once and for all, should govern and be governed. But since such a situation is not easily found, and since it is not the same here as among the inhabitants of India, where according to Scylax kings do differ so greatly from their subjects, clearly it is necessary, for many reasons, that all should share in the same way in ruling and in being ruled, by taking turns [*anankaion pantas homoiōs koinōnein tou kata meros archein kai archesthai*]" (*Politics*, VII, 14, 1332b 12–27). However, when it comes to the unconditionally best constitution, Aristotle attempts to reconcile the principle of rotation and the requirement that differences of function be based on nature. One thing permits such a reconciliation: age. The same individuals need to be ruled when nature most inclines them to that role, i.e. when they are young, and to be rulers when nature makes them more capable thereof, namely in later life. Aristotle adds that this alternation based on age satisfies the principle that "he who is destined to govern well must first have been well governed" *ibid.*, 1333a 3–4). So even when Aristotle is describing the best constitution, he remains attached to the principle that command is learned through obedience.

29

would affect the governed, because they knew, having experienced it for themselves, what it felt like to be governed and to have to obey. Furthermore, those in office had an incentive to take the views of the governed into account: the man giving the orders one day was discouraged from lording it over his subordinates, knowing that the next day he would be the subordinate. Admittedly, rotation was no more than a procedure; it did not dictate the content of decisions or determine what were just orders. But the procedure itself was nonetheless conducive to substantively just outcomes, creating as it did a situation in which it was both possible and prudent for the governors, when making decisions, to see the situation from the viewpoint of the governed.

In the theoretical outline that Rousseau put forward two thousand years later, justice was to be guaranteed by the universality of law: each citizen, voting on laws that would apply to himself as to everyone else, would be induced to will for others what he willed for himself. In the rotation procedure, a similar effect was produced through the medium of chronological succession: those who governed were led to decide by putting themselves in the place of their subjects, for it was a place they had known and would know again. The democrats of Athens were not content merely to preach justice, exhorting those in power to imagine themselves in the place of the governed: they gave them the means and the motivation to do so.

Rotation was of such importance to democrats that it was made a legal requirement. Not only was the power relationship reversible in principle; it was ineluctably reversed in fact. That was the purpose of the various restrictions mentioned above (e.g., the magistracies assigned by lot could not be held for more than one term, one could not be a member of the *boulē* more than twice). Because of these restrictions, several hundred new individuals had to be found each year to fill the posts of magistrate and councilor. It has been calculated that, among citizens aged thirty and over, one in two must have been a member of the *boulē* at least once in his life. Moreover, there was also a de facto rotation in attending the Assembly and the courts. The *ekklēsia* never assembled more than a fraction of the citizenry (averaging 6,000, as we mentioned, from a total of 30,000 citizens in the fourth century), and it is unlikely to have been the same citizens taking part each time. The Assembly was identified with the people not because all citizens attended, but because all of them *could* attend, and because its membership was constantly changing. As for the courts, we have clear archaeological proof to the effect that the *dikastai* changed a great deal.[55]

The Athenian democracy was thus to a large extent organized, in practice as well as in theory, around the principle of rotation. This fundamental principle made selection by lot a rational solution: since a substantial number of individuals were to be in office anyway, one day or another, the order in which they acceded to those offices might be left to chance. Moreover, the number of citizens being fairly small in relation to the number of posts to be filled, the rotation requirement made lot preferable to election. Election would in fact have reduced even further the number of potential magistrates by limiting it to people who were popular with their fellow-citizens. The Athenians, it might be said, could not afford to reserve the posts of magistrates and councilors for those citizens whom their peers judged sufficiently able or gifted to elect them: that kind of restriction would have inhibited rotation.

But we need to go even further: there was a potential conflict between the elective principle and rotation. The elective principle entails that citizens be free to choose those whom they place in office. Freedom to elect, however, is also freedom to re-elect. The citizens may want the same person to occupy a particular office year after year. It must even be assumed that if a citizen has succeeded in attracting votes once, he has a good chance of attracting them again. The only way to provide an absolute guarantee of rotation in an elective system is to limit the electorate's freedom of choice by deciding that certain citizens may not be elected because they have already been elected. This can be done, of course, but it means establishing a compromise between two principles implying potentially opposite consequences. By contrast, combining compulsory rotation with selection by lot presents no such danger: the rotation requirement carries no risk of thwarting the logic of the lot. The Athenians were aware of the potential conflict between the elective principle and the principle of rotation, which is why holding the same elective magistracy several times in succession was not prohib-

---

[55] Hansen, *The Athenian Democracy*, p. 313.

ited. The system of prohibitions applied only to those magistracies that were filled by lot. In the Athenian democracy, then, appointment by lot reflected above all the priority given to rotation.

Second, the combination of rotation and the drawing of lots stemmed from a deep distrust of professionalism. Most magistrates as well as all councilors and judges were not professionals but just ordinary citizens. The Athenians recognized the need for specialized professional skills in certain cases, but the general presumption was to the contrary: they reckoned that every political function was performable by non-specialists unless there were compelling reasons to think otherwise. The absence of experts or, at any rate, their restricted role was designed to safeguard the political power of ordinary citizens.[56]

The assumption was that if professionals intervened in government they would inevitably dominate. The Athenians probably sensed that, in collective decision-making, having knowledge and skills that others did not possess constituted by itself a source of power, giving those who possessed the skills an advantage over those who did not, no matter how their respective powers might be defined in law. A Council of professionals or professional magistrates would have a hold over the Assembly; the presence of experts in the courts would have reduced the importance of the other *dikastai*. Historians frequently assert that the chief objective of appointment by lot was to curtail the power of the magistrates.[57] However, the assertion is ambiguous and in any case applies to only one of the uses of lot, namely the selection of magistrates proper. In fact, appointment by lot did not affect the formal definition of functions or powers. The formal powers of magistrates were indeed limited, but this was because they were subject to constant monitoring by the Assembly and the courts. Selection by lot guaranteed more specifically that individuals serving as magistrates would not enjoy extra power by virtue of their expertise. Indeed, having the *dikastai* appointed by lot was not intended to reduce the formal power of the courts: they were invested with a power that was explicitly deemed decisive. That is why it is so important to look at

[56] Staveley, *Greek and Roman Voting*, p. 55.
[57] This is true of Staveley, *Greek and Roman Voting*, but also of Hansen, *The Athenian Democracy*, pp. 84, 235–7.

the courts in any analysis of how Athens utilized lot. In the courts, the use of lot to select judges and the complete absence of professionals were intended to guarantee that the voices of experts did not outweigh those of ordinary citizens.

In the final analysis, the Athenian democrats perceived a conflict between democracy and professionalism in political matters.[58] Democracy consisted in placing decisive power in the hands of amateurs, the people the Athenians called *hoi idiōtai*. Magistrates, when they came to render account, frequently pleaded lack of expertise in excuse for their mistakes.[59] That kind of rhetorical strategy obviously presupposed that those listening saw it as normal and legitimate that ordinary citizens should occupy magistracies. To gain public favor, even an orator and political leader of the stature of Demosthenes would on occasion, particularly in the early days of his career, present himself as "an ordinary person, like one of you [*idiōtēs kai pollōn humōn heis*]."[60]

The myth that Plato has Protagoras recount undoubtedly gives expression to a key element of democratic thinking. Plato, of course, had no sympathy for democracy and regarded Protagoras as an opponent whose ideas had to be refuted. However, he does seem to have felt a certain respect for Pericles's sophist friend. Moreover, the remarks he attributes to Protagoras accord too well with Athenian practice to have been a mere caricature designed to facilitate refutation. In the *Protagoras*, Socrates expresses surprise that the Assembly behaves very differently when dealing with buildings or ships to be constructed than when discussing the government of the city (*peri tōn tēs poleōs dioikēseōn*). In the former case, the Assembly calls builders or shipwrights, and, if anyone not regarded as an expert presumes to offer his opinion, the crowd makes fun of him and shouts him down. But when general city matters are under discussion, "we see the floor being taken indiscriminately by smiths, shoemakers, merchants, and seamen, rich and poor, high-born and commoners, and nobody thinks of rebuking them, as one would in the former case, for their attempt to give advice with no training obtained anywhere, under any teacher."[61] Protagoras has then

---

[58] Hansen, *The Athenian Democracy*, p. 308.   [59] *Ibid.*, p. 308.
[60] Demosthenes, *Prooemia*, 12. In some editions, this Prooemion is numbered 13.
[61] Plato, *Protagoras*, 319 D.

recourse to a myth to defend Athenian practice: Zeus granted political virtue to all men, for had it been reserved for some, as technical skills are, cities would be unable to survive; they would be torn apart by conflict, their members would be dispersed, and humanity would perish.[62] This myth constitutes a defense of the principle of *isēgoria*: so far as government is concerned, any citizen, no matter who, is sufficiently qualified for his opinion to merit at least a hearing.

Lot was also associated with the principle of equality, but this link is more difficult to interpret. Contemporary historians disagree on the subject. Some, like M. I. Finley, see the practice of drawing lots as an expression of the equality so dear to the Athenian democrats.[63] Others echo Hansen in claiming that it was chiefly authors hostile to democracy (Plato, Aristotle, Isocrates) who established a link between lot and the democratic ideal of equality, rather than the democrats themselves. Hansen further points out that the view of equality that these authors attributed to democrats did not correspond to the reality of Athenian democracy.[64]

Hansen's argument is hard to follow and conceptually weak. He uses the modern distinction between two conceptions of equality: equality of outcome, in which individuals have equal shares of everything, and equality of opportunity, in which everyone shares the same starting line, the final distribution being determined solely by individual merit.[65] Hansen demonstrates that the concept of equality actually championed by the Athenian democrats was not equality of outcome. Whatever Aristotle might have said, they did not claim that all must have equal shares in everything. Now the use of lot was not about equality of opportunity since it obviously did not distribute power in accordance with talent. Hansen infers that its only justification could be equality of outcome. Since this was not the view of equality held by democrats, the conclusion is that democrats did not defend lot in the name of their vision of equality.

The argument presupposes, however, that the distinction between

---

[62] Plato, *Protagoras*, 322 C 1–323 A 4.

[63] M. I. Finley, "The freedom of the citizen in the Greek world," in *Talanta: Proceedings of the Dutch Archaeological and Historical Society*, Vol. 7, 1975, pp. 9, 13.

[64] Hansen, *The Athenian Democracy*, pp. 81–5.   [65] *Ibid.*, p. 81.

equality of outcome and equality of opportunity, as understood today, exhausts the possibilities so far as concepts of equality are concerned. Certainly, talent played no part in selection by lot, but it does not follow that lot could embody only the notion of equality of outcome. It may be that the use of lot reflected a concept of equality that was neither equality of outcome nor equality of opportunity in the modern sense.

In fact, as Hansen himself acknowledges, it is not only in texts that are critical of or have reservations about democracy that the egalitarian nature of lot is stressed. It also appears in Herodotus, in the famous debate about constitutions (though this is not specifically about Athens), and above all in Demosthenes, who cannot be suspected of having been either hostile to Athens or unfamiliar with the city's political culture.[66] It would appear, then, that selection by lot was regarded as a particularly egalitarian procedure. The problem is knowing to which version of the complex notion of equality it was attached.

Greek culture distinguished two types of equality: arithmetical equality on the one hand, achieved when the members of a group all receive equal shares (whether of goods, honors, or powers), and geometrical or proportional equality on the other, which was reached by giving individuals shares whose value corresponded to the value of the individuals concerned, assessed according to a particular criterion, whatever it might be. To put it another way, if two individuals, A and B, had shares a and b in a particular asset assigned to them, arithmetical equality was said to obtain if a equaled b and geometrical equality if the ratio of values between the two individuals equaled the ratio of values between the shares ($A / B = a / b$).

Plato linked the drawing of lots to the arithmetical concept of equality in a passage in the *Laws* that merits attention because, in it, lot is not purely and simply rejected. Plato's position on the subject of democracy is not reducible to the emphatic attacks expressed in the *Republic*. In the *Laws* he attempts to combine monarchy and

---

[66] In the debate about constitutions, Otanes, who argues in favor of democracy, associates the use of lot with political equality (the word used is *isonomiē*): Herodotus, *Histories*, III, 80, 26. Demosthenes, for his part, speaks in one of his private orations of appointment to a post by lot as being something "shared by all equally [*koinou kai isou*]" (Demosthenes, *Against Boiotos*, I, XXXIX, 11).

35

democracy or rather, to be more precise, to find a middle way between those two forms of government.[67] Many analyses and commentaries have sought to account for this variation in Plato's political thinking. This is not the place to enter into such interpretative discussions, but whether the *Laws* reflects a chronological development of Plato's thought or whether that dialogue pursues a different objective than the *Republic*, the fact is that in the later work Plato is not unrelentingly critical of democracy.[68] Without showing any enthusiasm for the system, he concedes that it is probably prudent to pay a certain amount of attention to democratic views and institutions. This is particularly apparent in his remarks on lot. The Athenian Stranger starts by distinguishing two types of equality: equality of "measurement, weight, and number" and equality of "giving to each in proportion to his person." The first, he points out, is easily effected in distributions by lot. The second, which is more divine and the only real form of equality, requires the assistance of Zeus.[69] The founder of the city must aim primarily for true justice in the strict sense of the word, that is, proportional equality. "However," the Stranger adds, "the city as a whole must inevitably, on occasion, take these expressions in a somewhat altered sense as well if it wishes to avoid rebellions in any of its parts, for equity [*to epieikes*] and indulgence are always distortions of full exactness at the expense of strict justice; this makes it necessary to fall back on the equality of lot in order to avoid popular discontent [*duskolias tōn pollōn heneka*], once again calling upon divinity and good fortune that they may steer fate in the direction of the greatest justice." [70]

More amenable to democracy than Plato, Aristotle likewise associates lot with the arithmetical or numerical concept of equality.[71] He

---

[67] See, for instance, the passage in the *Laws* where the Athenian Stranger (the author's voice) justifies his proposed method of appointment for members of the Council: "Such a system of elections seems to fall midway between monarchy and democracy, and it is always between those two forms that the constitution must hold its course" (*Laws*, VI, 756 E 8–9).

[68] For one interpretation of the place occupied by the *Laws* in the body of Plato's political thought, see Glenn R. Morrow, *Plato's Cretan City. A Historical Interpretation of the Laws* (Princeton, NJ: Princeton University Press, 1960) esp. ch. V, pp. 153–240.

[69] Plato, *Laws*, VI, 757 B.   [70] *Ibid.*, 757 D–E.

[71] Aristotle, *Politics*, VI, 2, 1317b 18–1318a 10.

also, in his theory of justice, gives a more detailed philosophical elaboration of the distinction between arithmetical equality and geometrical or proportional equality. Aristotle considers that the true (most universal) definition of justice is geometrical equality, the arithmetical kind being simply one particular version of it, for individuals that are reckoned absolutely equal or equal in every respect. Indeed, if A and B are regarded as absolutely equal (A/B = 1), then application of proportional justice results in a distribution whereby a/b = 1, and hence in the arithmetical equality $a = b$.[72] Democrats, Aristotle declares, believe that since citizens are equal in one respect (all are freeborn), they are equal in every respect. The democratic conception of justice thus comes down, according to Aristotle, to arithmetical equality: democrats, deeming citizens absolutely equal (or equal from all points of view), define justice as "the fact of each person possessing an arithmetically equal share [*to ison echein apantas kat'arithmon*]."[73] Although this definition constitutes a particular version of the true concept of justice, Aristotle nevertheless calls it incorrect. The democrats' error, he says, is to exaggerate the implications of the actual equality: they are right to regard citizens as equal from a particular standpoint (that of free birth), but wrong to infer from this that citizens are equal in every respect.[74]

Isocrates, for his part, establishes a link between the drawing of lots and arithmetical equality, then rejects that concept of equality immediately on the basis of a somewhat rudimentary argument: arithmetical equality assigns the same thing to the good as to the

---

[72] Aristotle, *Politics*, III, 9, 1287a 7–25; see also *Nichomachean Ethics*, 1131a 24–8. For further discussion, see the analysis of the Aristotelian theory of justice presented by Cornelius Castoriadis in his essay: "Value, equality, justice, politics: from Marx to Aristotle and from Aristotle to ourselves," in *Les carrefours du labyrinthe*, (Paris: Seuil, 1978), pp. 249–316; English edition: *Crossroads in the Labyrinth* (Cambridge, MA: MIT Press, 1984), pp. 260–339.

[73] Aristotle, *Politics*, VI, 2, 1318a 5.

[74] *Ibid.*, III, 9, 1280a 7–25. According to Aristotle, oligarchs and aristocrats commit a symmetrical error: rightly considering citizens unequal on one point (wealth or virtue), they infer that the members of the city are unequal in every respect (and should therefore receive unequal shares). The conclusion that appears to flow from this argument is that, for Aristotle, citizens are equal in some respects and unequal in others, meaning that it is necessary to allow for both their equality and their inequality. This position justifies Aristotle's preference for a mixed constitution blending democratic characteristics with oligarchic or aristocratic characteristics.

wicked. In his view, geometrical equality alone constitutes true justice.[75]

The problem is knowing whether the association of lot with arithmetical equality was justified or whether it was simply a means of disqualifying the use of lot by contending that it sprang from an inferior conception of equality and justice. The question particularly arises in connection with the passage in the *Laws* just cited, where Plato concedes that room must be made for an institution beloved by democrats. This is even more so for Aristotle, whose concern was not merely to establish and defend the true conception of justice, but also to analyse and account for the different views of justice reflected by existing institutions in one place or another.

Granted, in one sense the phrase "an arithmetically equal share for all" [*to ison echein apantas kat'arithmon*], taken literally, does not entirely cover the use that the Athenian democracy made of lot. However, we need only inflect the phrase somewhat or make it slightly more specific to understand how Aristotle was able to see it as a reasonably accurate description of Athenian practice. First, we must recall a point that we have already looked at but that now assumes greater importance. The names drawn by lot were those of volunteers only. A person needed to be a "candidate" or to have presented himself outside the court in the morning for his name to be placed in the lottery machine. The system, in other words, did not exactly effect a distribution among all citizens without exception, but only among those who wished to hold office. But if selection by lot is looked at in conjunction with the principle of voluntarism, a crucial point emerges: the combination of lottery with voluntarism reflected the same concept of equality as *isēgoria* (the equal possibility of taking the floor in the Assembly or making a proposal), which was the key value of the political culture of democracy. In both cases, it was a question of guaranteeing anyone *who so desired* – the "first comer" – the chance to play a prominent part in politics.

Aristotle's portrayal of democratic equality, in that it omitted the voluntary element, was thus in a sense incomplete. However, there was not a huge difference between the principle of arithmetical

---

[75] Isocrates, *Areopagiticus*, VII, 20–3.

equality for everyone and that of arithmetical equality for everyone wishing to play a prominent political part. What is more, the Aristotelian expression usually translated as "an equal share" was actually, in Greek, a substantivized neuter adjective (*to ison*), that is, "something equal." One might, therefore, point out that there was some justification in using that "something" to mean the *possibility* of exercising power, in which case, the voluntary dimension was included in Aristotle's formula: it was quite correct to say that drawing lots made equally available to everyone the possibility of exercising power if they wished to do so.

But the notion of "arithmetically equal shares" applied to the use of lot invites even further refinement. It is clear that, when magistrates, councilors, or jurors were selected by lot, not everyone who presented himself obtained an equal share of power. Although it is true that rotation guaranteed all volunteers that one day they would fill the offices for which they stood, lot by itself (i.e. without regard to rotation), would on a given occasion elevate only some of them to office. In this respect there was a difference between lot and *isēgoria*. Any citizen might address the Assembly and submit a proposal if he so wanted. Speech and initiative were thus equally shared among all who cared to have them, though not in the case of magistrates or judges, where only some people acceded to the offices they sought. What was distributed equally by lot was not power exactly, but the (mathematical) probability of achieving power.

The Athenians were of course unaware of the mathematical concept of probability, which was not identified until the seventeenth century. The idea that chance might conform to mathematical necessity and random events be susceptible of calculation was alien to the Greek mind.[76] Yet it may not be out of the question that, even in the absence of the proper conceptual tools, thinking about the political use of lot may have led the Greeks to an intuition not unlike the notion of mathematically equal chances. It was true, in any case, that lot had the effect of distributing *something* equal in terms of number (*to ison kat'arithmon*), even if its precise nature eluded rigorous theorization. Since the state of mathematics did not

---

[76] See for example S. Sambursky, "On the possible and the probable in Ancient Greece," in *Osiris. Commentationes de scientiarum et eruditionis rationeque*, Vol. 12, Bruges, 1965, pp. 35–48.

make it possible to distinguish clearly, within numerical equality, equality of shares actually assigned and the equal probability of obtaining a desired object, Plato as well as Aristotle was naturally led to confuse equality of lot with the equality of shares actually distributed. In that sense but in that sense only their characterizations of lot are defective.

The equality achieved by the use of lot was certainly not equality of opportunity as we understand it today, since it did not distribute offices in accordance with talent and effort. Neither was it the same as what we call equality of outcome: it did not give everyone equal shares. However, this double difference does not prove that lot had nothing to do with equality, because equality may also assume a third form, which modern theories of justice overlook, namely the equal probability of obtaining a thing.

It is harder to explain why Aristotle saw election as an expression of geometrical or proportional equality and hence of the aristocratic or oligarchic conception of equality. One can point out, of course, that in an elective process the candidates do not all have equal chances of acceding to office because their election depends on their merits in the eyes of their fellow citizens and because they do not all possess the qualities others prize. An analogy thus appears between election and the aristocratic concept of justice, which would have goods, honors, and power assigned to each according to his value, seen from a particular viewpoint. Furthermore, the actual practice of election among the Athenians resulted, as we have seen, in elective magistracies usually going to the upper classes. So the intuition that election might be linked to oligarchy or aristocracy is understandable. Aristotle's formula gave expression to that intuition.

From a different angle, though, in an elective system in which citizens are at liberty to elect whomever they like (as was the case in Athens), there is no objective, fixed, universally accepted definition of what constitutes political value or merit. Each citizen decides according to his own lights what features make one candidate better qualified than another. The probability of his acceding to office will certainly depend upon his popularity; but unlike the criteria generally invoked by oligarchs or aristocrats (wealth or virtue), popularity does not exist independently of other people's esteem. It is a quality that only the free decision of all other people can confer. There is thus no obvious reason why the "first comer" should not be or become more popular than the other candidates, if the people so decide. It also follows that there is no obvious reason why, in a system in which elections are free, all citizens should not have equal chances of achieving that greater popularity. Establishing elections as an aristocratic procedure would have required demonstrating that, when people vote, preexistent objective criteria limit their choice and in fact prevent them from bestowing their favors on whomever they wish. Aristotle neither provided such proof, nor explained why the elective magistrates more often than not came from the higher social classes. Thus, his statement about the aristo- cratic or oligarchic nature of election was no more than an intuition, plausible and profound, but never explained.

Two main conclusions emerge. First, in the foremost example of "direct" democracy the assembled people did not exercise all powers. Substantial powers – sometimes greater than those of the Assembly – were assigned to separate, smaller bodies. However, their members were mainly appointed by lot. The fact that represen- tative governments have never used lot to assign political power shows that the difference between the representative system and "direct" systems has to do with the method of selection rather than with the limited number of those selected. What makes a system representative is not the fact that a few govern in the place of the people, but that they are selected by election only.

Second, selection by lot was not (contrary to what is sometimes stated even today) a peripheral institution in the Athenian democ- racy. It gave expression to a number of fundamental democratic values: it fitted in unproblematically with the imperative of rotation in office; it reflected the democrats' deep distrust of political professionalism; and above all, it produced an effect similar to that paramount principle of democracy *isēgoria* – the equal right to speak in the Assembly. The latter gave anyone who so wished an equal share in the power exercised by the assembled people. Lot guaranteed anyone who sought office an equal probability of exercising the functions that were performed by a smaller number of citizens. Even though they could not explain how it was so, democrats had the intuition that elections did not guarantee the same equality.

2

The triumph of election

Contrary to what is often thought today, the political use of lot was not peculiar to the Athenian democracy. Prior to the invention of representative government, most political systems where power was exercised by citizens, rather than by an hereditary monarch, had used lot in varying degrees and in a variety of forms. Lot played a part (albeit a limited one) in the assemblies (*comitia*) of the Roman people. The Italian republics of the Middle Ages and the Renaissance often chose their magistrates by lot. In Florence, the intellectual center of civic humanism and republican renewal, the selection of magistrates by lot was a key institution of the republican system. Finally, Venice – the Most Serene Republic whose stability and longevity fascinated observers – continued to practice a form of lot until its fall in 1797.[1] The new representative governments might call themselves republics (as the United States did from the beginning of the revolution, or as France did from 1792); they were nevertheless breaking with the republican tradition in finding no place for lot.

Yet that republican tradition was still alive in the political culture of the seventeenth and eighteenth centuries. At the very least, it was a subject of debate.[2] The Venetian republic had not yet collapsed. So, at the time when representative government was invented, it

---

[1] The first *doge* was appointed in 697.
[2] In a work that has since become a classic, John Pocock demonstrates the links between the republican tradition revived at the time of the Italian Renaissance and English and American political debates during the seventeenth and eighteenth centuries. See J. G. A. Pocock, *The Machiavellian Moment* (Princeton, NJ: Princeton University Press, 1975).

42

was not unknown that lot had been practiced in more places than just Athens and was in fact still in use. Political theorists reflected on the republican experiments past and present.

Harrington, a fervent admirer of Venice and an assiduous reader of Machiavelli, searched the republican tradition for models that might guide future free governments. Montesquieu concluded that republican government was a thing of the past and that the future belonged more to monarchies or to systems along the English lines. He reached this conclusion, however, only with something approaching nostalgia – he venerated Rome, in particular – and after a careful study of republican systems. Rousseau, for his part, was fond of recalling that he had been born a citizen of a republic and, his disputes with the Genevan authorities notwithstanding, retained a well-informed interest in and attachment to the institutions of his native city. He also knew Venice, having spent some time there as secretary to the French ambassador.[3] Finally, he was enthusiastic about Rome and proclaimed that: "every legitimate government is republican."[4] All three were familiar with the republican tradition, and none saw lot as being something odd, explicable only by the distinctive features of Greek culture. To them it was an institution capable of being analysed in a general way, and with relevance for other cultures and systems of government. Lot, in their eyes, was one of the tried and tested methods of conferring power in a non-hereditary manner. It fell into the same category as election, and they compared the characteristics and effects of the two institutions.

Republican models had in general either combined the two procedures or vacillated between them. Election had predominated in ancient Rome, as it did in Venice. The Venetian republic was even seen by seventeenth- and eighteenth-century observers as the archetype of the elective republic. The Florentine republicans had for a while hesitated between lot and election, bringing about an explicit debate about the respective merits of the two methods of appointment.

In comparing and contrasting the two practices, Harrington,

---

[3] Rousseau served as secretary to Count Montaigu, the ambassador of France in Venice, from September 1743 to August 1744. In that capacity, he wrote a series of diplomatic notes. See J.-J. Rousseau, "Dépêches de Venise," in *Oeuvres Complètes*, Vol. III (Paris: Gallimard, 1964), pp. 1045–1234.

[4] J.-J. Rousseau, *On the Social Contract*, Book II, ch. 6.

Montesquieu, and Rousseau were thus in keeping with the republican tradition. Their thoughts on lot and election are today treated as mere curiosities. Modern commentators grant them little or no attention. However, nothing but an uncritical projection of our own viewpoint onto the past gives any reason to suppose that Harrington, Montesquieu, or Rousseau themselves regarded their thoughts on lot and election as being peripheral. More important, the presence of these considerations in the works of authors whose influence is beyond doubt shows that the contrast between the two methods of appointment retained a measure of importance in the political culture of the seventeenth and eighteenth centuries. Propositions of a general nature concerning the properties of one or the other procedure were advanced by the intellectual authorities of the period. The cultivated elites that established representative government were certainly aware of them, which no doubt sheds some light on the beliefs and aspirations that moved those elites when the decision was made that modern political representation should be based solely on election.

LOT AND ELECTION IN THE REPUBLICAN TRADITION: THE LESSONS OF HISTORY

Rome

Rome was not a democracy, nor did anyone think it was. When an observer familiar with Greek political thought undertook to characterize the Roman system of government, he made no mention of democracy. The Greek writer Polybius, living in Rome in the second century BC, described the Roman political system not as a democracy but as a mixed constitution (*memigmenē politeia*). The government of Rome, Polybius argued, was a combination of monarchical, aristocratic, and democratic features. The consuls, and magistrates in general, constituted the monarchical element, the Senate the aristocratic element, and the popular assemblies (*comitia*) the democratic element. According to Polybius, it was the balance of these three institutions that gave Rome its exceptional stability. The three powers checked and balanced each other, thus avoiding the abuses of power that afflicted all pure constitutions (monarchy, aristocracy, or democracy) and doomed each of them to degenerate and subsequently give way to another in a recurrent cycle (*anakuklōsis tōn politeiōn*).[5]

Polybius is still one of our main sources of information about the Roman constitution. But, more important for present purposes, Polybius's work enjoyed great success in Rome and exercised enormous influence on Roman political thought. The Romans recognized themselves in the picture that this Greek had painted of their institutions. Indeed, the key political works of Cicero, *De Republica*, *De Legibus*, and *De Oratore*, bear the mark of the conceptualization put forward by Polybius.[6]

The influence of Polybius can also be observed in the way the Roman constitution was represented in the republican tradition, particularly among the political writers of the Italian Renaissance. It is striking, for example, how Machiavelli's *Discourses on Livy*, the work that did so much to revive interest in the Roman republic, echoes the Polybian interpretation of the stability of Rome almost word for word.[7] For Machiavelli, as for Polybius, the success of the most illustrious republic owed much to the fact that it was a mixed constitution. The notion of mixed government has largely been forgotten, yet it played a major part in the formation of Western political thought. It was in opposition to it that Bodin and Hobbes developed the modern theory of indivisible sovereignty.[8] In any case, it is surely not without significance that, in terms of constitutional theory, the Roman constitution passed into history under the heading of mixed government or mixed republic rather than under that of democracy.

Historians today characterize the Roman political system as a timocracy, that is, a system based on property qualifications. The citizens of Rome were classified according to a hierarchy of orders and classes that was revised regularly at the time of the *census*. A

[5]   Polybius, *Histories*, VI, ch. 10, 1–14 and chs. 11–18.
[6]   See Claude Nicolet, *Le métier de citoyen dans la Rome antique* (Paris: Gallimard, 1978), pp. 282–8; English edition: *The World of the Citizen in Republican Rome*, trans. P. S. Falla (Berkeley and Los Angeles: University of California Press, 1980), pp. 205–13.
[7]   Niccolò Machiavelli, *Discourses on the First Decade of Livy*, Book I, 2.
[8]   On the history of the idea of the mixed constitution, the best work is currently W. Nippel, *Mischverfassungstheorie und Verfassungsrealität in Antike und früher Neuzeit* (Stuttgart: Klett-Cotta, 1980).

citizen's wealth was not the sole criterion by which the censors gave him his place in the hierarchy. The *census* also took into consideration a person's physical (for military reasons), moral, and social qualities. But wealth played the key role; in the main, the amount of wealth a person had determined the extent of his political influence.

One way property determined power appeared in the organization of the popular vote. Even if in the late republic the poorest citizens were entitled to vote, their votes did not carry the same weight in the *comitia* as those of the rich, because of the system of voting by groups. The voting units that were counted for the final tally were not individuals but rather groups. The way individuals voted within each group determined the group vote, but the vote of each group had the same weight, regardless of its size. The voting groups consisted of centuries (military and fiscal divisions) in the case of centuriate assemblies (*comitia centuriata*)[9] and tribes (territorial divisions) in the case of tribal assemblies (*comitia tributa*). The advantage held by the propertied classes was particularly clear in the former, since the centuries of the lower classes comprised larger numbers of citizens than those of the upper classes. *Comitia tributa*, by contrast, had a more popular character.

The predominant role of wealth was also reflected in the reservation by law of magistracies for the upper classes of the census pyramid. In order to occupy a magistracy (except possibly the position of tribunes of the plebs), one had to be a member of the equestrian order and since senators had to be ex-magistrates the Senate was likewise the preserve of the equestrian order.

Most magistracies were elective (except for the position of *dictator*). None was assigned by lot. The people, assembled in tribes, elected the lower magistrates and the tribunes of the plebs. The people also appointed the higher magistrates (consuls, praetors, censors) when assembled in centuries. So it is possible to say, simplifying a complex system that changed and developed during

[9] Each century was seen as making an equal contribution to the life of the city: each had to supply the same number of men when an army was being raised, pay the same amount of tax, and contribute the same amount in the political assemblies (each had one vote). See C. Nicolet, *Rome et la conquête du monde méditerranéen, 264–227 BC.*, Vol. I, *Les structures de l'Italie romaine* (Paris: Presses Universitaires de France, 1979), p. 342.

the republican period, that in Rome the people elected the magistrates but could not themselves be magistrates. Since the *census* was regularly revised, social and political mobility was possible from generation to generation. The descendants of citizens belonging to the lower census categories could accede to magistracies if their wealth and status had increased sufficiently. However, at any given moment, the only power enjoyed by the lower classes was that of choosing among candidates from the upper classes.

Popular assemblies were not confined to electing magistrates. They also passed laws and tried certain cases. Most laws were passed by the *comitia tributa*, which historians today see as having been the essential organ of popular power. It should be pointed out, however, that the initiative belonged solely to the magistrates. An assembly of the Roman people could be summoned only by a magistrate with that responsibility. It was always a magistrate that convened the assembly and formulated the question to be put to it. "Every decision of the people," writes Claude Nicolet, "was a response."[10] The Roman constitution thus included an element of direct democracy, but the initiative was not, as in Athens, with "just anybody."

Although magistrates were appointed solely by election, lot nonetheless played a part in popular assemblies. So what could be the nature and meaning of lot in a largely oligarchic political system where wealth gave power? Lot was used to determine who should vote first in centuriate assemblies and which vote should be counted first in tribal assemblies.[11] In the former, the century that would vote first was drawn by lot. That century was known as the "prerogative century." It is on the significance and effects of drawing the prerogative century by lot that history provides the most information.

Centuriate assemblies comprised 193 centuries drawn from five census classes. Two factors made the propertied classes predomi-

---

[10] Nicolet, *Le métier de citoyen dans la Rome antique*, p. 345; English edition, pp. 254–5.

[11] On the organization and procedure of the *comitia* of the Roman people in general, see L. Ross Taylor, *Roman Voting Assemblies from the Hannibalic War to the Dictatorship of Caesar* (Ann Arbor: University of Michigan Press, 1966). See also E. S. Staveley, *Greek and Roman Voting* (Ithaca, NY: Cornell University Press, 1972); Nicolet, *Le métier de citoyen dans la Rome antique*, ch. 7, and *Rome et la conquête du monde méditerranéen*, ch. 9.

nant here. On the one hand, the first class, made up of the eighteen equestrian centuries and the eighty centuries of first-class infantry, commanded the majority of votes (98 out of 193) by itself. On the other, as we have seen, the centuries were not of equal sizes: the higher a century stood in the census hierarchy, the fewer citizens it contained. The centuries voted in hierarchical order, and votes were counted as they were cast. Counting stopped as soon as a majority had been obtained. So if the upper-class centuries all voted in the same way, the majority was reached and the ballot closed before the lower census classes had even been called. The latter played no part in decision-making except when there was disagreement and divergent voting among the higher categories. The lower orders could thus be said to have a power of arbitration in the event of conflict and division among the propertied elite. Clearly, the system encouraged the upper classes to maintain a certain political cohesion.

Around the end of the third century BC, centuriate assemblies underwent an important reform. The number of first-class infantry centuries dropped from eighty to seventy. Since the number of equestrian centuries remained at eighteen, this meant that from then on the votes of eight centuries of the second census class were needed to reach a majority. This was also the period in which the custom of drawing the prerogative century by lot was adopted. Prior to this reform, the eighteen equestrian centuries voted first. They may have been known collectively as the *primo vocatae*, the first called. After the reform, only one century was invited to vote first.[12] The prerogative century was determined by lot from among the first-class infantry centuries. The result of its vote was announced immediately, before the other centuries had begun voting (which they continued to do in hierarchical order, the equestrian centuries first, then the first-class infantry centuries, and so on).

The result of the lottery to select the prerogative century was taken as a sign from the gods (*omen*), and furthermore the way this century voted also assumed religious significance. This inaugural vote (so to speak) was regarded not merely as describing in advance the final outcome of the vote, but as prescribing how one should

---

[12] Hence its name, "prerogative century," from the Latin *praerogare*, to call first. This, of course, is the origin of the word and notion prerogative in English.

vote.[13] The decision of the prerogative century thus had a swaying effect on subsequent votes.

Today, historians agree in regarding the prerogative century and its selection by lot as an institution that promoted unity and agreement within the *comitia*. Some of them place the emphasis on the way it contributed towards maintaining political cohesion among the centuries at the top of the census hierarchy;[14] others highlight its unifying effect on the assemblies as a whole.[15] Given the order in which voting took place and the respective numbers of votes of the different census classes, the unifying effect probably operated in two distinct and successive ways. First of all, for the centuries of the first class, the vote of the prerogative century constituted a focal point that enabled them to coordinate how they would vote. The existence of a rallying point made salient by religion reinforced the predominance of the propertied classes in the centuriate assembly: if the centuries of the first class (and eight centuries of the second) followed the lead of the prerogative century, the final decision remained in the hands of the upper classes, for the centuries that came after them in the hierarchy would not be called upon to vote, a majority having already been attained. Dispersed voting among the first centuries, on the other hand, would have shifted the decisive votes down the census ladder. Thus the use of lot, together with the religious value it conferred on the prerogative century's vote, averted or mitigated any dissensions or rivalries that elections might have given rise to

---

[13] This point is given considerable emphasis by Christian Meier in his study entitled "Praerogativa Centuria" in *Paulys Realencyclopädie der Classischen Altertumswissenschaft*, Supplement Band VIII, (Munich: Alfred Druckenmüller Verlag, 1980) pp. 568–98; on this specific point, see pp. 595–6. The religious quality of the vote of the prerogative century appears to be firmly vouched for in the sources and acknowledged by all modern historians. See, for instance, Ross-Taylor, *Roman Voting Assemblies*, pp. 70–4; Nicolet, *Le métier de citoyen dans la Rome antique*, pp. 348, 355; English edition, pp. 257, 262.

[14] Examples are Meier in his "Praerogativa Centuria," pp. 583–4, and Staveley, *Greek and Roman Voting*, p. 155.

[15] An example is Nicolet, who points out that the institution of the prerogative century formed the object of slightly differing interpretations among Roman authors themselves. Those interpretations agree on one thing, however, namely that the initial vote cast by the prerogative century had a unifying effect on the assemblies. See Nicolet, *Le métier de citoyen dans la Rome antique*, p. 355; English edition, p. 262.

among the propertied classes and thereby weakened them.[16] The neutrality of the lot (in addition to its religious significance) further enhanced the efficacy of the rallying point: the first centuries were less reluctant to follow the path laid down by the initial vote because it appeared to have been traced, at least in part, by something external, neutral, and impartial.[17]

The second way in which lot contributed to the cohesion of the centuriate assemblies was a somewhat different effect on the lower classes. If the centuries of the higher classes had followed the lead offered by the gods in the vote of the prerogative century, as usually happened, the units lower down the census hierarchy did not vote; however, the fact that the final outcome appeared to flow from a neutral phenomenon and a supernatural sign must have made that outcome easier to accept for those who had not been balloted.

Lot also played a part in *comitia tributa*, though less is known about how it operated there. In such assemblies, lot was used differently depending on whether the meeting was passing laws or trying cases on the one hand, or electing the lower magistrates on the other. At legislative or judicial meetings of the *comitia tributa*, the tribes voted one after another. It was therefore necessary to determine which tribe should vote first. The others would vote in a fixed sequence (*ordo tribuum*), about which little seems to be known except that it was not hierarchical. Lot in fact determined at which the point in the *ordo tribuum* voting should begin. The tribe voting first was identified by a particular term (*principium*) and was in a way the equivalent of the prerogative century in centuriate assemblies.[18] The result of each tribe's vote was announced soon after it had finished voting, but while the others were still casting their votes. Balloting halted as soon as a bill or verdict had been decided upon by a majority of tribes (i.e. eighteen votes, since there were thirty-five tribes). Consequently, for legislative and judicial votes in the tribal assemblies, the use of lot must have produced the same effects as in centuriate assemblies: the religious quality and neutrality of lot encouraged voting to crystallize around the first vote

[16] See Meier, "Praerogativa Centuria," p. 584.

[17] The unifying effect of the neutrality of lot is particularly emphasized in Staveley, *Greek and Roman Voting*, p. 155.

[18] Nicolet, *Le métier de citoyen dans la Rome antique*, pp. 383–4; English edition, pp. 283–4

while making it easier for the tribes that had not been balloted to accept the result. However, unlike the outcome of the centuriate assemblies, in this case the cohesive effect did not redound to the benefit of any particular class.

When, on the other hand, the *comitia tributa* elected magistrates, all tribes voted simultaneously, so there was no need to determine which tribe should vote first. However, lot was used to decide which tribe's vote should be counted first. A candidate was declared elected as soon as he had obtained eighteen votes: the count was then stopped. As it happened, certain peculiarities of the voting procedure meant that the order of counting was not unimportant: it could lead to declaring the election of a candidate who, if all the votes had been counted, would have obtained fewer votes than another. Here again, the religious quality of the lot, as well as its neutrality, played a part, helping to make the result acceptable to those whose votes had not been counted.

Unlike the Athenians, then, the Romans did not use lot for its egalitarian properties. In the census-based Roman republic, lot chiefly had the effect of drawing votes together and promoting political cohesion, first among the propertied classes and then among the people as a whole, because of its neutrality and the religious interpretation that was placed on it.

The Italian city-republics

The early Italian communes founded in the eleventh and twelfth centuries used lot to select their magistrates.[19] In the initial period the methods for selecting members of the councils and other offices were subject to constant experiment. Three procedures appear to have been used most frequently: indirect election, that is, a system whereby the first selection determined the personnel of the electors who made the final choice; designation by the outgoing councilors or officials; and finally sortition, often called "election by lot." "The intention both of indirect election and of lot," writes Daniel Waley, "was to hinder the domination of city politics by cliques, who might prolong their control by securing the choice of members of their

[19] On the Italian communes in general, see Daniel Waley, *The Italian City Republics*, 3rd edn (London: Longman, 1988).

51

own faction."[20] Throughout the history of the Italian city-republics, the political scene was dominated by factionalism. But the phenomenon of factions cannot be separated from the high value that citizens attached to political office. Citizens ardently strove to reach the "honors and benefits" of office, and the conflicts between factions turned primarily on office-holding. The desire for office may be seen in an idealized way as an expression of a certain idea of human excellence: man fulfills his nature as a political animal by holding office.[21] But in more mundane terms, the consuming desire for office fueled factional conflicts. The history of the Italian city-republics can also be read as the bitter experience of the divisions generated by the desire for public office.

It was to overcome the disrupting effects of factions that, in the early thirteenth century, most communes established a *podestà*, that is, a single executive magistrate, more specifically entrusted both with judiciary and policing powers. A Genoese chronicler wrote in 1190: "*Civil discords and hateful conspiracies and divisions* had arisen in the city on account of the mutual envy of the many men who *greatly wished to hold office* as consuls of the commune. So, the sapientes and councillors of the city met and decided that from the following year the consulate of the commune should come to an end and they almost all agreed that they should have a *podestà*."[22] The most notable characteristic of the *podestà* was that he had to come from outside the city, and preferably not from a neighboring commune, in order to be "neutral in its discords and conspiracies."[23] The use of lot in the early Italian communes should primarily be seen in this light.

There is a striking formal analogy between the institution of the *podesteria* and the practice of lot, even though the *podestà* was elected and not selected by lot. The common element is that in both cases recourse was made to something external and neutral to overcome factional strife. In the Italian cities, the crucial property of lot appears to have been that it shifted the allocation of offices to a procedure that was not subject to human influence. On the one

---

[20] Waley, *The Italian City Republics*, p. 37.
[21] This is the overall interpretation put forward by Pocock in his book, *The Machiavellian Moment, passim.*
[22] Waley, *The Italian City Republics*, p. 41. My emphasis.
[23] *Ibid.*

hand, an outcome determined by lot was more acceptable to conflicting factions on account of its conspicuous impartiality. On the other hand, placing the decision beyond reach prevented the divisive effects of open competition among factions. The practice of sortition and the institution of the *podesteria* can thus be seen as variations on a common theme: the peacekeeping potential of externality. In any case, that the use of lot came to be seen as a solution to the problem of factions (whether or not it was introduced for that reason) is borne out by the following comment by Leonardo Bruni on the introduction of lot in fourteenth-century Florence: "Experience has shown that this practice [selection of magistrates by lot] was useful in eliminating the struggles that so frequently erupted among the citizens competing for election ..."[24] Bruni continues, in the same passage of his *Histories of the Florentine People* (1415–21), by criticizing the use of lot, because when citizens must compete for election and "openly put their reputation on the line," they have an incentive to conduct themselves well. This incentive is of course removed when office-holders are selected by lot, and Bruni deplores the absence of this incentive. But his ultimate opposition to the use of sortition serves to underscore the principal merit he recognizes in this practice.

The search for external and neutral mechanisms in the appointment of office-holders appears as a constant feature of Italian republican thought. Another instance of this quest can be found in the "Discorso di Logrogno" by Francesco Guicciardini (1512). In this reflection on the government of Florence, Guicciardini proposes to extend the membership in the Great Council (the body electing the magistrates) to a greater number of citizens (compared to the actual membership of the Florentine Great Council). Both the specific content of Guicciardini's proposal and its justification deserve particular notice. He proposes in fact to extend the membership in the Great Council to citizens who would *not* be eligible for office: these citizens, he argues, would constitute impartial arbiters whose judgment could not possibly be swayed by their personal ambitions.[25] According to Guicciardini, elections are divisive, and when

[24] Cited in John M. Najemy, *Corporatism and Consensus in Florentine Electoral Politics 1280–1400* (Chapel Hill: University of North Carolina Press, 1982), pp. 308–9.
[25] "Del modo di ordinare il governo popolare" [1512] (this text is commonly called

the electors can themselves be elected factional interest prevails, since the judges are also interested parties. In order to promote the common good, Guicciardini argues, the citizens, or at least part of them, should not have a personal and direct interest in the outcome of the electoral competition; they should only judge, from outside, the comparative merits of men that come forward as candidates. Like Bruni, Guicciardini was not in favor of lot; he too preferred elections. His proposal aims precisely at combining the beneficial effects of elections and the impartiality of an external and therefore neutral agency. Guicciardini's proposal is remarkable for its rather unexpected (but potentially far-reaching) justification of the extension of voting rights, but more importantly in its search for neutral institutions that could mitigate the divisive effects of competition for office. Within this central problematic of the political culture of the Italian city-republics, lot appeared as one external and neutral device.

Florence

Florentine constitutional history brings to light more precisely the different dimensions of the use of lot.[26] The Florentines used lot to select various magistrates and the members of the *Signoria* during the republican periods. Actually, Florentine institutions went through many developments and upheavals between the fourteenth and sixteenth centuries. So, a brief chronological outline may be in order.

To simplify, two republican periods can be distinguished. The first extended from 1328 to 1434. The Florentine republic had been

the "Discorso di Logrogno"), in F. Guicciardini, *Dialogo e discorsi del Reggimento di Firenze*, a cura di R. Palmarocchi (Bari: Laterza, 1931), pp. 224–5.

[26] On Florence, see N. Rubinstein, "I primi anni del Consiglio Maggiori di Firenze (1494–1499)," in two parts in *Archivio Storico Italiano*, 1954, Issue 403, pp. 151 ff. and Issue 404, pp. 321 ff. N. Rubinstein, "Politics and constitution in Florence at the end of the fifteenth century," in Ernest F. Jacob (ed.), *Italian Renaissance Studies* (London: Faber & Faber, 1960); Gene A. Brucker, *Florentine Politics and Society 1342–1378* (Princeton, NJ: Princeton University Press, 1962); Nicolai Rubinstein, "Florentine constitutionalism and Medici ascendancy in the fifteenth century," in N. Rubinstein (ed.), *Florentine Studies: Politics and Society in Renaissance Florence*, (Evanston, IL: Northwestern University Press, 1968); Gene A. Brucker, *The Civic World of the Early Renaissance Florence* (Princeton, NJ: Princeton University Press, 1977); Najemy, *Corporatism and Consensus*.

in existence since the thirteenth century, but certain important reforms were adopted in 1328, and a relatively stable (though not untroubled) republican institutional system emerged that lasted until the Medici first came to power in 1434. From then until 1494, the Medici kept up an appearance of republican structure but in fact controlled the government with the aid of their clients and various subterfuges. Consequently, the regime that functioned during that sixty-year period is not generally regarded as republican. The republic was resurrected with the revolution of 1494, in which Savonarola played a key role, and remained in place until 1512. In that year the Medici returned to power and again dominated the city for another fifteen years. The republic was briefly revived one last time between 1527 and 1530 before finally collapsing and giving way to an hereditary form of government, the Medici-controlled duchy of Tuscany. To simplify the analysis, we shall here consider the institutions that functioned from 1494 to 1512 and then from 1527 to 1530 as forming a single period, which we shall call the second republican system.[27]

In both the first and second republican systems, the citizens had to be approved by a scrutiny (*squittinio*). The names of those who received more than a certain number of favorable votes were placed in bags (*borsellini*) from which the names of those who would accede to magistracies were then drawn at random (in particular, the nine magistrates of the *Signoria*, the twelve *Buoni Huomini*, and the sixteen *Gonfalonieri*, the magistrates of the different Florentine districts). In scrutinies, voting was secret. The names that were submitted to the *squittinio* had themselves been chosen by a preselection committee whose members were known as *nominatori*. It was in the methods used for this nomination and for the scrutiny that the institutions of the first and second republican periods differed.

Another feature of both republican periods was the existence of provisions which guaranteed rotation in office, the *divieti*. These were prohibitions which prevented the same office from being assigned to the same person or to members of the same family several times in succession during a given period. The members of

---

[27] The best source of information about this second republican system is Donato Giannotti, "Discorso intorno alla forma della repubblica di Firenze" [1549], in *Opere Politiche e Letterarie*, 2 vols. (Firenze: Le Monnier, 1850), Vol. I, pp. 17–29.

the *Signoria* were replaced every two months; the other magistrates' terms of office lasted a bit longer. The Florentine republic thus echoed the kind of combination of lot and rotation that typified the Athenian democracy.

In the fourteenth century, access to the magistracies was in part controlled by the *Ottimati*, the aristocracy of large merchant families and leaders of the major corporations. It was possible for non-aristocrats (e.g. middle-ranking merchants or artisans) to rise to office, but only if they had been approved by the elites of wealth and birth, who dominated the committee which decided who would be "scrutinized." [28] By contrast, the body that, through the *squittinio*, approved or rejected the names put forward was more open. It numbered some hundred members (*arrotti*) elected by citizens who had themselves been drawn by lot.[29] Thus, the names that were finally placed in the bags after the *squittinio* had been approved twice: once by the aristocracy, and once by a wider circle.

At the end of the fourteenth century, this complex system was regarded as guaranteeing impartiality in the selection of magistrates and as guarding against factions. Its very complexity appeared to shield it from manipulation by individuals and clans: no one could control every stage of the process or steer the result as he wished.[30] The part played in the final stage by the neutral, unmanipulable mechanism of lot was largely responsible for generating this feeling

---

[28] The composition of this preselection committee in the fourteenth century is analysed in detail by Najemy, *Corporatism and Consensus*, p. 122. In the fourteenth century, the *nominatori* might choose the names put forward for the *squittinio* without restriction from among all citizens of Florence, i.e. all male taxpayers who had reached their majority (they alone being considered *cittadini* in the full sense, the rest being simply "inhabitants of Florence"). The total population of Florence fluctuated during the fourteenth century between 50,000 and 90,000 (including women and children); see Najemy, *Corporatism and Consensus*, p. 177. In the 1350s, around 3,500 names were put forward for the *squittinio*. In 1382, that number rose to 5,350, and in 1433, one year before the Medici first seized power, it reached 6,354 (see Najemy, *Corporatism and Consensus*, pp. 177, 273, 275).

[29] The procedure was to select by lot twelve consuls from the twelve major guilds and fifty-five citizens whose names had been approved on the occasion of earlier scrutinies for different offices (the Priorate, the twelve *Buoni Huomini*, the *Gonfalonieri*). These sixty-seven persons designated by lot subsequently chose the 100 electors (*arrotti*) who voted in the scrutiny. On the composition of the body that carried out the *squittinio* in the fourteenth century, see Najemy, *Corporatism and Consensus*, p. 122.

[30] *Ibid.*

of impartiality. Florence was no different, in this respect, from the other Italian republics.

However, the Florentine experiment reveals a further dimension in the use of lot. The procedure had been introduced in Florence for the first time in 1291, but this initial experiment proved short-lived. The combination of scrutiny and lot that became one of the cornerstones of Florentine republicanism was actually established by the ordinances of 1328. The prologue to the new ordinances described the object of the reform (and hence also of the use of lot) as follows: "Those citizens of Florence, who shall be approved by the favourable consensus of the good and law-abiding citizens as worthy and sufficient in their life and customs, may *in a fair measure* achieve and ascend to the honours [of political office]."[31] The Florentines had no more desire than the Athenians to be governed by incompetent or unworthy citizens. The *squittinio* served to eliminate these (while of course also lending itself to partisan ends). In Florence, therefore, it was the judgment of others and not, as in Athens, voluntarism combined with the prospect of sanctions, that was meant to ensure the elimination of the incompetent. But among those considered worthy and capable of holding office (i.e. those who had obtained the required number of votes in the scrutiny), lot was deemed to effect a more equitable distribution. That is why the 1328 ordinances were presented as guaranteeing greater equality of access to public office and would be remembered as such.[32] The belief, however, in the egalitarian and democratic character of lot did not establish itself at one stroke, nor was it as unquestionable in Florence as it was in Athens. For some time, indeed, until the very last years of the fifteenth century, the actual properties of lot (and of elections) remained problematic. One can see hesitations, fluctuations, and reversals on this subject in Florentine political debates.

Although lot was explicitly associated with political equality in 1328, no such association was made when lot was introduced for the first time in 1291.[33] Bruni's aforementioned comment suggests that at that time lot was seen primarily as a neutral and external

[31] Quoted in Najemy, *Corporatism and Consensus*, p. 102 (my emphasis).
[32] On this point, see also Rubinstein, "Florentine constitutionalism and Medici ascendancy in the fifteenth century," in N. Rubinstein (ed.), *Florentine Studies*, p. 451.
[33] Najemy, *Corporatism and Consensus*, pp. 31–2.

mechanism that would obviate factional strife. After 1328, and for the rest of the fourteenth century, the corporations, which constituted the popular element of the Florentine social and political system, showed a particular attachment to lot.[34] A century later, however, when the republic was reestablished following the first Medici period (1434–94), there was a new period of doubts and hesitations concerning the effects of lot.

The major innovation of the revolution of 1494 was the establishment of a Great Council on the Venetian model. It was decided at that time that all members of the Great Council should participate in the selection of magistrates and would themselves be eligible for office.[35] Preselection of the names put forward for election was retained, but the aristocracy lost its control: the *nominatori* were henceforth chosen by lot from among the members of the Great Council.[36] The big question, however, was deciding what selection procedure the Great Council should use. Should they keep the combination of *squittinio* and lot that had operated during the first republican period (with all names receiving more than a set number of votes being placed in the bags from which they would be drawn at random), or should a new system be adopted that made no use of lot but assigned magistracies to those who had obtained *the most votes in favor* (*le più fave*) at the time of the *squittinio*?[37] The second

---

[34] After the defeat of the Ciompi revolt, certain leaders of the popular movement suggested abolishing the practice of drawing lots in order to prevent aristocrats hostile to the people from being nominated to the *Signoria*. When the guilds were consulted, it emerged that their base did not follow them on this point. See Najemy, *Corporatism and Consensus*, pp. 257–9.

[35] The reform of 1494 decided two things: (1) the Great Council should henceforth include all whose names had been approved by *squittinio* for the most prestigious executive magistracies (the *Signoria*, the twelve *Buoni Huomini*, the sixteen *Gonfalonieri*) or whose fathers or grandfathers had been approved by *squittinio* for those same offices; (2) on the other hand, every three years the Great Council should choose sixty citizens from among those who paid taxes and belonged to families with members who had held office in the past. Those sixty citizens would then themselves become members of the Great Council. Around the year 1500, the Great Council had just over 3,000 members out of a population of approximately 70,000 (including women and children); see Felix Gilbert, *Machiavelli and Guicciardini: Politics and History in Sixteenth Century Florence* (Princeton, NJ: Princeton University Press, 1965), p. 20.

[36] See Donato Giannotti, "Discorso intorno alla forma della repubblica di Firenze" [1549], in Giannotti, *Opere Politiche e Letterarie*, Vol. I, p. 20.

[37] Voting was done with black and white beans; hence the expression *le più fave*.

system clearly constituted an election. A debate was thus launched concerning the relative merits of election and lot.

The revolution of 1494, which overthrew the Medici, was achieved through an alliance between a section of the *Ottimati* and the *Popolani* (the lower classes, comprising artisans, small merchants, and shopkeepers). The key problem during the last years of the fifteenth century was knowing which of these two groups would have the upper hand in the new republican regime. Those involved believed that the answer to the question depended on what procedure the Great Council was going to employ. Remarkably, for some years the principal actors appear to have been uncertain about the respective effects of lot and election. Each of the two camps wondered which method of selection would be to its advantage. In his fascinating articles, Nicolai Rubinstein has documented in detail the fluctuations and hesitations of those involved in this debate.[38]

This crucial episode of Florentine constitutional history may be roughly divided into three brief periods. In the first (Nov. 9–Dec. 2 1494), the decision was made to restore the institutions of the first republican system. In other words, it was decided, after a brief transitional period, to go back to selection by lot. The *Ottimati* seem to have believed at that point that the combination of scrutiny and lot would restore the predominant influence that they had enjoyed in the fourteenth century. Their preference for lot may also have reflected their attachment to established and traditional procedures. Last, the *Ottimati* were afraid that elections might bring back to power the clients of the Medici. In a second period (December 9–23, 1494), in response to the dissatisfaction of the *Popolani* with the first reform, steps were taken in the direction of a more popular government. This second period saw the peak of Savonarola's influence and culminated in the radical reform of December 22–3, when the Great Council was created. Another aspect of the reform, however, was the substitution of election for lot in the appointment to the *Signoria*. Savonarola appears to have played a key role in this second decision. He strongly favored elections, which he regarded as integral to popular government.[39] At this point, then, the popular

---

[38] Rubinstein, "I primi anni del Consiglio Maggiori di Firenze (1494–1499)", parts I and II, and Rubinstein, "Politics and constitution in Florence."

[39] *Ibid.*, p. 178.

movement apparently believed that elections would operate in its favor. Yet simultaneously the *Ottimati* altered their position. They accepted the elective method in the belief that their connections, prestige, and talents would enable them to carry the day in any electoral competition. One observer, who was sympathetic to the *Ottimati*, went so far as to say that the new system (election rather than lot) "had no other end than to give back the state to the nobility."[40] Thus there was still, in December 1494, some uncertainty regarding the probable effects of election compared to those of lot. It was this uncertainty that enabled the reform to go through: each camp believed the change would work to its favor. Initially, experience seemed to vindicate the expectations of the popular movement. In the popular enthusiasm for the Great Council, "new men" (*gente nuova*) and partisans of the popular movement were elected to high offices in the first elections. But after a while things changed. "The novelty gradually wore off," Rubinstein writes, "and the prestige and influence of the *Ottimati* came increasingly into their own again ... Thus we find once more a considerable proportion of the highest offices going to the families which had been used to hold them under the Medici and before."[41] At this point there was a change of opinion among the popular elements, which came to believe that lot was more in their favor. The *Ottimati*, for their part, in view of their success at getting themselves elected, became increasingly satisfied with the system of elections. Finally, during a third period (1495–7), pressure from the popular movement ensured that election was gradually abandoned in favor of lot.

The developments that occurred in the second period (the elections of 1494–5) obviously constitute the crucial turning point. This decisive episode seems to have stabilized once and for all the system of beliefs regarding the respective effects of election and lot. Thereafter, elections were systematically associated with *governo stretto* ("narrow" or aristocratic government) and lot with *governo largo* ("open" or popular government). These beliefs were to find their most brilliant and authoritative expression in the writings of Guic-

[40] The observer in question was Parenti. On this point, see Rubinstein, "I primi anni del Consiglio Maggiori di Firenze (1494–1499)," p. 324, and Rubinstein, "Politics and constitution in Florence," p. 179.

[41] *Ibid.*, p. 179.

ciardini. A member of one of the great *Ottimati* families and one of the most influential defenders of aristocratic republicanism, Guicciardini was the author of two speeches on the respective merits of election and lot.[42]

The first speech states the case for election (the *più fave* system), while the second advocates the combination of scrutiny (the *squittinio*) and lot. Although Guicciardini, following the rules of an established rhetorical *genre*, champions first one and then the other procedure, a number of discreet but unambiguous signs reveal that his own preference is for election. The advocate of elections argues that in the framing of a republic two ends must be kept in view: "the first one and the main one [is] that they are so constituted that every citizen must be equal before the law, and that in this no distinction should be made between rich and poor, between the powerful and the impotent, in such a way that their person, property and standing cannot be damaged." The other political end to be kept in view is that public offices should be arranged so as to be "as open as possible to everyone, such that the greatest possible number of citizens participate in them."[43] Equality before the law and equal access to public office were the core values of Florentine republicanism, and Guicciardini's speech formulates a common theme of republican thought. A century earlier, in his "Funeral Oration for Nanni degli Strozzi" Bruni had defined republican equality in the following terms: "This, then, is true liberty, this equality in a republic (*res publica*): not to have to fear violence or wrongdoing from anybody, and to enjoy equality among citizens before the law and in the participation in public office."[44] Guicciardini, however, ranks the two objectives. Whereas the first (equality before the law) must be realized without restrictions, Guicciardini goes on, the second (equal access to public office) should be sought only within certain limits, for the fate of the city must not be left in the hands of those who are merely adequate. This is where election

---

[42] "Del modo di eleggere gli uffici nel Consiglio Grande," in Guicciardini, *Dialogo e discorsi del Reggimento di Firenze*, pp. 175–85.

[43] *Ibid.*, pp. 175–6.

[44] Leonardo Bruni, "Funeral Oration for Nanni degli Strozzi" [1428], quoted by Hans Baron, *The Crisis of the Early Italian Renaissance* [1955] (Princeton, NJ: Princeton University Press, 1966), p. 419 (Baron reproduces the Latin text on p. 556).

is seen to be superior to lot. Election ensures that magistrates are "as select [*scelti*] as possible."[45] It has the further virtue of preventing just anybody from "raising himself to a prominent position [*si fare grande*]." In an elective system, eminence is conferred by others, not by oneself. And at the same time voters are able to distinguish the truly great from those who affect greatness.[46] Against such a system, Guicciardini concedes, the sole objection that might validly be advanced would be that "the number of those who obtain the magistracies grows smaller [*gli uffici vanno stretti*]." The answer to that objection consists in a question: If the people prefers to keep official functions within chosen circles, what is wrong with that? And if the objector persists, pointing out that, with an elective system, deserving citizens may remain excluded from public office while the people constantly re-elects the same persons, a different reply may be given: "Whether someone is meritorious is not a matter for a private individual to decide but for the people, who has a better judgement than anyone else, because it is prince and without passion. [The people] knows each of us better than we do ourselves and has no other end than to distribute things to those who are seen to merit them."[47] The notion that the people is capable of judging what is put to it, whether persons or decisions, but incapable of governing itself forms a recurring subject in Guicciardini's thought. Elections are thus preferable to lot since they select the best while still leaving it up to the people to discern who are the best. This value judgment aside, the way in which Guicciardini describes the respective properties of election and lot seems to reflect fairly precisely the common view of the two models that became established after 1495–7.

So having introduced lot to combat factionalism, the Florentines ended up rediscovering through experience the enigmatic idea of the Athenian democrats that lot is more democratic than election. Although Guicciardini did not explain, any more than had Aristotle, *why* elections tended to make public office the preserve of the elite,

---

[45] The Italian word *scelti* means both selected and select (as in the select few). Guicciardini is clearly playing on the double meaning here.

[46] Here again Guicciardini is using the many connotations of the expression *si fare grande* to take in not only those who proclaim themselves to be important but also those who act the part and those who affect importance.

[47] "Del modo di eleggere gli uffici nel Consiglio Grande," pp. 178–9.

he had no doubt that it was the case, and the Florentine republicans in general thought similarly. Florentine republicanism would in turn exercise a considerable influence on later developments of republican thought, particularly in England and the United States.[48] Thus there is reason to believe that the theorists and political actors of the seventeenth and eighteenth centuries, who were familiar with the Florentine republican experiment, knew that the belief in the aristocratic nature of elections was not unique to Greek political culture.

Venice

Venice, too, used lot, but in a quite different way.[49] The Venetians perfected an extraordinarily complicated and subtle system for appointing magistrates that became famous among political authors all over Europe.[50] Harrington was to recommend its adoption for his ideal republic of Oceana.[51] Lot intervened within the Venetian system only in the selection of members of the committees that nominated candidates to be considered by the Great Council (the *nominatori*). Those committees were appointed through a multi-stage procedure that involved a combination of lot and elections.[52] Lot was therefore not, as in Florence, used to select the magistrates themselves. The Venetian *nominatori* proposed several names for each office to be filled. The names proposed were then *immediately* put to vote in the Great Council.[53] For each magistracy, it was the

[48] This influence of Florentine political thought has been solidly documented by Hans Baron, Felix Gilbert and John Pocock.

[49] On Venice, see William J. Bouwsma, *Venice and the Defense of Republican Liberty: Renaissance Values in the Age of the Counter-Reformation* (Berkeley: University of California Press, 1968); Frederic Lane, *Venice: A Maritime Republic* (Baltimore, MD: Johns Hopkins University Press, 1973). The main reference work on the Venetian constitution is Giuseppe Maranini, *La Costituzione di Venezia*, 2 vols. (Florence: La Nuova Italia, 1974) [1st edn 1927].

[50] The Venetian appointment system is described as a whole in Maranini, *La Costituzione di Venezia*, Vol. II, pp. 106–24.

[51] J. Harrington, "The manner and use of the ballot," in J. G. A. Pocock (ed.), *The Political Works of James Harrington* (Cambridge: Cambridge University Press, 1977), pp. 361–7.

[52] The combination of lot and election in the appointment of *nominatori* concerned only the election of the doge. For the other magistracies, the committee of *nominatori* was simply appointed by lot. On the procedure specific to the election of the doge, see Maranini, *La Costituzione di Venezia*, Vol. I, pp. 187–90.

[53] This procedure was not, however, used for all magistracies. For some of the most important offices, the Senate (*Consiglio dei Pregadi*) both nominated and elected,

candidate who obtained the most votes that was appointed.[54] The system was thus based primarily on election, not only because the candidates were in the end elected by the Great Council, but also because the names of the candidates proposed were those who had collected *the most votes* in the preselection committee.

The use of lot for the selection of nominators made it all but impossible for cliques to influence the nominating process: the members of the Great Council simply did not know in advance whose job it would be to propose the candidates. As a further precaution, the vote was taken as soon as the candidates were announced, so there was no point in campaigning within the Council. "The selection of the nominating committee by lot and the immediacy of the nominating and the voting were *expressly* devised to prevent candidates from campaigning for office by appeals that would inflame factions."[55] Another feature of the system, one that intrigued observers, worked in the same direction: voting in the Great Council was by secret ballot. The Venetians went to quite extraordinary lengths to ensure that voting in the Great Council be completely secret: the balls used for voting were even wrapped in cloths to silence their fall when they were dropped into the urn. Here again, the object was to hinder action by organized groups: when voting, each member of the Council must be as isolated as possible from group and factional pressure.

Even if the essential aim of lot was to dissociate elections from the intrigues and divisive campaigns that usually went with them, some authors (notably Gasparo Contarini, the most famous theorist of the Venetian constitution) also credited it with a "popular" aspect in that it gave more people a role.[56] However, this egalitarian dimension meant only that all the members of the Great Council had an equal chance of being "important": an equal chance, that is, to be a nominator, but not to attain office.[57] The fact remains that in Venice too the use of lot was associated with the popular dimension of

with the Great Council playing no part. And for the magistrates elected by the Great Council, candidates were in some instances proposed from above by the *Signoria* or by the Senate. See Lane, *Venice*, pp. 258–9.

[54] See Maranini, *La Costituzione di Venezia*, Vol. II, p. 118.
[55] Lane, *Venice*, p. 110 (my emphasis).
[56] Gasparo Contarini, *De Magistratibus et Republica Venetorum* (Paris, 1543).
[57] Lane, *Venice*, p. 259.

government and with the notion of equal access, even if these related only to a limited and highly specialized function.

It did not escape the more perceptive observers, notably Harrington and Rousseau, that in reality the top magistracies usually remained in the hands of a few eminent families who formed a much smaller group than the Great Council. Rousseau, for example, in the chapter of his *Social Contract* devoted to elections, wrote: "It is a mistake to see the government of Venice as a true aristocracy. Even though the people has no part in the government there, the nobility themselves are of the people. A multitude of poor Barnabites [poor members of the Venetian nobility inhabiting the district of Saint Barnabas] never came close to holding any magistracy, and all they get out of their nobility is the empty title 'Excellence' and the right to attend the Great Council."[58] As Rousseau saw it, the Venetian nobility was the equivalent of the bourgeoisie that formed the General Council in Geneva, and Venice was "no more aristocratic" than his native republic. Both cities, in his eyes, constituted "mixed governments."[59]

Granted, the Venetian Great Council included only a small fraction of the population. Membership was hereditary, and members were the descendants of those who had been admitted at the time of the 1297 reform (the *Serrata* or "closing" of the Council). In the mid-sixteenth century, the Council comprised 2,500 members. The Great Council thus constituted the Venetian nobility. And these nobles only enjoyed political rights: they alone were the citizen body. It was not, however, the hereditary and closed character of the Venetian Great Council that most attracted the attention of Rousseau or Harrington, but the fact that only a small fraction of even that restricted group could become magistrates. This additional restriction occurred without any limitations being placed on the freedom of elections.

In a somewhat cryptic passage, Harrington, who was a careful observer and keen admirer of Venice, portrays this feature as the great enigma of the Venetian government:

---

[58] J.-J. Rousseau, *On the Social Contract* [1762], Book IV, ch. 3; English translation by J. Masters, *On the Social Contract* (New York: St. Martin's Press), p. 112. For Harrington's comments on the same subject, see *The Prerogative of Popular Government*, in Pocock (ed.), *The Political Works of James Harrington*, p. 458.

[59] J.-J. Rousseau, *Social Contract*, Book IV, 3.

Riddle me, riddle me, what this is? The magistracies in Venice (except such as are rather of ornament than of power) all are annual, or at most biennial. No man whose term is expired can hold his magistracy longer, but by a new election. The elections are most of them made in the Great Council, and by the ballot, which is the most equal and impartial way of suffrage. And yet the greater magistracies are perpetually wheeled through a few hands. If I be worthy to give advice unto a man that would study the politics, let him understand Venice: he that understands Venice right shall go nearest to judge (notwithstanding the difference that is in every polity) right of any government in the world.[60]

Harrington did not give an explicit answer to the riddle, but the reader could discover it without difficulty: even when elections are free and fair, electors tend to vote repeatedly for the same prominent individuals or distinguished families. Harrington further suggested that the impact of this mysterious rule of politics extended well beyond Venice.

By limiting intrigue among the members of the Great Council, lot helped to maintain the remarkable cohesiveness of the Venetian nobility. And doubtless that cohesiveness was one of the causes of the astonishing stability of the republic. While the other Italian city-republics witnessed popular uprisings in which a section of the upper strata of the population allied itself with the lower strata, the powerful internal unity of the Venetian nobility enabled it effectively to exclude the other classes from power, thus avoiding disturbances that would have undermined the status quo.

Venice's stability, past victories over the Turks, wealth, and flourishing in the arts gave her an almost mythic status (*il mito di Venezia*).[61] The city also had a reputation as a paradigm of elective government. This must have suggested that somehow a link existed between republican success and the use of election, an impression that could only be reinforced by the case of Ancient Rome, another exceptionally long-lived and successful elective republic. Meanwhile, the experience of Florence kept alive the old Athenian idea that drawing lots was more egalitarian than voting. The fraction of the population enjoying political rights was almost as small in

---

[60] Harrington, *The Prerogative of Popular Government*, p. 486.
[61] On the "myth of Venice" as seen by observers, see Pocock, *The Machiavellian Moment*, pp. 100–2, 112–13, 284–5, 319–20, 324–5, 327–8.

Florence as it was in Venice, but the Florentine republicans perceived that, within such limits, lot could promote equality in the distribution of offices. It was the experiences of these ancient and contemporary republics that seventeenth- and eighteenth-century political thinkers had in mind when they thought about election and lot.

THE POLITICAL THEORY OF ELECTION AND LOT IN THE SEVENTEENTH AND EIGHTEENTH CENTURIES

Harrington

Harrington, that great champion of republicanism under Cromwell's protectorate, noted that Athens was brought to ruin because, with its Council (*boulé*) appointed by lot, the city lacked "a natural aristocracy." Athens was imperfect, Harrington wrote, "in regard that the senate, chosen at once by lot, not by suffrage, and changed every year not in part but the whole, consisted not of the natural aristocracy nor, sitting long enough to understand or be perfect in their office, had sufficient authority to withhold the people from that perpetual turbulence in the way was ruin in the end."[62] The same theory is repeated in *The Prerogative of Popular Government*: the fact that the Council (or Senate) was chosen by lot deprived Athens of "the natural and necessary use of an aristocracy."[63] There was no doubt in Harrington's mind that election, unlike lot, selected preexisting elites. When men are left free, he argued, they spontaneously recognize their betters.

> Twenty men, if they not be all idiots – perhaps if they be – can never come together, but there will be such a difference between them that about one third will be wiser, or at least less foolish, than all the rest ... These upon acquaintance, though it be but small, will be discovered and (as stags as have the largest heads) lead the herd; for while the six, discoursing and arguing one with another, show the eminence of their parts, the fourteen discover things that they never thought on, or are cleared in diverse truths which formerly perplexed them.[64]

[62] J. Harrington, *Oceana* [1656], in *The Political Works of James Harrington*, p. 184.
[63] Harrington, *The Prerogative of Popular Government*, p. 477.
[64] Harrington, *Oceana*, p. 172.

This comment occurs in the passage in the Preliminaries to *Oceana*, in which Harrington is discussing the election of his ideal Senate, but it is put forward as a general characteristic of human nature. Presumably, then, Harrington saw it as applying to any type of election. It is to permit the free recognition of this natural aristocracy that the author of *Oceana* advocates use of the election.

So Harrington rejected the use of lot in the selection of office-holders. Yet his name remains associated with praise for rotation in office. Pocock in particular stresses the importance of the idea of rotation in Harrington's thought, showing how it reflected his attachment to the cardinal principle of civic humanism: man achieves the full flowering of his nature through participation in politics.[65] Traditionally, however, the principle of rotation was associated with the practice of lot. How was Harrington able to advocate both election and rotation of office if it is true, as we noted above, that freedom to elect is also freedom to reelect, and that potentially, therefore, the elective principle and the ideal of rotation are in conflict? Here we need to take a close look at the institutional arrangements or "orders" in *Oceana*.[66]

At the parish level (the smallest political subdivision in Harrington's system), the "elders" elect a fifth of their number each year: "the persons so chosen are deputies of the parish for the space of one year from their election and no longer, nor may they be elected *two years together*."[67] Each elder, Harrington assumes, is thus a

---

[65] Notably in *The Machiavellian Moment*, and the detailed "Historical Introduction" to his edition of *The Political Works of James Harrington*, pp. 1–152. Pocock even sees rotation, as advocated by Harrington, as an institution transcending the distinction between representatives and represented. "The entire citizen body," he writes, "in its diverse capacity as horse and foot [the two property classes that Harrington proposes to establish], constantly 'poured itself' into government ... Indeed, if the whole people could be involved in rotation, parliament itself would be transcended and the freely choosing people would itself be the constantly successive government; even the 'prerogative tribe' [the popular assembly elected by the lower property class] or representative assembly would be renewed so frequently that all distinction between representative and represented would disappear" (Pocock, "Historical Introduction" in *The Political Works of James Harrington*, p. 69).

[66] Note that the idiomatic use of the term "orders" to refer to institutions is peculiar to Harrington. This neologism is one of countless manifestations of the debt Harrington owes to Machiavelli. The author of the *Discourses on the First Decade of Livy* uses the term *ordini* to denote institutions.

[67] Harrington, *Oceana*, "Fifth Order," p. 215 (my emphasis).

deputy of the parish every five years. At this level, therefore, rotation is complete, since all the elders will be deputies in turn.[68] However, the parish deputies are merely *electors* to the supreme assemblies of Oceana (the Senate and the Prerogative Tribe). The deputies of the different parishes meet in an assembly that Harrington calls the "galaxy" to elect knights (members of the Senate) and deputies (members of the Prerogative Tribe). At this level, the regulations are different: "A knight, a deputy of the galaxy having fulfilled his term of three years, shall not be re-elected unto the same or any other tribe, *till he has also filled his three years' vacation.*"[69] In other words, there is nothing to prevent the members of the Senate and the deputies from being reelected a number of times; they are merely forbidden to succeed themselves. They must wait until the end of the next legislative term before becoming eligible again. Given the numbers of parish deputies and the size of the assemblies governing Oceana, rotation was thus not necessarily complete at this second level. Certain electors, delegated by the parishes, might never be elected to the Senate or to the Prerogative Tribe. There was no arrangement in Oceana to compare with the Athenian rule that prohibited a citizen from being a member of the *boulē* more than twice in his life.

Harrington makes this point even clearer in a passage of the *Prerogative of Popular Government* (which he wrote as a defense of *Oceana*). He draws a clear distinction between two types of rotation, that of electors and that of persons elected:

> This rotation [of electors to the national assemblies], being in itself annual, comes in regard of the body of the people to be quinquennial, or such as in the space of five years gives every man his turn in the power of election. But though every man be so capable of being an elector that he must have his turn, yet every man is not so capable of being elected in those magistracies that are sovereign or have the

---

[68] In reality, complete rotation of parish deputies does not necessarily follow from the above mentioned regulations. Under the stipulated rules, 60 percent of the voters could form a coalition to ensure that three subgroups of 20 percent each rotated in office. Harrington, then, seems to have miscalculated the effects of the provisions he recommended, for he explicitly claimed, in *The Prerogative of Popular Government*, that they secured a complete rotation of deputies at the parish level (see the passage cited below at note 70). I am indebted to Jon Elster for this observation.

[69] Harrington, *Oceana*, "Twelfth Order," p. 227 (my emphasis).

leading role of the whole commonwealth, that it can be safe to lay a necessity that every man must take his turn in these also; but it is enough that every man, who in the judgement and conscience of his country is fit, may take his turn. Wherefore, upon the conscience of the electors (so constituted as hath been shown), it goes to determine who shall partake of sovereign magistracy or be, at the assembly of a tribe, elected into the Senate or Prerogative Tribe.[70]

The institutions of Oceana no doubt guarantee a certain rotation in the Senate and in the Prerogative Tribe, since their members cannot carry out two mandates consecutively. However, that rotation may be confined to the restricted circle of those whom "the judgement and conscience" of the electors have found worthy of such offices.

In another passage, Harrington writes that "a parliament man in Oceana may in twelve years have borne his magistracy six, notwithstanding the necessity of his vacations."[71] The passage from *The Prerogative of Popular Government* quoted above even shows that Harrington explicitly wished this to happen. Harrington's rotation is thus of two types: full or absolute rotation for electors (each citizen being an elector every five years), and limited rotation among those elected, that is, among the natural aristocracy, as recognized by the electors. "The Senate and the Prerogative Tribe – or representative assembly of the people – being each of the same constitution, amount to four thousand experienced leaders, *ready upon new election to resume their leading.*"[72] There is thus no conflict in Harrington between the principle of rotation and the elective principle, since rotation applies in absolute terms only to the electors and not to those they elect.[73]

Montesquieu

Montesquieu, a reader of Machiavelli, Harrington, and probably also of Guicciardini, established a close link between lot and democracy on the one hand and election and aristocracy on the other. "Selection by lot [*le suffrage par le sort*]," he writes, "is in the nature of democracy, selection by choice [*le suffrage par choix*] is in

---

[70] Harrington, *The Prerogative of Popular Government*, p. 487.
[71] *Ibid.*, p. 493.   [72] *Ibid.*, p. 494 (my emphasis).
[73] So we cannot agree with Pocock when he states that in Oceana the whole people "constantly 'pours itself'" into government.

the nature of aristocracy. The lot is a way of selecting [*une façon d'élire*] that offends no one; it leaves to each citizen a reasonable expectation of serving his country." [74] The first thing to note is the strength of the link established between selection procedures and types of republican governments. [75] The social scientist in search of the "necessary relationships deriving from the nature of things" posits as a constant, universal rule that democracy goes with lot and aristocracy with election. [76] The two methods are not described as appertaining to particular cultures or resulting from the "general spirit" of a given nation; they stem from the very nature of democracy and aristocracy. Furthermore, Montesquieu sees them as forming part of the "fundamental laws" of a republic (in the same way as the extension of the franchise, the secret or public character of voting, or even the allocation of legislative power). [77]

Admittedly, Montesquieu regards lot as "defective in isolation." [78] However, he goes on to say that its most obvious fault (the possibility of incompetent individuals being selected) can be corrected, which is what the greatest legislators set out to do. Montesquieu then proceeds to a brief analysis of the use of lot in Athens, crediting Solon with having hedged lot about with other arrangements that averted or reduced its undesirable aspect. "However, to correct lot," Montesquieu writes, "he [Solon] ruled that selection might be effected [i.e. lots drawn] only among those who presented themselves: that the person selected should be examined by judges, and that anyone might accuse him of being unworthy of selection: this implied both lot and choice. On completing his term, a magistrate had to undergo a further judgment as to the manner in which he had conducted himself. People without ability must have been very reluctant to put their names forward for selection by lot." [79] The historical perspicacity of Montesquieu's analysis is astonishing.

[74] Montesquieu, *De l'Esprit des Lois* [1748], Book II, ch. 2.
[75] The reader is reminded that, in Montesquieu's work, democracy and aristocracy are the two forms a republic can take. "Republican government," he writes, "is that in which the people as a body or only a section of the people has sovereign power" (*Spirit of the Laws*, Book II, ch. 1).
[76] Montesquieu, *Spirit of the Laws*, Book I, ch. 1.
[77] "Since in a republic the division of those who have the right to vote is a fundamental law, the way of arriving at that division is likewise a fundamental law" (*Spirit of the Laws*, Book II, ch. 2).
[78] *Spirit of the Laws*, Book II, ch. 2.   [79] *Spirit of the Laws*, Book II, ch. 2.

Whereas later historians (notably, Fustel de Coulanges) were to wonder whether there was at Athens a preselection of the names submitted for selection by lot, Montesquieu already saw what the most recent historical research confirms, namely, that lots were drawn only from among the names of those who offered themselves. In addition, he grasped that the combination of the voluntary nature of candidacy for selection by lot with the prospect of sanctions must have led to a self-selection of candidates.

Two characteristics of lot make it necessary for a democracy. It neither humiliates nor brings disgrace upon those who are not selected for magistracies (it "offends no one"), since they know that fate might equally well have chosen them. And at the same time it obviates envy and jealousy toward those who are selected. In an aristocracy, Montesquieu remarks, "selection should not be by lot; one would have only its drawbacks. Indeed, in a government that has already established the most offensive distinctions [*les distinctions les plus affligeantes*], though a man might be chosen by lot, he would be no less detested for it; it is the noble that is envied, not the magistrate."[80] On the other hand, lot accords with the principle that democrats cherish above all others, namely equality, because it gives each citizen a "reasonable" chance of exercising a public function.[81]

Does this mean that for Montesquieu election does not give everyone a "reasonable" chance of holding office? He is not as explicit about the aristocratic nature of election as he is about the democratic properties of lot. He, too, fails to explain why elections are aristocratic. Yet a number of his observations regarding "selection by choice" suggest strongly that election does in fact elevate to magistracies certain kinds of people. Montesquieu's praise for "the natural ability of the people to discern merit" shows first that he, like Harrington, believed that the people will spontaneously choose the truly superior.[82] Furthermore, the examples cited in support of

---

[80] *Spirit of the Laws*, Book II, ch. 3.

[81] "In a democracy, love of the republic is love of democracy; love of democracy is love of equality" (*Spirit of the Laws*, Book V, ch. 3).

[82] "Should anyone doubt the natural ability of the people to discern merit, he need only look at the continuous succession of astonishing choices made by the Athenians and the Romans; no one, presumably, will attribute that to chance" (*Spirit of the Laws*, Book II, ch. 2).

this theory lead to the conclusion that Montesquieu did not draw a firm distinction between a natural aristocracy based on aptitude alone and the upper strata of society as defined by birth, wealth, and prestige.

> We know that in Rome, though the people had given itself the right to elevate plebeians to office, it could not bring itself to elect them; and although in Athens it was possible, by virtue of the law of Aristides, for magistrates to be drawn from any class, Xenophon tells us it never happened that the common people asked for themselves those magistracies that might affect its safety or its glory.[83]

"The people," Montesquieu had written in an earlier passage, "is admirable in its ability to choose those to whom it must entrust some part of its authority. It has only to decide on the basis of things it cannot ignore and of facts that are self-evident."[84] But let us look at the examples he cites to illustrate this proposition: the soldier who is elected general because he was successful on the battlefield; the assiduous and honest judge whom his fellow-citizens elevate to the praetorship; the citizen chosen as a councilor for his "munificence" or "riches." Here again, the examples of qualities that lead to a person's being elected range from purely personal merit (success in war), through a combination of moral virtue and social status (the zeal, honesty, and authority of the worthy judge), to something that may simply have been inherited (wealth). Montesquieu claims that

---

[83] *Spirit of the Laws*, Book II, ch. 2. This sentence should be compared with the following passage from the *Discourses on Livy*, at the end of which Machiavelli quotes the Roman historian: "The Roman people, as I have already said, came to look on the office of consul as a nuisance, and wished this office to be thrown open to plebeians, or, alternatively, that the authority of the consuls should be reduced. To prevent the authority of the consuls from being sullied by the adoption of either of these alternatives, the nobility suggested a middle course, and agreed to the appointment of four tribunes with consular power who might be either plebeian or nobles. With this the plebs were content, since it was tantamount to abolishing the consulate, and in the highest office of the state they had a share. An event then took place which is noteworthy. When it came to electing these tribunes, though they might have elected plebeians in all cases, all those the Roman people elected were nobles. On this Titus Livy remarks that 'the outcome of these assemblies shows that the attitude adopted in the struggle for liberty and honour was different from that adopted when the struggle was over and gave place to unbiased judgment.' " Machiavelli, *Discourses on the First Decade of Titus Livy*, Vol. I, 47, trans. L. J. Walker (London: Penguin, 1983), p. 225 (translation modified).

[84] Montesquieu, *Spirit of the Laws*, Book II, ch. 2.

the people elect the best, but the best may well be located among the upper classes.

Rousseau

Rousseau too, in the *Social Contract*, links lottery with democracy and election with aristocracy. Lot and election are presented as the two procedures that might be used to choose the "Government." In Rousseau's vocabulary, remember, the "Government" (also called the "Prince") stands for the executive branch. Legislation always remains in the hands of the people (the "Sovereign"). Consequently, no selection takes place at that level. But in selecting executive magistrates, a choice has to be made between one method of selection or the other. In a passage addressing this question, Rousseau starts by quoting Montesquieu and states his agreement with the idea that "selection by lot is of the nature of democracy." He adds, however, that the reasons why this is so are not those put forward by Montesquieu (prevention of jealousy, equal distribution of offices).

> Those are not reasons. If it is carefully noted that the selection of leaders [*l'élection des chefs*] is a function of Government, and not of Sovereignty, it will be seen why the drawing of lots is more in the nature of democracy, in which the administration is better to the extent that its acts are fewer. In every true democracy, the magistracy is not a benefit but a burdensome responsibility, which cannot fairly be placed on one particular individual rather than another. The law alone can impose this responsibility on the one to whom it falls by lot. For then, as the condition is equal for all, and the choice is not dependent on any human will, there is no particular application that alters the universality of the law.[85]

This complex reasoning becomes intelligible only if one realizes that the whole argument rests on a key notion that is not explicitly stated in the passage. For Rousseau, the allocation of magistracies ("the selection of leaders"), whether by lot or election, is a *particular* measure. Distribution of offices concerns individuals identified by name rather than all citizens. It cannot, therefore, be something

---

[85] Rousseau, *Social Contract*, Book IV, ch. 3. The quotation from Montesquieu referred to is the passage cited above, from *Spirit of the Laws*, Book II, ch. 2.

done by the people as Sovereign. Indeed, one of the key principles of the *Social Contract* is that the Sovereign can act only through the laws, that is, through general rules affecting all citizens equally. Particular measures are the province of Government. Consequently, if the people appoints magistrates, it can do so only in its capacity as Government ("the selection of leaders is a function of Government, and not of Sovereignty").[86] But two problems arise here.

First, according to Rousseau, democracy is defined precisely by the fact that in it the people are both the Sovereign (as in every legitimate political system) and the Government: in a democracy, the people make the laws and execute them. Rousseau further supposes that, even when the people wield executive power collectively, the different magistracies must be assigned to different citizens. Given this definition of democracy, it might seem that election ("selection by choice") is especially suitable for democratic regimes, since in such systems the people may also act *qua* Government. That is not, however, what Rousseau concludes; at this point, a different argument enters his reasoning. Popular exercise of both legislative and executive functions gives rise to a major danger: the decisions of the people *qua* Sovereign (the laws) may be infected by the particular views it must adopt when operating *qua* Government. "It is not good for him who makes the laws to execute them," Rousseau writes in his chapter on democracy, "nor for the body of the people to turn its attention away from general considerations to particular objects."[87] Men being less than perfect, this danger constitutes a major defect of democracy. This is one of the reasons why Rousseau concludes his chapter on democracy with the frequently cited words: "If there were a people of Gods, it would govern itself democratically. Such a perfect government is not suited to men." Gods would be able to separate in their minds the general views they must hold when they act as the Sovereign, from the particular ones they must adopt as executors of the laws, and avoid the adulteration of the former by the latter. But this is beyond human capacity. Therefore, a democratic government works best, when the people, who, above all, are the Sovereign, have the fewest possible occasions to make particular decisions as the Government.

---

[86] Rousseau, *Social Contract*, Book IV, ch. 3.   [87] *Ibid.*, Book III, ch. 4.

This is why Rousseau states in the passage cited above that in democracies "the administration is better to the extent that its acts are fewer."[88] Lot then solves this first problem. When the magistrates are selected by lot, the people have only one decision to make: they need only establish that magistrates will be selected by lot. Clearly, such a decision is a general rule or law, which they may therefore pass in their capacity as Sovereign. No further particular intervention is required of them as Government. If, on the other hand, the democracy is elective, the people must intervene twice: first, to pass the law instituting elections and how they shall be conducted, and then as the Government in order to elect the magistrates. It can be argued, along Rousseauian lines, that in this case their first decision would run the risk of being influenced by the prospect of the second one: they may, for example, frame the general electoral law with a view to making the election of certain individuals more or less likely.

But there is also a second problem. Even supposing that, in a democracy, the people manage not to let their decisions as Sovereign be affected by the particular views they need to adopt in order to govern, the fact remains that, when it comes to choosing magistrates, particular considerations of personality will influence their choice. When the members of the Government (in this case, all citizens) parcel out the offices of government among themselves, they assign each office to one individual rather than another (each magistracy has to be "placed on one particular individual rather than another"). Even if that distribution of magistracies is carried out in accordance with a general law, questions of personality will inevitably intervene between the law and the assignment of a function to a person, giving rise to the risk of partiality.[89] In this respect, lot presents a second advantage: it is a rule of distribution that does not require any further decision in order to be applied to particular cases. If the allocation of offices is done by lot, there is no

---

[88] *Social Contract*, Book IV, ch. 3.

[89] Rousseau finds it necessary to add that, in a "true" democracy, the exercise of a magistracy is essentially regarded as "a heavy burden" and that, in consequence, political justice consists in spreading costs, not benefits. However, this idea is not indispensable to the logic of his argument. The risk of injustice in any particular application of the rule of distribution of public offices would exist even if magistracies were regarded as benefits.

room for any particular will ("there is no particular application that alters the universality of the law"). Conditions are then rigorously the same for all members of the Government, since they are all equal before the law regulating the allocation of magistracies and since it is that law itself, so to speak, that assigns them particular offices.

So whether it is a question of limiting the number of occasions on which the people need to adopt particular views, or the risk of partiality in the distribution of offices, lot is the right selection method for democracy because it allocates magistracies without the intervention of any *particular will*. Furthermore, Rousseau adds, the condition of the citizens in a democracy is such that we can disregard the objection to the use of lot (selection of incompetent or unworthy citizens): "Selection by lot [*l'élection par sort*] would have few disadvantages in a true democracy where, all things being equal, both in mores and talents as well as in maxims and fortune, the choice would become almost indifferent."[90]

Elections, by contrast, are suited to aristocracy. "In an aristocracy the Prince chooses the Prince; the Government preserves itself, and it is there that voting is appropriate."[91] In an aristocracy, election presents no danger, since by definition the body that does the selecting (the "Prince" or "Government") is not the same as the one that makes the laws. When the Government chooses magistrates from among its number, it may resort to elections, which necessarily imply particular views and intentions. Here, there is no risk of those particular views affecting the creation of laws – especially the electoral law – since legislation is in any case in other hands. A footnote by Rousseau confirms this interpretation. In an aristocracy, he points out, it is vital that the rules governing elections remain in the hands of the Sovereign. "It is of great importance that *laws* [i.e. decisions by the Sovereign] should regulate the form of the election of magistrates, for if it is left to the will of the Prince [the government], it is impossible to avoid falling into a hereditary aristocracy."[92] If those who have the power to choose the magistrates also have the power to decide how the magistrates will be chosen, they will decide on the method most favorable to their interests – in this case, heredity. On the other hand, aristocracy is *the*

[90] *Social Contract*, Book IV, ch. 3.   [91] *Ibid.*, Book IV, ch. 3.
[92] *Ibid.*, Book III, ch. 5. (note by Rousseau; my emphasis).

system in which differences and distinctions among citizens can manifest themselves freely. And those differences can be utilized for political ends.

> In addition to the advantage of the distinction between the two powers [Sovereign and Government], it [aristocracy] has that of the choice of its members. For in popular government all citizens are born magistrates; but this type of government [aristocracy] limits them to a small number, and they become magistrates only by *election*, a means by which probity, enlightenment, experience, and all the other reasons for public preference and esteem are so many guarantees of being well governed.[93]

Because it is possible, in an aristocracy, to make political use of differences in talent and worth, elective aristocracy is the best form of government.[94]

While Montesquieu's discussion of lot in the *Spirit of the Laws* is remarkable for its historical insight, it is rigor of argument that stands out in Rousseau's *Social Contract*. Indeed, Rousseau himself regarded Montesquieu's account of the democratic properties of lot as poorly argued, though basically sound. His own account, however, for all its subtlety and impeccable logic, owed more to the idiosyncratic definitions and principles laid down in the *Social Contract* than to historical analysis. It might be pointed out that, given its complexity, the precise reasoning by which Rousseau linked lot to democracy probably exercised only the most limited influence on political actors. That may well be so, but the important points lie elsewhere.

The first thing to note is that, even as late as 1762, a thinker who undertook to lay down the "Principles of Political Right" (as the *Social Contract* was subtitled) would make a place for lot in his political theory. Both Montesquieu and Rousseau were fully aware that lot can select incompetents, which is what strikes us today, and explains why we do not even think of attributing public functions by lot. But both writers perceived that lot had *also* other properties or merits that at least made it an alternative worthy of serious

---

[93] *Social Contract*, Book III, ch. 5 (my emphasis; the term "election" here means election in the modern sense – what in other contexts Rousseau calls "selection by choice [*l'élection par choix*]."
[94] *Ibid.*, Book III, ch. 5.

consideration, and perhaps justified that one should seek to remedy the obvious defect with other institutions.

The other notable fact is that political writers of the caliber of Harrington, Montesquieu, and Rousseau should, each from his own standpoint and in his own manner, have advanced the same proposition, namely that election was aristocratic in nature, whereas lot is *par excellence* the democratic selection procedure. Not only had lot not disappeared from the theoretical horizon at the time representative government was invented, there was also a commonly accepted doctrine among intellectual authorities regarding the comparative properties of lot and election.

Scarcely one generation after the *Spirit of the Laws* and the *Social Contract*, however, the idea of attributing public functions by lot had vanished almost without trace. Never was it seriously considered during the American and French revolutions. At the same time that the founding fathers were declaring the equality of all citizens, they decided without the slightest hesitation to establish, on both sides of the Atlantic, the unqualified dominion of a method of selection long deemed to be aristocratic. Our close study of republican history and theory, then, reveals the sudden but silent disappearance of an old idea and a paradox that has hitherto gone unnoticed.

THE TRIUMPH OF ELECTION: CONSENTING TO POWER RATHER THAN HOLDING OFFICE

What is indeed astonishing, in the light of the republican tradition and the theorizing it had generated, is the total absence of debate in the early years of representative government about the use of lot in the allocation of power. The founders of representative systems did not try to find out what other institutions might be used in conjunction with lot in order to correct its clearly undesirable effects. A preliminary screening, along the lines of the Florentine *squittinio*, aiming to obviate the selection of notoriously unqualified individuals, was never even considered. One could also argue that by itself lot gives citizens no control over what magistrates do once in office. However, a procedure for the rendering of accounts, coupled with sanctions, would have provided some form of popular control over the magistrates' decisions; such a solution was never discussed either. It is certainly not surprising that the founders of representative government did not consider selecting rulers endowed with full freedom of action by drawing lots from among the entire population. What is surprising is that the use of lot, even in combination with other institutions, did not receive any serious hearing at all.

Lot was not completely forgotten, however. We do find the occasional mention of it in the writings and speeches of certain political figures. In the debates that shaped the United States Constitution, for instance, James Wilson suggested having the President of the United States chosen by a college of electors, who were themselves drawn by lot from among the members of Congress. Wilson's proposal was explicitly based on the Venetian model and aimed to obviate intrigues in electing a president.[95] It provoked no discussion, however, and was set aside almost immediately. In France, a few revolutionaries (Siéyès before the revolution, Lanthenas in 1792) thought of combining lot with election. And in 1793 a member of the French Convention, Montgilbert, suggested replacing election by lot on the grounds that lot was more egalitarian.[96] But none of these suggestions met with any significant level of debate within the assemblies of the French revolution. In 1795 the Thermidorians decided that each month the seating arrangement within the representative assemblies (the *Cinq Cents* and the *Anciens*) would be determined by lot.[97] The measure was aimed at inhibiting the formation of blocs – in the most physical sense. Lot was still associated with preventing factionalism, but in an obviously minor way. In any case, the rule was never observed.

The revolutionaries invoked the authority of Harrington, Montesquieu, and Rousseau, and meditated on the history of earlier republics. But neither in England, nor America, nor France, did anyone, apparently, ever give serious thought to the possibility of

[95] See M. Farrand (ed.), *The Records of the Federal Convention of 1787* [1911], 4 vols. (New Haven, CT: Yale University Press, 1966), Vol. II, pp. 99–106. I owe this reference to Jon Elster, who has my thanks.

[96] The suggestions of Siéyès and Lanthenas, together with the pamphlet written by Montgilbert, are quoted by P. Guéniffey in his book *Le Nombre et la Raison. La révolution française et les élections* (Paris: Editions de l'Ecole des Hautes Etudes en Sciences Sociales, 1933), pp. 119–20.

[97] See Guéniffey, *Le Nombre et la Raison*, p. 486.

assigning any public function by lot.[98] It is noteworthy, for example, that John Adams, one of the founding fathers who was most widely read in history, never considered selection by lot as a possibility, not even for the purposes of rejecting it.[99] In the lengthy descriptive chapters of his *Defense of the Constitutions of Government of the United States of America* devoted to Athens and Florence, Adams briefly notes that those cities chose their magistrates by lot, but he does not reflect on the subject. When representative systems were being established, this method of choosing rulers was not within the range of conceivable possibilities. It simply did not occur to anyone. The last two centuries, at least up until the present day, would suggest that it had disappeared forever.

To explain this remarkable, albeit rarely noted, phenomenon, the idea that first springs to mind is that choosing rulers by lot had become "impracticable" in large modern states.[100] One can also argue that lot "presupposes" conditions of possibility that no longer obtained in the states in which representative government was invented. Patrice Guéniffey, for example, contends that lot can create a feeling of political obligation only within small communities in which all members know one another, which he argues is "an indispensable prerequisite for their accepting a decision in which they have played no part or only an indirect one."[101] Selection by lot also requires, the same author continues, that political functions

---

[98] This claim ought to be accompanied by a caveat. I certainly have not consulted all the historical works available, let alone all the original sources relating to the three great modern revolutions. Moreover, the political use of lot has so far received a very limited amount of scholarly attention; it cannot be ruled out, therefore, that future research may reveal additional cases of lot being discussed. Nonetheless it seems to me reasonable, given what I know at present, to maintain that selecting rulers by lot was not contemplated in any major political debate during the English, American, and French revolutions.

[99] This is true at least of his three main political works, namely *Thoughts on Government* [1776], *A Defense of the Constitutions of Government of the United States of America* [1787–8], and *Discourses on Davila* [1790]. See C. F. Adams (ed.), *The Life and Works of John Adams*, 10 vols. (Boston, MA: Little Brown, 1850–6), Vols. IV, V, and VI.

[100] It is odd that Carl Schmitt, one of the few modern authors to devote any attention to the selection of rulers by lot, should adopt this point of view. Schmitt comments that lot is the method that best guarantees an identity between rulers and ruled, but he immediately adds: "This method has become impracticable nowadays." C. Schmitt, *Verfassungslehre*, § 19 (Munich: Duncker & Humblot, 1928), p. 257.

[101] Guéniffey, *Le Nombre et la Raison*, p. 122.

be simple and not need any special competence. And finally, Guéniffey claims, for it to be possible to select rulers at random, an equality of circumstances and culture must "pre-exist among the members of the body politic, in order that the decision may fall on any one of them indifferently."[102]

Such comments contain grains of truth, but they are defective in that they obscure the element of contingency and choice that is invariably present in every historical development, and that certainly played a part in the triumph of election over lot. In the first place – and this point has been made before, but it bears repeating – lot was not totally impracticable. In some cases, such as England, the size of the electorate was not as large as some might think. It has been calculated, for example, that in 1754 the total electorate of England and Wales numbered 280,000 persons (out of a population of around 8 million).[103] There was nothing practical preventing the establishment of a multiple step procedure: lots could have been drawn in small districts, and a further drawing of lots could then have taken place among the names selected by lot at the first level. It is even more remarkable that no one thought of using lot for local purposes. Towns, or even counties of the seventeenth and eighteenth centuries could not have been much larger or more populous than ancient Attica or Renaissance Florence. Local political functions presumably did not present a high degree of complexity. Yet neither the American nor the French revolutionaries ever contemplated assigning local offices by lot. Apparently, not even in the towns of New England (which de Tocqueville was later to characterize as models of direct democracy) were municipal officials chosen by lot in the seventeenth and eighteenth centuries; they were always picked by election.[104] In those small towns of homogeneous popula-

---

[102] Guéniffey, *Le Nombre et La Raison*, p. 123.

[103] See J. Cannon, *Parliamentary Reform 1640–1832* (Cambridge: Cambridge University Press, 1973), p. 31.

[104] Here again, the assertion needs to be advanced with caution. I have not consulted all the historical studies dealing with the local government system in New England during the colonial and revolutionary periods. Moreover, instances of the use of lot may have escaped the attention of historians. It seems, however, that even if the practice existed here and there, it was certainly neither widespread nor salient. On this question, see J. T. Adams, *The Founding of New England* (Boston, MA: Little Brown, 1921, 1949), ch. 11; Carl Brindenbaugh, *Cities in Revolt. Urban Life in America 1743–1776* (New York: A. A. Knopf, 1955); E. M. Cook Jr, *The Fathers of the Towns: Leadership and Community Structure in Eighteenth-century*

tion and limited functions, where common affairs were discussed by all the inhabitants in annual town meetings, conditions today put forward as necessary for the use of lot must have been approximated. The difference between the city-republics of Renaissance Italy and the towns of colonial and revolutionary New England did not lie in external circumstances, but in beliefs concerning what gave a collective authority legitimacy.

It is certainly true that political actors in the seventeenth and eighteenth centuries did not regard selecting rulers by lot as a possibility. Electing them appeared as the only course, as indicated by the absence of any hesitation about which of the two methods to use. But this was not purely the deterministic outcome of external circumstances. Lot was deemed to be manifestly unsuitable, *given* the objectives that the actors sought to achieve and the dominant beliefs about political legitimacy. So whatever role circumstances may have played in the eclipse of lot and the triumph of election, we have to inquire into which beliefs and values have intervened to bring this about. In the absence of any explicit debate among the founders of representative government as to the relative virtues of the two procedures, our argument inevitably remains somewhat conjectural. The only approach possible is to compare the two methods with ideas whose force is otherwise attested in the political culture of the seventeenth and eighteenth centuries. This will allow us to determine what kinds of motivation could have led people to adopt election as the self-evident course.

There was indeed one notion in the light of which the respective merits of lot and election must have appeared widely different and unequal, namely, the principle that all legitimate authority stems from the consent of those over whom it is exercised – in other words, that individuals are obliged only by what they have consented to. The three modern revolutions were accomplished in the name of this principle. This fact is sufficiently established for there to be no need to rehearse the evidence at length here.[105] Let us look at a few illustrative examples. In the Putney debates (October 1647)

New England (Baltimore, MD: Johns Hopkins University Press, 1976). The analysis by de Tocqueville to which I refer may be found in *Democracy in America*, Vol. I, part 1, ch. 5.

[105] On the role of the idea of consent in Anglo-American political culture in the eighteenth century, see among others, J. P. Reid, *The Concept of Representation in*

between the radical and conservative wings of Cromwell's army, which constitute one of the most remarkable documents on the beliefs of the English revolutionaries, the Levellers' spokesman Rainsborough declared: "Every man that is to live under a government ought first by his own consent to put himself under that government; and I do think that the poorest man in England is not at all bound in a strict sense to that government that he hath not had a voice to put himself under." Replying to this, Ireton, the chief speaker of the more conservative group, did not dispute the principle of consent but argued that the right of consent belonged solely to those who have a "fixed permanent interest in this kingdom." [106] One hundred and thirty years later, the American Declaration of Independence opened with the words: "We hold these truths to be self-evident, that all men are created equal, that they are endowed by their Creator with certain inalienable Rights, that among these are Life, Liberty, and the pursuit of Happiness, – That to secure these rights, Governments are instituted among Men, deriving their just powers from the consent of the governed." [107] Finally, in France, a key figure in the early months of the revolution, Thouret, published at the beginning of August 1789 a draft declaration of rights that included the following article: "All citizens have the right to concur, individually or through their representatives, in the formation of the laws, and to submit only to those to which they have freely consented." [108]

This belief that consent constitutes the sole source of legitimate authority and forms the basis of political obligation was shared by all Natural Law theorists from Grotius to Rousseau, including Hobbes, Pufendorf, and Locke. This too has been sufficiently established, and we may confine ourselves to a single illustration. It is taken from Locke, the intellectual authority who enjoyed the

---

[106] the *Age of the American Revolution* (Chicago: University of Chicago Press, 1989), esp. ch. 1, "The concept of consent."

[106] "The Putney debates," in G. E. Aylmer (ed.), *The Levellers in the English Revolution* (Ithaca, NY: Cornell University Press, 1975), p. 100.

[107] "Declaration of Independence" [4 July 1776], in P. B. Kurland and R. Lerner (eds.), *The Founders' Constitution*, 5 vols. (Chicago: University of Chicago Press, 1987), Vol. I, p. 9.

[108] Thouret, "Projet de déclaration des droits de l'homme en société" [1789], in S. Rials (ed.), *La déclaration des droits de l'homme et du citoyen* (Paris: Hachette, 1988), p. 639.

greatest ascendancy in England, America, and France alike.[109] In his *Second Treatise of Government*, Locke wrote: "Men being, as has been said, by Nature, all free, equal, and independent, no one may be taken from this Estate and subjected to the Political Power of another but by his own *consent*." He further wrote: "And thus that, which begins and actually *constitutes any Political Society*, is nothing but the consent of any number of Freemen capable of a majority to unite and incorporate themselves into such a Society. And this is that and that only which did, or could give *beginning* to any *lawful Government* in the World." [110]

Once the source of power and the foundation of political obligation had been located in this way in the consent or will of the governed, lot and election appeared in a completely new light. However lot is interpreted, whatever its other properties, it cannot possibly be perceived as an expression of consent. One can establish, to be sure, a system in which the people consent to have their leaders designated by lot. Under such an arrangement, the power of those selected for office at a particular in time would be ultimately founded on the consent of the governed. But in this case, legitimation by consent would only be indirect: the legitimacy of any particular outcome would derive exclusively from the consent to the procedure of selection. In a system based on lot, even one in which the people have once agreed to use this method, the persons that happen to be selected are not put in power through the will of those over whom they will exercise their authority; they are not put in power by anyone. Under an elective system, by contrast, the consent of the people is constantly reiterated. Not only do the people agree to the selection method – when they decide to use elections – but they also consent to each particular outcome – when they elect. If the goal is to found power and political obligation on consent, then obviously elections are a much safer method than lot. They select the persons who shall hold office (just as lot would), but at the same time they legitimize their power and create in voters a feeling of

---

[109] For an excellent presentation of the ideas of the Natural Law School, see R. Derathé, *J.-J. Rousseau et la science politique de son temps* [1950] (Paris: Vrin, 1970), *passim*, esp. pp. 33 ff., 180 ff.

[110] J. Locke, *The Second Treatise of Government*, ch. VIII, §§ 95, 99, in Locke, *Two Treatises of Government*, ed. P. Laslett (Cambridge: Cambridge University Press, 1960), pp. 330, 333 (original emphasis).

obligation and commitment towards those whom they have appointed. There is every reason to believe that it is this view of the foundation of political legitimacy and obligation that led to the eclipse of lot and the triumph of election.

The link between election and consent was not in fact a complete novelty at the time representative government was established. Nor was it the invention of modern natural law theorists to hold that what obligates all must have been consented to by all. The expression of consent through election had already proved itself as an effective way of generating a sense of obligation among the population. The convening of elected representatives for the purpose of fostering this sense, particularly in regard to taxation, had been used successfully for several centuries. The "Assemblies of Estates" and the "Estates-General" of the Middle Ages (and the modern period) were based on this principle. Some historians stress the differences between the medieval "Assemblies of Estates" and the representative assemblies that became the locus of power in the wake of the three great revolutions. The differences are indeed substantial. However, they should not obscure the elements of continuity. The fact is that the English Parliament after the revolutions of 1641 and 1688 was also the descendant of the Parliament of the "ancient constitution" – and was seen as such. The American colonies, too, had experience of elected representative assemblies, and the slogan of the 1776 revolution ("no taxation without representation") testifies to the prevalence of the ancient belief that the convening of elected representatives was the only legitimate way to impose taxation. In France, the break may have been more abrupt, nonetheless it was a financial crisis that led the monarchy to convene the Estates-General, reviving an institution which was known to be effective at creating a sense of obligation. Moreover, there are good grounds for thinking that the electoral techniques employed by representative governments had their origins in medieval elections, both those of "Assemblies of Estates" and those practiced by the Church (rather than in the elections of the Roman republic, for example).[111]

---

[111] See especially Léo Moulin, "Les origines religieuses des techniques électorales modernes et délibératives modernes," in *Revue Internationale d'Histoire Politique et Constitutionelle*, April–June 1953, pp. 143–8; G. de Lagarde, *La Naissance de l'esprit*

In the Middle Ages, the use of election went hand in hand with the invocation of a principle that, according to all evidence, crucially affected the history of Western institutions. This was the principle of Roman origin: *Quod omnes tangit, ab omnibus tractari et approbari debet* ("What touches all should be considered and approved by all"). Following the reemergence of Roman law in the twelfth century, both civil and Canon lawyers spread this principle, though reinterpreting it as applying to public matters, whereas in Rome it belonged to private law.[112] The principle Q.O.T. was invoked by Edward I in his writ summoning the English Parliament in 1295, but recent research has shown that by the late thirteenth century the phrase already had wide currency. The expression was also used by the French king Philip IV when he summoned the Estates-General in 1302, and by Emperor Frederick II when he invited the cities of Tuscany to send delegates (*nuntii*) with full powers.[113] Popes Honorius III and Innocent III likewise made quite frequent use of it. One should note that the authorities who thus called for the election of representatives usually insisted that they be invested with full powers (*plenipotentiarii*) – that is to say, that the electors should consider themselves bound by the decisions of the elected, whatever those decisions may be. The involvement of the will and consent of

laïque à la fin du Moyen Age (Leuven/Louvain: E. Nauvelaerts, 1956); L. Moulin, "'Sanior et Major pars', Étude sur l'évolution des techniques électorales et délibératives dans les ordres religieux du VIème au XIIIème siècles," in *Revue Historique de Droit Français et Etranger*, 3–4, 1958, pp. 368, 397, 491–529; Arthur P. Monahan, *Consent, Coercion and Limit, the Medieval Origins of Parliamentary Democracy* (Kingston, Ontario: McGill-Queens University Press, 1987); Brian M. Downing, *The Military Revolution and Political Change. Origins of Democracy and Autocracy in Early Modern Europe* (Princeton, NJ: Princeton University Press, 1992).

[112] The formulation of this principle (usually known as "Q.O.T." for short), found in Justinian's *Codex* of 531 (*Cod.*, 5, 59, 5, 2), became the source for medieval commentators, such as Gratian, who mentions it in the *Decretum* (*circa* 1140; *Decretum*, 63, post c.25). On the original meaning of "Q.O.T.," see G. Post, "A Roman legal theory of consent, *quod omnes tangit* in medieval representation," in *Wisconsin Law Review*, Jan. 1950, pp. 66–78; Y. Congar, "Quod omnes tangit, ab omnibus tractari et approbari debet" [1958], in Y. Congar, *Droit ancien et structures ecclésiales*, (London: Variorum, 1982), pp. 210–59. On other developments of this legal principle, see A. Marongiu, "Q.O.T., principe fondamental de la démocratie et du consentement au XIVème siècle," in *Album Helen Maud Cam*, 2 vols. (Leuven/Louvain: Presses Universitaires de Louvain, 1961), Vol. II, pp. 101–15; G. Post, "A Romano-canonical maxim, 'Quod omnes tangit' in Bracton and early parliaments," in G. Post, *Studies in Medieval Legal Thought* (Princeton,NJ: Princeton University Press, 1964), pp. 163–238.

[113] See Monahan, *Consent, Coercion and Limit*, pp. 100 ff.

the governed in the selection of delegates gave to the resolutions of the representative assemblies a binding force that the decisions of men selected by lot would not have possessed. Once the delegates had given their consent to a particular measure or tax, the king, pope, or emperor could then turn to the people and say: "You consented to have representatives speak on your behalf; you must now obey what they have approved." There was in election something like a promise of obedience.

Invoking the Q.O.T. principle did not imply that the consent of the governed was deemed the sole or principal source of legitimacy – a basic difference from modern representative assemblies. Rather it meant that a wish from "above" had to meet with approval from "below" in order to become a fully legitimate directive that carried obligation.[114] Nor did the principle entail any notion of choice among candidates by the people or proposals by the assembly. It was rather that the people were being asked to give their seal of approval to what the authorities (civil or ecclesiastical) had proposed. Often that approval took the form of a mere "acclamation."[115] But even in this form, the principle implied, at least in theory, that approval could be withheld. Repeated use of the Q.O.T. formula undoubtedly helped to propagate and establish the belief that the consent of the governed was a source of political legitimacy and obligation.

At this point, we should open a brief parenthesis. It has been claimed on occasion that the Church took the lead in bringing the practice of lot to an end by banning its use in the selection of bishops and abbots at a time when the procedure was still current in the Italian city-republics.[116] It is true that Honorius III did, by a decretal promulgated in 1223 (*Ecclesia Vestra*, addressed to the chapter of Lucca), prohibit the use of lot in ecclesiastical

---

[114] On the combination of the "ascending" and "descending" conceptions of authority in medieval thought and practice, the basic works remain those of Walter Ullmann; see in particular his *Principles of Government and Politics in the Middle Ages* (London: Methuen, 1961).

[115] On the essentially acclamatory nature of elections of representatives in pre-revolutionary England, see M. Kishlansky, *Parliamentary Selection: Social and Political Choice in Early Modern England* (Cambridge: Cambridge University Press, 1986), esp. ch. 2.

[116] Moulin, "Les origines religieuses des techniques électorales modernes et délibératives modernes," p. 114.

appointments.[117] Previously lot had occasionally been employed in filling episcopal positions.[118] But it was understood to manifest God's will. And it was the use of lot as an appeal to divine providence that *Ecclesia Vestra* banned. The decretal can be found in the *Liber Extra*, under the heading *De sortilegiis* (Of Sortileges) (Tit. XXI) among prohibitions of other divinatory practices deemed superstitious. So, the Church voiced no objections to the purely secular use of lot, that is, where it was not given supernatural significance. This interpretation of the Church's prohibition finds confirmation in the *Summa Theologiae*.[119] In a detailed argument (that merits no elaboration here), Thomas Aquinas distinguishes a number of possible uses of lot: distributive lot (*sors divisoria*), consultative lot (*sors consultatoria*), and divinatory lot (*sors divinatoria*). The important point is that, according to Aquinas, the distributive use of lot to assign "possessions, honours, or dignities" does not constitute a sin. If the outcome of lot is seen as no more than the product of chance (*fortuna*), there is no harm in resorting to it "except that of possibly acting in vain [*nisi forte vitium vanitatis*]." So there is no doubt that the Church was not opposed to the use of lot for assigning offices, provided that no one accorded any religious significance to the procedure. This explains, in fact, why the highly Catholic Italian republics continued to use lot after *Ecclesia Vestra* without the practice giving rise to any controversy

[117] *Corpus Juris Canonici*, E. Friedberg edition, 2 vols. (Tauschnitz, 1879–81), Vol. II, p. 823 (*Liber Extra*, Tit. XXI, cap. III). I owe this reference to Mr. Steve Horwitz of California, an expert in canon law and antique books, with whom I got in touch via electronic mail on the Internet and whom I should like to thank here. Léo Moulin (in the article referred to in note 116 above) mentions the existence of the decretal but without giving either a precise reference or an analysis of its content. My questions to a number of experts on canon law as well my own research in the *Corpus Juris Canonici* had proved fruitless. Paul Bullen, whom I should also like to thank, then suggested that I put the problem to a group of experts on medieval and canon law who subscribed to the Internet. In this way I was eventually able to consult the text of the decretal, the precise content of which is important, as we shall see. Possibly I should also pay homage to the technology which has today extended the republic of letters to cover the entire planet!

[118] See Jean Gaudemet, "La participation de la communauté au choix de ses pasteurs dans l'Eglise latine: esquisse historique," in J. Gaudemet, *La société ecclésiastique dans l'Occident médiéval* (London: Variorum, 1980), ch. 8. Gaudemet indicates that in 599 the Council of Barcelona decided, "among the two or three candidates that the clergy and the people have chosen by agreement," the bishop might be appointed by lot (*La société ecclésiastique*, pp. 319–20).

[119] Thomas Aquinas, *Summa Theologiae*, IIa IIae, qu. 95, art. 8, I. Again, my thanks to Paul Bullen for drawing this passage to my attention.

with the ecclesiastical authorities. If the medieval Church contributed to the decline in the political use of lot, it was purely in so far as it propagated the principle of consent, not because it prohibited the assignment of "dignities" by lot.

The seventeenth- and eighteenth-century authors familiar with the history of republics realized that the appointment of representatives by election owed more to feudal than to republican tradition. On this point too, Harrington, Montesquieu, and Rousseau were in agreement. Commenting on the use of lot to choose the prerogative century in Rome, Harrington wrote: "But the Gothic prudence, in the policy of the third state [stage of history], runs altogether upon the collection of a representative by the *suffrage* of the people [election]."[120] Harrington, for all his republicanism, preferred election to lot (as we have seen). Thus, election was probably the only principle of "Gothic prudence" to be retained in a scheme wholly oriented towards reviving the principles of "Ancient prudence." Montesquieu's famous phrase about the origins of the English government points in the same direction: "This marvellous system was found in the woods" – the woods of *Germania*, that is, which had also given birth to "Gothic" customs and the feudal system.[121] Finally, it would be wrong to read only invective in the well-known passage of the *Social Contract*: "The idea of representatives is modern: it comes to us from feudal government, from that iniquitous and absurd government in which the human race is degraded and the name of man dishonoured. In the old republics, and even in monarchies, the people never had representatives."[122] The expression, the "name of man," refers, with impressive if implicit historical accuracy, to the feudal oath by which the vassal made himself his lord's "man" by pledging allegiance to him. For Rousseau, it was a

---

[120] Harrington, *The Prerogative of Popular Government*, p. 477 (original emphasis).

[121] Montesquieu, *Spirit of the Laws*, Book XI, ch. 6. A passage in the *Pensées* confirms that Montesquieu saw a close link between the laws of England and the Gothic system: "Regarding what Mr. Yorke told me about a foreigner being unable to understand a single word in Lord Cook and in Littleton, I told him I had observed that, as regards the feudal laws and the ancient laws of England, it would not be very hard for me to understand them, any more than those of all other nations, because since all the laws of Europe are Gothic they all had the same origin and were of the same nature" (Pensée 1645, in *Oeuvres complètes*, 3 vols. (Paris: Nagel, 1950), Vol. II, p. 481).

[122] *Social Contract*, Book III, ch. 15.

dishonor to the human race to associate its name to an act of subordination.

At the time when representative government was established, medieval tradition and modern natural right theories converged to make the consent and will of the governed the sole source of political legitimacy and obligation. In such a situation, election suggested itself as the obvious method for conferring power. At the same time, however, the question of legitimacy very much obscured (or at least relegated to the background) the problem of distributive justice in the allocation of political functions. Henceforth, it no longer mattered whether public offices were distributed equally among citizens. It was much more important that those who held office did so through the consent of the rest. It was the manner in which power was distributed that made the outcome acceptable, whatever it was. To be sure, the concern for distributive justice in the allocation of offices had not entirely disappeared. But election as a method for conferring power was seen as substantially fairer and more egalitarian than the principle that had been in place, namely, that of heredity. Compared to the gap that separated election and heredity, the difference between the distributive effects of the two non-hereditary procedures (lot and election) appeared negligible. Since in other respects the notion of legitimacy gave clear preference to one of the two non-hereditary methods, it is understandable that even the most egalitarian revolutionaries never seriously contemplated introducing lot. The difference between the respective distributive effects of lot and election was something that educated leaders, whether conservative or radical, were certainly aware of. Yet it failed to arouse controversy because conservatives were (secretly or not so secretly) quite happy about it, and radicals were too attached to the principle of consent to defend lot.

Admittedly, external circumstances also helped relegate to the background the problem of distributive justice in the allocation of offices. In the large states of the seventeenth and eighteenth centuries, the sheer ratio between the number of offices to be filled and the size of the citizen body effectively meant that, whatever the method of selection, any given citizen had only a minute chance of attaining those positions. The fact remains, however, that if Aristotle, Guicciardini, or Montesquieu were right, lot would have distributed equally that minute probability, whereas election did so unequally. One can also argue that, this probability being so low, the distribution of offices became a less pressing and politically urgent problem, since the stakes were smaller than in fifth-century Athens or fifteenth-century Florence, even assuming that the value placed on office-holding was the same in each case. It is certainly true that from the standpoint of an individual eighteenth-century citizen, it did not much matter whether his odds were slightly higher or slightly lower than those of his fellow-citizens (since in any case they were quite small). It does not follow, however, that the difference in the distribution of offices achieved by one or the other of the two procedures was inconsequential. It is not, for example, a matter of indifference that a governing assembly contains more lawyers than farmers, even if it is a matter of relative indifference to each individual farmer that a lawyer should have more chance than himself of entering assembly.

Whatever the respective roles that circumstance and belief may have played, when representative government was established, concern for equality in the allocation of offices had been relegated to the background. Here lies the solution to the paradox, noted earlier, of a method known for distributing offices less equally than lot (election) prevailing without debates or qualifications, at the moment political equality among citizens was being declared. By the time representative government arose, the kind of political equality that was at center stage was the equal right to consent to power, and not – or much less so – an equal chance to hold office. This means that a new conception of citizenship had emerged: citizens were now viewed primarily as the source of political legitimacy, rather than as persons who might desire to hold office themselves.

Noting this change opens up a new perspective on the nature of representative government. Two hundred years after modern political representation was established, viewing citizens as the source of power and as the assigners of office appears today as the natural way of envisioning citizenship. Not only do we share the viewpoint that prevailed at the end of the eighteenth century, but we are no longer aware that we are thereby giving precedence to a particular conception of citizenship over another. We have almost completely forgotten that, even under conditions where it is not possible for everyone to participate in government, citizens can also be seen as desirous of reaching office. We do not even think, therefore, of inquiring into how offices, seen as scarce goods, are distributed among citizens by representative institutions. The history of the triumph of election suggests that by doing so we would deepen our comprehension of representative government.

3

The principle of distinction

As we have seen, the founders of representative government were not concerned that elections might result in an inegalitarian distribution of offices; their attention was concentrated on the equal right to consent that this method made possible. Another inegalitarian characteristic of representative government, however, was deliberately introduced after extensive discussion, namely that the representatives be socially superior to those who elect them. Elected representatives, it was firmly believed, should rank higher than most of their constituents in wealth, talent, and virtue. The fraction of the population constituting the electorate varied from country to country at the time representative government was established. For example, in England only the upper strata of the society could vote, whereas in the United States and in revolutionary France the right to vote extended to more popular elements. But whatever the threshold was, measures were taken to ensure that representatives were well above it. What counted was not only the social status of representatives defined in absolute terms, but also (and possibly more importantly) their status relative to that of their electors. Representative government was instituted in full awareness that elected representatives would and should be distinguished citizens, socially different from those who elected them. We shall call this the "principle of distinction."

The non-democratic nature of representative government in its early days is usually seen to lie in the restricted character of the electoral franchise. In post-civil war England the right to vote was indeed reserved to a small fraction of the population. The French

Constituent Assembly also drew a distinction between "active" and "passive" citizens, with only the former being entitled to vote. In America, the Constitution left it to the states to make these decisions: it stipulated that the qualifications for voting in federal elections would be the same as those applying in each state for elections to the lower house. Since in 1787 most states had established a property or tax qualification for the electors, the decision of the Philadelphia Convention entailed in practice a somewhat restricted franchise for federal elections.[1]

The limits on the right of suffrage in early representative government are well known, and the attention of historians has usually been concentrated on the gradual disappearance of those limits during the nineteenth and twentieth centuries. What has been less noticed and studied, however, is that, independent from these restrictions, there existed also a number of provisions, arrangements, and circumstances which ensured that the elected would be of higher social standing than the electorate. This was achieved by different means in England, France, and America. One can generally say that superior social standing was guaranteed in England by a mix of legal provisions, cultural norms, and practical factors, and in France by purely legal provisions. The American case is more complicated, but also, as we shall see, more revealing.

ENGLAND

It is a commonplace to say that in seventeenth- and eighteenth-century Britain membership in the House of Commons was reserved to a small social circle. Since the beginning of the twentieth century, so many studies have documented this fact that it is unnecessary to underline it yet again.[2] The first revolution to some extent opened the political game, in the sense that, during the revolutionary period contested elections occurred more frequently than before. A recent study has shown that prior to the civil war, parliamentary selection was part of a global and integrated pattern of authority. Returning a

---

[1] See J. R. Pole, *Political Representation in England and the Origins of the American Republic* (Berkeley: University of California Press, 1966), p. 365.

[2] For a general view of this field, with bibliographical references, see J. Cannon, *Parliamentary Reform 1640–1832* (Cambridge: Cambridge University Press, 1973).

Member was a way of honoring the "natural leader" of the local community. Elections were seldom contested. It was seen as an affront to the man or to the family of the man who customarily held the seat for another person to compete for that honor. Electoral contests were then feared, and avoided as much as possible. Elections were usually unanimous, and votes rarely counted.[3] The civil war deepened religious and political divisions among the elites, and thus made electoral contests more frequent. Elections then assumed the form of a choice, but one between divided and competing elites. Even during the revolutionary period, the social component of selection, although in retreat, never disappeared.[4] Furthermore, after the years of turmoil, the late seventeenth century even witnessed "a consolidation of gentry and aristocracy." "While the social groups that comprised the electorate expanded," Mark Kishlansky writes, "the social groups that comprised the elected contracted."[5] This was even more true after the mid-eighteenth century, when the number of contested elections markedly decreased.[6]

Two key factors account for this aristocratic or oligarchic nature of representation in England. First, there was a cultural climate in which social standing and prestige were exceptionally influential. Respect for social hierarchy profoundly imbued people's thinking: voters tended to take their cue from the most prominent local figures and considered it a matter of course that these prominent figures alone could be elected to the House of Commons. This distinctive feature of British political culture later came to be termed "deference." The term was coined by Walter Bagehot in the late nineteenth century, but the phenomenon to which it referred had long been typical of English social and political life.[7] The second factor was the exorbitant cost of electoral campaigning, which increased steadily following the civil war and throughout the eighteenth century. Members themselves complained in their private correspondence and in parliamentary debates that elections were

---

[3] See M. Kishlansky, *Parliamentary Selection: Social and Political Choice in Early Modern England* (Cambridge: Cambridge University Press, 1986), esp. chs. 1–4.
[4] *Ibid.*, pp. 122–3.
[5] *Ibid.*, p. 229.   [6] Cannon, *Parliamentary Reform*, pp. 33–40.
[7] On the role of "deference" in nineteenth-century elections, see David C. Moore, *The Politics of Deference. A Study of the Mid-nineteenth Century English Political System* (New York: Barnes & Noble, 1976).

too expensive. Historical studies confirm beyond any doubt that electioneering was a rich man's pursuit. This fact was largely due to peculiarities of the English elections. Polling stations were few, which often required voters to travel great distances. And it was customary for each candidate to transport favorable voters to the polling place and to entertain them during their travel and stay. The combination of deference and electoral expenses thus "spontaneously" restricted access to the House of Commons, despite the absence of explicit legal provisions to that effect.

In 1710, a further factor came into play. A formal property qualification was then established for MPs, that is, a property qualification different from and higher than that of the electors. It was enacted (9 Anne, c.5) that knights of the shire must possess landed property worth £600 per annum, and burgesses £300 per annum.[8] The measure was passed by a Tory ministry, and was intended to favor the "landed interest." But the "moneyed interest" (manufacturers, merchants, and financiers) could still buy land, however, and in fact did so. The Whigs, after their victory in 1715, made no attempt to repeal the Act.[9] Indeed, they had long been thinking themselves of introducing a specific property qualification for the elected. In 1679, Shaftesbury, the Whig leader who played a prominent role during the Exclusion crisis, had introduced a bill to reform elections. The bill contained various provisions which aimed at securing the independence of the Parliament from the Crown. The most famous of these provisions affected the franchise: Shaftesbury proposed that in the shires only householders and inhabitants receiving £200 in fee could vote (instead of the forty-shilling franchise, the value of which had been dramatically eroded since its establishment in 1429). The objective of this provision was to reserve voting rights to men who had enough "substance" to be independent from the Crown, and therefore less susceptible to its corruptive endeavors.[10] But the bill also contained a provision establishing a

---

[8] By "worth" is meant the amount of rent a property was capable of generating, according to assessments by the fiscal authorities.

[9] See Cannon, *Parliamentary Reform*, p. 36; Pole, *Political Representation*, pp. 83, 397. Pole remarks that if the measure was passed and kept, it might have been because the expected "natural" differences between electors and elected were no longer so obvious.

[10] On the bill of 1679, see J. R. Jones, *The First Whigs, The Politics of the Exclusion Crisis 1678–1683* (London: Oxford University Press, 1961), pp. 52–5.

specific property (and age) qualification for the representatives, different from that of the electors. In an unpublished tract (found among his papers after his death), Shaftesbury wrote in defense of his bill:

> As the persons electing ought to be men of substance, so in a *proportioned degree* ought also the Members elected. It is not safe to make over the estates of the people in trust, to men who have none of their own, lest their domestic indigencies, in conjunction with a foreign temptation [the king and the court], should warp them to a contrary interest, which in former Parliaments we have sometimes felt to our sorrow.[11]

Shaftesbury proposed that representatives be chosen only from among the members of the gentry "who are each worth in land and moveables at least £10,000, all debts paid" (and of forty years of age).[12]

Even in England, then, where the franchise was already severely limited, additional restrictions applied to elected representatives. Whigs and Tories agreed, albeit for different reasons, that the elected should occupy a higher social rank than the electors.

FRANCE

In France, the Constituent Assembly established early on a markedly wider franchise. By today's standards, of course, it appears restricted. To qualify as an "active citizen" one had to pay the equivalent of three days' wages in direct taxes. In addition, women, servants, the very poor, those with no fixed abode, and monks had no vote, on the grounds that their position made them too dependent on others for them to have a political will of their own. The exclusion of these "passive citizens" from the franchise attracted a

---

[11] Antony Ashley Cooper, First Earl of Shaftesbury, "Some observations concerning the regulating of elections for Parliament" (probably 1679), in J. Somers (ed.), *A Collection of Scarce and Valuable Tracts*, 1748, First coll., Vol. I, p. 69. My emphasis.

[12] Shaftesbury, "Some observations concerning the regulating of elections for Parliament," p. 71. The sum of £10,000 seems enormous and almost implausible. This is, however, what I found in the copy of the 1748 edition which I have seen, but it could be a misprint (£1,000 would appear more plausible). I have been unable as yet to further check this point. In any case, the exact amount is not crucial to my argument. The essential point is that Shaftesbury proposes a higher property qualification for the elected than for the electors, on which the author is perfectly clear.

great deal of attention from nineteenth- and early twentieth-century historians. It was certainly not without importance, for it implied that in the eyes of the Constituents, political rights could legitimately be dissociated from civil rights, with the latter only being enjoyed indistinctly by all citizens. Recent studies show, however, that the franchise established by the Constituent Assembly was actually quite large given the culture of the time (which regarded women as part of a marriage unit), and in comparison with contemporary practice elsewhere (notably in England), or later practice in France under the restored monarchy (1815–48). It has been calculated that the French electorate under the qualifications set in 1789 numbered approximately 4.4 million.[13] The decrees of August 1792 establishing "universal" suffrage certainly enlarged the electorate, but this was primarily the result of lowering the voting age from 25 to 21. (Women, servants, and those with no permanent place of residence remained excluded.)[14] Although the proclamation of universal manhood suffrage was perceived as historic, the actual change was limited. After 1794, the Thermidorians, without reviving the politically unfortunate terms "active" and "passive" citizens, returned to an electoral system not unlike that of 1789, while still making the right to vote conditional on the ability to read and write. (The argument being that secret voting required the ability to cast written ballots.) The electorate following Thermidor was still large, probably numbering 5.5 million citizens.[15]

In France, then, the debate over how popular representative government should be did not center on who could vote. Rather, it centered on who could be voted for. In 1789 the Constituent Assembly decreed that only those who could meet the two conditions of owning land and paying taxes of at least one *marc d'argent* (the equivalent of 500 days' wages) could be elected to the National Assembly. It was this *marc d'argent* decree that constituted the focus of controversy and opposition. Whereas the three days' labor tax qualification for the electors disfranchised only a relatively small number of citizens, the *marc d'argent* qualification for deputies seems

---

[13] P. Guéniffey, *Le Nombre et la Raison. La révolution française et les élections* (Paris: Editions de l'Ecole des Hautes Etudes en Sciences Sociales, 1933), pp. 44–5. This figure represented something like 15.7 percent of the total population and 61.5 per cent of the population of adult males (Guéniffey, *Le Nombre et la Raison*, pp. 96–7).

[14] *Ibid.*, p. 70.   [15] *Ibid.*, p. 289.

to have been very restrictive (although there is some uncertainty about where the line of exclusion actually lay).[16] One could say, to use non-contemporary but convenient terminology, that the members of the Constituent Assembly considered the vote a "right," but the holding of office a "function." Since a function was said to be performed on behalf of society, society was entitled to keep it out of unqualified hands. The goal was to reserve the position of representatives for members of the propertied classes, and the Constituent Assembly chose to achieve it by explicit legal means.

The decree provoked immediate objections. Some Constituents argued that the quality of representative should be determined only by the votes and the trust of the people. "Put trust in the place of the *marc d'argent*," one deputy (Prieur) declared;[17] and Siéyès, normally an opponent of democracy, concurred. But such voices were ignored. In 1791, faced with the threat of a radicalization of the revolution and a rising tide of opposition, the Assembly was finally forced to abandon the *marc d'argent* rule. The arrangement that took its place was designed to achieve the same objective by different means. In 1789, the Constituent Assembly had established a system of indirect election that was explicitly conceived of as a mechanism of filtration, which would secure the selection of eminent citizens. It had been decided that voters should gather in "primary assemblies" (*assemblées primaires*) at the *canton* level, and there choose electors (one for every 100 active citizens) for the second stage; these would then meet at the *département* level to elect the deputies.[18] In 1789, the Constituent Assembly had also laid down an intermediate qualification for second-stage electors, namely payment of a tax equivalent of ten days' labor. In 1791, the Assembly dropped the *marc d'argent* rule and the property qualification for representatives, but it retained the system of indirect election and raised the intermediate tax qualification. It was then resolved that only those paying the

---

[16] Guéniffey estimates that only around 1 percent of the population met that condition (*Le Nombre et la Raison,* p. 100).

[17] Quoted in *ibid.,* p. 59.

[18] Note that the small size of *cantons* (64 sq km) and their large number (4,660) were explicitly designed to limit the distance voters needed to travel to reach their polling place (in the main town of the canton); see Guéniffey, *Le Nombre et la Raison,* p. 276. England probably constituted the countermodel here.

equivalent of forty days' wages could be elected as second-stage electors,[19] a fairly high threshold.[20] Some people denounced "a hidden transfer of the *marc d'argent.*"[21] The measure indeed amounted to shifting the barrier of entry from one step of the electoral hierarchy to another. The tacit assumption was that propertied second-stage electors would usually elect representatives from among their ranks, while it could be retorted to the popular movement that these electors were free to select meritorious persons regardless of class. The new regulation did in fact succeed in significantly reducing the number of persons eligible at the second stage (if not in "bringing the revolution to an end," as its promoters hoped). In 1792, any kind of property or tax qualification was abolished, but the principle of indirect election was retained.[22] The Thermidorians went back to the 1791 system: no property or tax qualification for deputies, but a restrictive one for second-stage electors.

Nevertheless, statistical studies confirm that throughout the course of the revolution, including in 1792, second-stage electoral assemblies were dominated by the wealthy classes.[23] This was reflected in the composition of the national representative assembly. The Convention itself was "an assembly of lawyers (52 percent of members) elected by peasants."[24]

The socially selective effect of elections was undoubtedly much less marked than in England, but it was present all the same. In France too, the founders of representative government aimed to establish a system in which the elected would generally be wealthier and more prominent than those who elected them. But whereas in England this result was partly achieved through the silent operation of social norms and economic constraints, in France a similar outcome was achieved by wholly explicit institutional arrangements: the tax qualification for second-stage electors and the principle of indirect election. The system of indirect election, which was

[19] P. Guéniffey, *Le Nombre et la Raison*, p. 61.
[20] On the statistical effects of the forty days' labor wage qualification, see *Ibid.*, pp. 101–2.
[21] The expression was used by Brissot in his journal, *Le Patriote Français*. See Guéniffey, *Le Nombre et la Raison*, p. 61.
[22] *Ibid.*, p. 70.
[23] *Ibid.*, pp. 411–13.   [24] *Ibid.*, p. 414.

seen as a "filtration of democracy," [25] deserves particular mention because it was retained throughout the revolution.

THE UNITED STATES

Philadelphia

In regard to the franchise, the Philadelphia Convention took a position similar to that of the French in opting for the most open of the solutions considered. The clause of the Constitution alluded to earlier stipulating that "the electors in each state shall have the qualifications requisite for electors of the most numerous Branch of the State Legislature" (Art. I, Sec. 2, cl. 1), applied only to elections to the House of Representatives. For under the draft Constitution of 1787, senators were to be chosen by the legislatures of the different states (Art. I, Sec. 3, cl. 1) and the President was to be chosen by an "electoral college" appointed by the state legislatures (Art. II, Sec. 1, cl. 2). The Presidency and the Senate thus did not require any further decisions concerning the franchise. The most significant debates regarding elections and how they affected the nature of representation focused on elections to the lower chamber. It should also be borne in mind that state franchise qualifications were set by the different state *constitutions*. The federal clause therefore did not amount to leaving regulation of the franchise to the individual state legislatures.

The members of the Philadelphia Convention were fully aware that in some states there were significant franchise restrictions, which meant, in turn, restrictions in the election of federal representatives. However, the decision that the Convention eventually reached needs to be placed in context: it was in fact the most open or, as James Wilson said in the Pennsylvania ratification debate, the most "generous" of the options discussed in Philadelphia. For there was also among the delegates a current in favor of a federal *property* qualification for congressional electors, which would have narrowed the franchise in some states (such as Pennsylvania), where only a

---

[25] Guéniffey, *Le Nombre et la Raison*, p. 41.

low *tax* qualification was in force for state elections.[26] Gouverneur Morris, for example, asked for a property qualification that would have restricted electoral rights to freeholders. His argument was that propertyless people would be particularly susceptible to corruption by the wealthy and would become instruments in their hands. He presented his motion as a guard against "aristocracy,"[27] and on this point, he won the support of Madison. "Viewing the matter on its merits alone," Madison argued, "the freeholders of the Country would be the safest depositories of Republican liberty." As a matter of principle, then, Madison favored the introduction of a freehold qualification. But at the same time he feared popular opposition to such a measure. "Whether the Constitutional qualification ought to be a freehold, would with him depend much on the probable reception such a change would meet with in States where the right was now exercised by every description of people."[28] Madison's speech reveals a certain hesitation and, on the basis of the *Records*, it seems that in the end he advocated a property qualification, but not in the form of landed property. In any case, neither Morris nor Madison carried the day, and the general tenor of the speeches pronounced on that occasion shows that a majority of delegates opposed any restrictions other than those applied by the states. The principal argument seems to have been that the people were strongly attached to the right of suffrage and would not

---

[26] The radical Pennsylvania constitution of 1776 had abolished the former property qualification for state elections and extended the right of suffrage to all tax-paying adult freemen who had resided one year in their constituencies, which amounted to a large franchise (small tradesmen, independent artisans, and mechanics could vote). In Virginia, by contrast, the right of suffrage was reserved to freeholders, which of course excluded independent artisans and mechanics. The constitution of Massachusetts, to mention another example, had set up a whole hierarchy of property qualifications, but its actual effect was a fairly large franchise (two out of three, or three out of four adult males were enfranchised). See on this, Pole, *Political Representation*, pp. 272, 295, 206.

[27] *The Records of the Federal Convention of 1787*, ed. M. Farrand [1911], 4 vols. (New Haven, CT: Yale University Press, 1966), Vol. II, pp. 202–3. In what follows, references to the Farrand edition will be given as: *Records*, followed by volume and page numbers.

[28] *Records*, Vol. II, pp. 203–4. It should be noted that, when Madison prepared his notes on the Federal Convention for publication (probably in 1821), he revised the speech on the franchise that he had delivered in Philadelphia on August 7, 1787, explaining that his viewpoint had since changed. The foregoing quotations are taken from the original speech. The revised version of 1821, generally known by the title "Notes on the right of suffrage," is an extremely important document to which we shall be returning.

"readily subscribe to the national constitution, if it should subject them to be disfranchised."[29] But no one in Philadelphia proposed that the federal franchise be *wider* than those of the individual states. Clearly, then, the Convention opted for the widest version of the electoral franchise under consideration at the time.

Turning now to the qualifications for representatives, which are more important for our purposes, we find the following clause in the Constitution: "No Person shall be a Representative who shall not have attained the Age of twenty-five Years, and been seven Years a Citizen of the United States, and who shall not, when elected, be an Inhabitant of that State in which he shall be chosen" (Art. I, Sec. 2, cl. 2). These requirements are obviously not very stringent and contain no trace of what I have called the principle of distinction. A more egalitarian culture and a more homogeneous population on this side of the ocean perhaps gave representative government a different character from the one in the Old World, marked as it was by centuries of hierarchical organization. However, a close reading of the *Records* shows that behind the closed doors of the Convention the debates on the qualifications for representatives were actually very complex.

On July 26, 1787, George Mason proposed a motion asking that the Committee of Detail (the body that prepared the work of plenary sessions) be instructed to devise a clause "requiring certain qualifications of landed property and citizenship in members of the legislature and disqualifying persons having unsettled accounts with or being indebted to the US."[30] During the debate, Mason cited the example we discussed earlier (see p. 97) of the parliamentary qualifications adopted in England in the reign of Queen Anne, "which [he said] had met with universal approbation."[31] Morris replied that he preferred qualifications for the right of suffrage. Madison suggested deleting the word "landed" from Mason's motion, pointing out that "landed possessions were no certain evidence of real wealth" and further arguing that commercial and manufacturing interests should also have an "opportunity of making their rights be felt and understood in the public Councils";

---

[29] The formulation is Oliver Ellsworth's (*Records*, Vol. II, p. 201), but it sums up the general tone of a number of speeches.
[30] *Records*, Vol. II, p. 121.   [31] *Records*, Vol. II, p. 122.

landed property should not be granted any special treatment.[32] Madison's motion was adopted by an overwhelming majority of ten to one.[33] The Committee of Detail was therefore asked to draft a clause laying down an unspecified property qualification for representatives.

Discussion within the Convention thus focused purely on the *type* of property that ought to be required for representatives. This hesitation aside, all the delegates apparently agreed that a property qualification of one sort or another was proper. Whereas the Convention had opted for the most liberal course regarding the electors, it clearly leaned in the opposite direction with respect to the elected. Two main arguments were advanced. First, it seemed of the greatest importance to guarantee that representatives had sufficient economic independence to be immune to all corruptive influences, especially that of the executive branch. The weight of this concern (to protect the independence of the legislature in relation to the executive) is also reflected in the clause forbidding senators and representatives from holding federal office during their term (Art. 1, Sec. 6, cl. 2). This latter clause was obviously devised to guard against a "place system" along English lines, which was so odious to eighteenth-century republicans. More generally, the idea that economic independence offered one of the best guarantees against corruption was a central tenet of republican thought, and hence the views of the Philadelphia delegates were in keeping with a wider trend of thought.[34] In the second place, a property qualification for representatives appeared justified since the right of property was seen by all delegates as one of the most important rights, and its protection a principal object of government. It therefore seemed necessary to take specific precautions to ensure that representatives would particularly take to heart the rights and interests of property. In any case, whether property was regarded as a bulwark of republican freedom or as a fundamental right, the federal Convention felt that representatives should be property owners, and consequently of higher social rank than those who elected them, since no such qualification was

---

[32] *Records*, Vol. II, pp. 123–4.

[33] In the *Records*, votes are counted by states. Ten "Ayes" and one "No" mean that ten delegations voted in favor and one against.

[34] See J. G. A. Pocock, *The Machiavellian Moment*, (Princeton, NJ: Princeton University Press, 1975), *passim*.

required for the right of suffrage. Thus it appears that the principle of distinction was present in Philadelphia too. The question is: why was it not translated into a constitutional provision?

Let us return to the debates to seek an answer. A few weeks later, the Committee of Detail submitted the following clause to the plenary assembly: "The Legislature of the United States shall have authority to establish such uniform qualifications of the members of each House, with regard to property, as to the said Legislature shall seem expedient."[35] The Committee (as explained by two of its members, Rutledge and Ellsworth) had been unable to agree on any precise property requirement, and had decided consequently to leave the matter for future legislatures to settle. Two obstacles prevented the Committee from reaching agreement. First, as Rutledge stated, the members of the Committee had been "embarrassed by the danger on one side of displeasing the people by making them [the qualifications] high, and on the other of rendering them nugatory by making them low." Second, according to Ellsworth, "the different circumstances of different parts of the US and the probable difference between the present and future circumstances of the whole, render it improper to have either *uniform* or *fixed* qualifications. Make them so high as to be useful in the Southern States, and they will be inapplicable to the Eastern States. Suit them to the latter, and they will serve no purpose in the former."[36] The proposed clause may have solved the internal problems of the Committee of Detail, but in plenary session it encountered a major objection: leaving the matter to legislative discretion was extremely dangerous, since the very nature of the political system could be radically altered by simple manipulation of those conditions.[37] Wilson, albeit a member of the Committee, also pointed out that "a *uniform* rule would probably be never fixed by the legislature," and consequently moved "to let the session go out."[38] The vote was taken immediately after Wilson's

[35] *Records*, Vol. II, Report of the Committee of Detail, p. 165. The Committee of Detail consisted of Gorham, Ellsworth, Wilson, Randolph, and Rutledge: see J. H. Hutson, *Supplement to Max Farrand's The Records of the Federal Convention of 1787* (New Haven, CT: Yale University Press, 1987), pp. 195–6.

[36] *Records*, Vol. II, p. 249; original emphasis.

[37] The objection was advanced by Madison, *Records*, Vol. II, pp. 249–50.

[38] *Records*, Vol. II, p. 251; my emphasis.

intervention, and the Committee's proposal was rejected by seven to three. The Constitution would include no property qualification for representatives.

This episode shows that the absence of property qualifications in the 1787 constitution was not due to reasons of principle, but of expediency. The delegates did favor the principle of a property qualification, but they simply could not agree on any uniform threshold that would yield the desired result in both the northern and southern states, in both the undeveloped agrarian states of the west and in the wealthier mercantile states of the east. Thus the absence of any property requirements for representatives in the Constitution, which strikingly departs from the English and French pattern, must be seen as a largely unintentional result. Admittedly, when casting their last vote, the delegates were, in all likelihood, conscious that they were abandoning the very principle of property qualifications, and thus the result was not strictly speaking unintentional. It is clear, nevertheless, that the delegates had been led by external circumstances to make a final vote that was different from (and indeed contrary to) their initial and explicit intention. Furthermore, there is no evidence that they had changed their minds on the point of principle in the meantime. One is tempted to say that the exceptionally egalitarian character of representation in the United States owes more to geography than to philosophy.

The members of the Philadelphia Convention made two further decisions regarding elections. The House of Representatives was to be elected every two years, a term short enough to secure proper dependence on their electors. Paramount was the fear of long parliaments which, on the basis of the English experience, were seen as the hallmark of tyranny. Some delegates argued for annual elections, but by and large the agreement on a two-year term was reached without much difficulty. The Convention also resolved that: "The number of Representatives shall not exceed one for every thirty thousand [inhabitants], but each State shall have at least one Representative" (Art. I, Sec. 2, cl. 3). It was decided that the House would comprise sixty-five members until the first census was taken. The ratio between electors and elected was set with a view to keeping the size of the House within manageable limits, even when the expected (and hoped for) increase in the population would occur. A vast majority of the delegates were determined to avoid the "confusion" of large assemblies. The Committee of Detail had initially proposed a ratio of one representative for every 40,000 eligible voters.[39] Some delegates, most notably Mason, Gerry, and Randolph, objected to the small size of the representative assembly.[40] But on the whole it seems that this question did not provoke a major debate in the Convention, as Gerry himself was to admit in his correspondence.[41] The delegates were apparently more concerned with the relative weights of the individual states in future federal legislatures than with the ratio between electors and elected.[42]

The ratification debate

Whereas the question of the size of the House of Representatives did not give rise to significant arguments at the Philadelphia Convention, it turned out to be a major point of contention in the ratification debates. Indeed, as Kurland and Lerner note, in the matter of representation, "eclipsing all [other] controversies and concerns was the issue of an adequate representation as expressed in the size of the proposed House of Representatives."[43] The question of the size of the representative assembly (which in some ways was a technical problem of the optimal number for proper deliberation) assumed

---

[39] *Records*, Vol. I, p. 526.

[40] *Records*, Vol. I, p. 569 (Mason and Gerry); Vol. II, p. 563 (Randolph).

[41] Elbridge Gerry to the Vice President of the Convention of Massachusetts (January 21, 1788), in *Records*, Vol. III, p. 265.

[42] I entirely leave out here the debate on the *basis* for representation and the question of the apportionment of seats, although both figured prominently in the debates of the Convention. The debate about the basis for representation had far-reaching implications, for it entailed a decision on *what* was to be represented. The major question in this respect was: should the apportionment of seats (and hence representation) be based on *property* or *persons*? As J. R. Pole has shown in detail, the final decision to base the apportionment of seats primarily on numbers (even allowing for the "federal ratio" according to which a slave, considered a form of property, was to be counted as three-fifths of a person) "gave a possibly unintentional but nevertheless unmistakable impetus to the idea of political democracy" (*Political Representation*, p. 365). Those who advocated a specific or separate representation of property were thus ultimately defeated. This aspect of the debate, however, has been studied by Pole with all desirable clarity and persuasiveness. His conclusions are presupposed in the present chapter.

[43] P. B. Kurland and R. Lerner (eds.), *The Founders' Constitution*, 5 vols. (Chicago: University of Chicago Press, 1987), Vol. I, p. 386, "Introductory note."

enormous political importance; it involved the relationship between representatives and represented, that is, the very core of the notion of representation. The argument revolved almost exclusively around the consequences of the ratio between elected and electors. Neither the extension of the franchise nor the legal qualifications for representatives was in question, since the Anti-Federalists (those who rejected the plan prepared in Philadelphia) had no objection to the former, and the Constitution did not contain any of the latter. Another point deserves to be stressed: the debate opposed two conceptions of representation. The Anti-Federalists accepted the need for representation: they were not "democrats" in the eighteenth-century sense of the term, as they did not advocate direct government by the assembled people. This has rightly been emphasized in a recent essay by Terence Ball.[44]

The principal objection that the Anti-Federalists raised against the Constitution was that the proposed ratio between elected and electors was too small to allow the proper *likeness*. The concepts of "likeness," "resemblance," "closeness," and the idea that representation should be a "true picture" of the people constantly keep recurring in the writings and speeches of the Anti-Federalists.[45]

Terence Ball's analysis of the two conceptions of representation that were in conflict in the ratification debates is not entirely satisfactory. Using categories developed by Hanna Pitkin, Ball characterizes the Anti-Federalist view of representation as the "mandate theory," according to which the task of the representative is "to mirror the views of those whom he represents" and "to share their attitudes and feelings." By contrast, Ball claims, the Federalists saw representation as the "independent" activity of "a trustee who must make his own judgements concerning his constituents' interests and how they might best be served."[46] Clearly, the Anti-Federalists thought that representatives ought to share the circum-

---

[44] T. Ball, "A Republic – If you can keep it," in T. Ball and J. Pocock (eds.), *Conceptual Change and the Constitution* (Lawrence: University Press of Kansas, 1987), pp. 144 ff.

[45] On the importance of this notion of "likeness" among the Anti-Federalists, see H. J. Storing (ed.), *The Complete Anti-Federalist*, 7 vols. (Chicago: University of Chicago Press, 1981), Vol. I, *What the Anti-Federalists were for?*, p. 17.

[46] Ball, "A Republic – If you can keep it," p. 145. The work to which Ball refers is H. Pitkin, *The Concept of Representation* (Berkeley: University of California Press, 1967).

stances, attitudes, and feelings of those whom they represented. It is also true that this concern was virtually absent from Federalist thinking. However, the focus of the debate was not exactly, as is implied by the contrast between "independence" and "mandate," the freedom of action of the representatives with regard to the wishes of their constituents. The charge that the Anti-Federalists repeatedly leveled was not that under the proposed Constitution representatives would fail to act as instructed, but that they would not be *like* those who elected them. The two questions are obviously not unrelated, but they are not the same. The ratification debate did not turn on the problem of mandates and instructions, but on the issue of similarity between electors and elected.

Brutus, for example, wrote:

> The very term representative, implies, that the person or body chosen for this purpose, should *resemble* those who appoint them – a representation of the people of America, if it be a true one, must be *like* the people ... They are the sign – the people are the thing signified ... It must then have been intended that those who are placed instead of the people, should possess their sentiments and feelings, and be governed by their interests, or in other words, should bear the strongest *resemblance* of those in whose room they are substituted. It is obvious that for an assembly to be a true *likeness* of the people of any country, they must be considerably numerous.[47]

For his part, Melancton Smith, Hamilton's chief adversary at the New York ratification convention, declared in a speech on the proposed House of Representatives: "The idea that naturally suggests itself to our minds, when we speak of representatives, is that they *resemble* those they represent; they should be a *true picture* of the people: possess the knowledge of their circumstances and their wants; sympathize in all their distresses, and be disposed to seek their true interests."[48] The tireless insistence on the need for identity or resemblance between electors and elected is among the most striking features of Anti-Federalist pamphlets and

---

[47] Brutus, Essay III, in Storing (ed.), *The Complete Anti-Federalist*, Vol. II, 9, 42; my emphasis. Hereafter references to Anti-Federalist writings and speeches will be given as: *Storing*, followed by the three numbers employed by the editor, the roman numeral denoting the volume.

[48] Melancton Smith, "Speech at the New York ratification convention" (June 20, 1788), *Storing*, VI, 12, 15.

speeches.[49] Certainly the Anti-Federalists did not form an intellectually homogeneous current. However, although some were conservative, others radical, they were virtually unanimous in their demand that representatives resemble those they represented.

The idea that political representation should be conceived as a reflection or picture, the main virtue of which should be resemblance to the original, had found in the first years of independence one of its most influential expressions in John Adams's *Thoughts on Government*. And although Adams did not participate in the constitutional debate of 1787, his influence on Anti-Federalist thinking can hardly be doubted. "The principal difficulty lies," Adams had written in 1776, "and the greatest care should be employed in constituting this representative assembly. [In the preceding passage, Adams had shown the need for representation in large states.] It should be in miniature an exact portrait of the people at large. It should think, feel, reason and act like them."[50] To use Hanna Pitkin's categories, one could say that the Anti-Federalists were defending a "descriptive" conception of representation. In such a view, the aim is for the assembly, as the people in miniature, to act as the people themselves would have acted, had they been assembled. In this sense, the objectives of the "descriptive" view and of the "mandate" theory of representation are the same. However, in the latter case, identity between the will of the representatives and the will of the people is secured through formal legal provisions (instructions or imperative mandates); while the "descriptive" conception supposes that the representatives will *spontaneously* do as the people would have done since they are a reflection of the people, share the circumstances of their constituents, and are close to them in both the metaphorical and spatial senses of the term.

When Anti-Federalists spoke of "likeness" or "closeness," they meant it primarily in a social sense. Opponents of the Constitution claimed that several classes of the population would not be properly represented, because none of their number would sit in the assembly. Samuel Chase wrote:

[49] See The Federal Farmer, Letter II, *Storing*, II, 8, 15; Minority of the Convention of Pennsylvania, *Storing*, III, 11, 35; Samuel Chase, Fragment 5, *Storing*, V, 3, 20; Impartial Examiner, III, *Storing*, V, 14, 28–30.

[50] J. Adams, *Thoughts on Government* [1776], in C. F. Adams (ed.), *The Life and Works of John Adams*, 10 vols. (Boston: Little Brown, 1850–6), Vol. IV, p. 195.

It is impossible for a few men to be acquainted with the sentiments and interests of the US, which contains many different classes or orders of people – merchants, farmers, planters, mechanics and gentry or wealthy men. To form a proper and true representation each order ought to have an opportunity of choosing from each a person as their representative ... Only but ... few of the merchants and those only of the opulent and ambitious will stand any chance. The great body of planters and farmers cannot expect any of their order – the station is too elevated for them to aspire to – the distance between the people and their representatives will be so great that there is no probability of a farmer or planter being chosen. Mechanics of every branch will be excluded by a general voice from a seat – only the gentry, the rich, the well born will be elected.[51]

Given the diversity of the population of America, only a large assembly could have met the requirements of an "adequate" representation. In a truly representative assembly, Brutus noted, "the farmer, merchant, mechanick and other various orders of people, ought to be represented according to their respective weight and numbers; and the representatives ought to be intimately acquainted with the wants, understand the interests of the several orders in the society, and feel a proper sense and becoming zeal to promote their prosperity."[52] The Anti-Federalists did not demand, however, that all classes without exception have members sitting in the assembly. They wished only that the main components of society be represented, with a special emphasis on the middling ranks (freeholders, independent artisans, and small tradesmen).

They had no doubt, however, that representation as provided for in the Constitution would be skewed in favor of the most prosperous and prominent classes. This was one of the reasons why they denounced the "aristocratic" tendency of the Constitution (another focus of their fear of "aristocracy" being the substantial powers granted to the Senate). When the Anti-Federalists spoke of "aristocracy," they did not mean, of course, hereditary nobility. Nobody ever questioned that America would and should be without a nobility, and the Constitution explicitly prohibited the granting of titles of nobility (Art. I, Sec. 9, cl. 9). What the Anti-Federalists envisioned was not legally defined privilege, but the social super-

---

[51] Samuel Chase, Fragment 5, *Storing*, V, 3, 20.
[52] Brutus, Essay III, *Storing*, II, 9, 42.

iority conferred by wealth, status, or even talent. Those enjoying these various superiorities composed what they called "the natural aristocracy" – "natural" here being opposed to legal or institutional. As Melancton Smith put it in the New York ratification debate:

> I am convinced that this government is so constituted, that the representatives will generally be composed of the first class of the community, which I shall distinguish by the name of natural aristocracy of the country ... I shall be asked what is meant by the natural aristocracy – and told that no such distinction of classes of men exists among us. It is true that it is our singular felicity that we have no legal or hereditary distinction of this kind; but still there are real differences. Every society naturally divides itself into classes. The author of nature has bestowed on some greater capacities than on others – birth, education, *talents* and wealth create distinctions among men as visible and of as much influence as titles, stars and garters. In every society, men of this class will command a superior degree of respect – and if the government is so constituted as to admit but a few to exercise the powers of it, it will, *according to the natural course of things*, be in their hands.[53]

For his part, Brutus noted:

> *According to the common course of human affairs*, the natural aristocracy of the country will be elected. Wealth always creates influence, and this is generally much increased by large family connections ... It is probable that but few of the merchants, and those of the most opulent and ambitious, will have a representation of their body – few of them are characters sufficiently conspicuous to attract the notice of electors of the state in so limited a representation.[54]

As the Pennsylvania Minority stressed: "Men of the most elevated rank in life, will alone be chosen."[55] The Anti-Federalists were not radical egalitarians, denouncing the existence of social, economic, or personal inequalities. In their view, such inequalities formed part of the natural order of things. Nor did they object to the natural

---

[53] Melancton Smith, speech of June 20, 1788, *Storing*, VI, 12, 16; my emphasis. It is noteworthy that Smith places talents, birth, and wealth on the same footing. This is not the place to embark on the philosophical debates that such categorization might raise, but it is worth highlighting.

[54] Brutus, Essay III, *Storing*, II, 9, 42; my emphasis. On the notion that only the "natural aristocracy" would be elected, see also The Federal Farmer, Letter IX, *Storing*, II, 8, 113.

[55] The Address and Reasons of Dissent of the Minority of the Convention of Pennsylvania to Their Constituents, *Storing*, III, 11, 35.

aristocracy playing a specific political role. But they did not want it to monopolize power.

The Anti-Federalists did not develop a detailed explanation, let alone a clear and simple one, that could be successfully used in public debate, regarding why only the rich and the prominent would be elected. Their ideas had rather the form of profound but incompletely articulated intuitions. The larger the electoral districts, they claimed, the greater the influence of wealth would be. In small settings, common people could be elected, but in large ones a successful candidate would have to be particularly conspicuous and prominent. Neither proposition was self-evident, but the opponents of the Constitution were unable to explain them any further. This lack of articulation explains in part the weakness of their case when confronted with the clear and compelling logic of the Federalists. The Anti-Federalists were fully aware of the argumentative strength of their adversaries' case. And in the end they fell back on the simple but rather short assertion that the Federalists were deceiving the people. In a statement that captures both the core of the Anti-Federalist position and its argumentative weakness, the Federal Farmer wrote:

> the people may be electors, if the representation be so formed as to give one or more of the natural classes of men in the society an undue ascendancy over the others, it is imperfect; the former will gradually become masters, and the latter slaves ... It is deceiving the people to tell them they are electors, and can choose their legislators, if they cannot *in the nature of things*, choose men among themselves, and genuinely *like themselves*.[56]

The accusatory tone and rhetorical exaggeration could not mask the lack of substantial argument. The Anti-Federalists were deeply convinced that representatives would not be like their electors, but they were unable to explain in simple terms the enigmatic "nature of things" or "common course of human affairs" that would lead to this result.

Such a position lay entirely vulnerable to Madison's lightning retort. We are told, Madison declared in an equally rhetorical passage, that the House of Representatives will constitute an oligarchy, but:

[56] The Federal Farmer, Letter VII, *Storing,* II, 8, 97; my emphasis.

114

Who are to be the electors of the federal representatives? Not the rich, more than the poor; not the learned, more than the ignorant; not the haughty heirs of distinguished names, more than the humble sons of obscure and unpropitious fortune. The electors are to be the great body of the people of the United States ... Who are to be the objects of popular choice? Every citizen whose merit may recommend him to the esteem and confidence of his country. No qualification of wealth, of birth, or religious faith, or of civil profession is permitted to fetter the judgement or disappoint the inclination of the people.[57]

The Anti-Federalists had no objections to the federal franchise, and they admitted that there were no property or tax qualifications for representatives in the Constitution. Thus, they had no effective counterargument.

After this first defense, the gist of Madison's argument in "Federalist 57" states that the Constitution provides every guarantee that representatives will not betray the trust of the people. Because representatives will have been "distinguished by the preference of their fellow citizens," Madison argues, there are good reasons to believe that they will actually have the qualities for which they were chosen and that they will live up to expectations. Moreover, they will know that they owe their elevation to public office to the people; this cannot "fail to produce a temporary affection at least to their constituents." Owing their honor and distinction to the favor of the people, they will be unlikely to subvert the popular character of a system that is the basis of their power. More importantly, frequent elections will constantly remind them of their dependence on the electorate. Finally, the laws they pass will apply as much to themselves and their friends as to the society at large.[58]

Given all these guarantees, Madison turns the tables on the Anti-

---

[57] Madison, "Federalist 57," in A. Hamilton, J. Madison, and J. Jay, *The Federalist Papers* [1787–8], ed. C. Rossiter (New York: Penguin, 1961), p. 351. On the qualifications for election as a representative, see also "Federalist 52." There Madison recalls the three qualifications laid down in the Constitution (twenty-five years of age, seven year citizenship in the US, and residence in the state where the candidate runs for Congress) before adding: "Under these reasonable limitations, the door of this part of the federal government is open to merit of every description, whether native or adoptive, whether young or old, and without regard to poverty or wealth, or to any particular profession of religious faith" (p. 326). Hereafter references to *The Federalist Papers* will indicate only the essay number and the page in the Rossiter edition.

[58] Madison, "Federalist 57," pp. 351–2.

Federalists and indirectly casts suspicion on their attachment to republican or popular government by asking:

> What are we to say to the men who profess the most flaming zeal for republican government, yet boldly impeach the fundamental principle of it [the right of the people to elect those who govern them]; who pretend to be champions for the right and capacity of the people to choose their own rulers, yet maintain that they will prefer those only who will immediately and infallibly betray the trust committed to them?[59]

Madison implies that these professed republicans in fact harbor doubts about the right of the people to choose for rulers whom they please and their ability to judge candidates. Although Madison stresses to great effect the popular or republican dimension of representation under the proposed scheme, nowhere in his argumentation does he claim that the Constitution will secure likeness or closeness between representatives and represented. He too knows that it will not.

Madison develops instead an altogether different conception of what republican representation could and should be:

> The aim of every political constitution is, or ought to be, first to obtain for rulers men who possess most wisdom to discern, and most virtue to pursue, the common good of the society; and in the next place, to take the most effectual precautions for keeping them virtuous whilst they continue to hold their public trust. The elective mode of obtaining rulers is the characteristic policy of republican government. The means relied on in this form of government for preventing their degeneracy are numerous and various. The most effectual one is such a limitation of the term of appointment as will maintain a proper responsibility to the people.[60]

In this characterization of republican government, it is worth noting, there is not the slightest mention of any likeness between representatives and represented. Indeed, representatives should be different from their constituents, for republican government requires as any other that power be entrusted to those who possess "most wisdom" and "most virtue," that is, to persons who are superior to, and different from, their fellow citizens. This is one of the clearest formulations of the principle of distinction in Federalist thinking,

---

[59] Madison, "Federalist 57," p. 353. [60] Madison, "Federalist 57," pp. 350–1.

but Madison expresses the same idea on numerous occasions. In the famous passage of "Federalist 10," in which Madison sets out his conception of the differences between a democracy and a republic, he notes first that the defining characteristic of a republic is "the delegation of the government ... to a small number of citizens elected by the rest ... The effect of [which] is, on the one hand, to refine and enlarge the public views by passing them through the medium of a *chosen body of citizens,* whose wisdom may best discern the true interest of their country and whose patriotism and love of justice will be least likely to sacrifice it to temporary or partial considerations."[61] What distinguishes a republic from a democracy, then, is not merely the existence of a body of representatives, but also the fact that those representatives form a "chosen body." Like Guicciardini before him, Madison is clearly playing on two senses of the term "chosen": the representatives are chosen, in the literal sense, since they are elected, but they also constitute the "chosen Few." Thus the complete characterization of the republican mode of designating rulers is that it leaves it to the people to select through election the wisest and most virtuous.

Madison's republicanism, however, is not content with providing for the selection of the wisest and most virtuous; there is no blind faith in wise and virtuous elites. Representatives should be kept on the virtuous path by a system of constraints, sanctions, and rewards. The "most effectual precaution to keep them virtuous" is to subject them to frequent election and reelection. The constant prospect of an upcoming election, combined with the desire for continuing in office, will guarantee their proper devotion to the interests of the people. If, in republican government, the selected and select few serve the common good rather than their own interest, it is not on account of any resemblance to their constituents, but primarily because they are held responsible to the people through regular elections. The Anti-Federalists thought that in order for the representatives to serve the people, the former had to be "like" the latter. Madison responds that representatives may well be different from the people, indeed they ought to be different. They will nonetheless serve the people because they will be kept duly dependent on them

---

[61] Madison, "Federalist 10," p. 82; my emphasis.

by institutional means. Recurring elections, and not social likeness or closeness, are the best guardians of the people's interests. The full scope of the divergence between the two conceptions of representation is now apparent. The Anti-Federalists did not question the need for recurring elections, but to them, this was only a necessary condition for a genuine representation; similarity and proximity were also required. The Federalists, on the other hand, saw elections as both a necessary and sufficient condition for good representation.

Faced with the objection that the Constitution was aristocratic, the Federalists replied by stressing the difference between aristocracy pure and simple and "natural aristocracy" and by arguing moreover that there was nothing objectionable in the latter. An example of this line of argument can be found in the speeches of James Wilson during the Pennsylvania ratification debate. His defense of the Constitution on this point is particularly significant, because of all the Federalist leaders, he was certainly the most democratically minded. For example, he praised the Constitution for its "democratic" character, something which Madison (much less Hamilton) would never do. Nevertheless, when confronted with the objection that the proposed Constitution leaned in the direction of aristocracy, Wilson was prepared to justify government by a natural aristocracy.

> I ask now what is meant by a natural aristocracy. I am not at a loss for the etymological definition of the term; for when we trace it to the language from which it is derived, an aristocracy means nothing more or less than a government of the best men in the community or those who are recommended by the words of the constitution of Pennsylvania, where it is directed that the representatives should consist of those most noted for wisdom and virtue. [It should be kept in mind that the 1776 Pennsylvania constitution was widely seen as one of the most "democratic" state constitutions; and it constitued anyway a reference for Wilson's audience.] Is there any danger in such representation? I shall never find fault that such characters are employed ... If this is meant by natural aristocracy, – and I know no other – can it be objectionable that men should be employed that are most noted for their virtue and talents?[62]

---

[62] J. Wilson, speech of December 4, 1787, in John Elliot (ed.), *The Debates in the Several State Conventions on the Adoption of the Federal Constitution as recommended by the General Convention at Philadelphia*, 5 vols. (New York: Burt Franklin, 1888) Vol. II, pp. 473–4.

In his definition of natural aristocracy, Wilson made no mention of wealth, which made his position easier to defend and rendered his argument somewhat more common, but not to the point of triviality. For the argument must be seen in the context of the whole debate and in the light of the other side's accusations. From this perspective, Wilson's argument, in that it explicitly conceded two points made by the Anti-Federalists, is significant. First, representatives would not be *like* their electors, nor should they be. It was positively desirable that they be more talented and virtuous. Second, the representative assembly would consist primarily, if not exclusively, of the natural aristocracy.

After this defense of natural aristocracy, Wilson stressed how greatly it differed from aristocracy proper. An "aristocratic government," he continued, is a government

> where the supreme power is not retained by the people, but resides in a select body of men, who either fill up the vacancies that happen, by their own choice and election, or succeed on the principle of descent, or by virtue of territorial possession, or some other qualifications that are not the result of personal properties. When I speak of personal properties, I mean the qualities of the head and the disposition of the heart.[63]

When confronted with the same objection about the aristocratic character of the Constitution, Hamilton responded first by ridiculing his adversaries' conception of aristocracy.

> Why, then, are we told so often of an aristocracy? For my part, I hardly know the meaning of this word, as it is applied ... But who are the aristocracy among us? Where do we find men elevated to a perpetual rank above their fellow-citizens, and possessing powers independent of them? The arguments of the gentlemen [the Anti-Federalists] only go to prove that there are men who are rich, men who are poor, some who are wise, and others who are not; that indeed every distinguished man is an aristocrat ... This description, I presume to say is ridiculous. The image is a phantom. Does the new government render a rich man more eligible than a poor one? No. It requires no such qualification.[64]

Hamilton came back again and again to the Federalists' favorite

---

[63] J. Wilson, speech of December 4, 1787, p. 474.
[64] Hamilton, speech of June 21, 1788, in Elliot (ed.), *The Debates* ..., Vol. II, p. 256.

argument: the people had the right to choose whomever they pleased as their rulers. But he went even further, acknowledging that wealth was bound to play an increasingly important part in elections: "As riches increase and accumulate in a few hands, as luxury prevails in society, virtue will be in greater degree considered as only a graceful appendage of wealth, and the tendency of things will be to depart from the republican standard. This is the real disposition of human nature: it is what neither the honorable member [Melancton Smith] nor myself can correct."[65] And although Hamilton lamented this ineluctable development, something more than mere resignation sounded in the following remarks:

> Look through the rich and the poor of the community, the learned and the ignorant. Where does virtue predominate? The difference indeed consists, not in the quantity, but kind, of vices which are incident to various classes; and here the advantage of character belongs to the wealthy. Their vices are probably more favorable to the prosperity of the state than those of the indigent, and partake less of moral depravity.[66]

More than any other Federalist, Hamilton was prepared to advocate openly a certain role for wealth in the selection of representatives. Rome fascinated him and his paramount objective was that the young nation become a great power, perhaps an empire. He saw economic power as the main road to historical greatness, hence he wished the country to be led by prosperous, bold, and industrious merchants. At Philadelphia, in his speech against the plan put forward by the New Jersey delegation, he had stressed the need for attracting to the government "real men of weight and influence."[67] In *The Federalist* he replied to the Anti-Federalists that "the idea of an actual representation of all classes of the people by persons of each class" was "altogether visionary," adding: "Unless it were expressly provided in the constitution that each different occupation should send one or more members, the thing would never take place in practice."[68] Once again, the point was being conceded to the Anti-Federalists: the numerical importance of each of the various classes of society would never find spontaneous reflection in the representative assembly.

[65] Hamilton, speech of June 21, 1788, p. 256.   [66] *Ibid.*, p. 257.
[67] *Records*, Vol. I, p. 299.   [68] Hamilton, "Federalist 35," p. 214.

Mechanics and manufacturers will always be inclined, with few exceptions, to give their votes to merchants in preference to persons of their own professions or trades. Those discerning citizens are well aware that the mechanic and manufacturing arts furnish the materials of mercantile enterprise and industry ... They know that the merchant is their *natural* patron and friend; and they are aware that however great the confidence they may justly feel in their own good sense, their interests can be more effectually promoted by the merchants than by themselves.[69]

The difference was that Hamilton, unlike the Anti-Federalists, welcomed this "natural" state of affairs.

Not all Federalists shared Hamilton's point of view on the role of commerce and wealth, as the debates and conflicts of the next decade would show. In the 1790s Madison and Hamilton found themselves in opposing camps: Hamilton, then in office, continued to stand up for commercial and financial interests and to defend a strong central power; while Madison joined Jefferson in denouncing what they took to be the corruption associated with finance and commerce, as well as the encroachments of the federal government. The Federalists, however, all agreed that representatives should not be like their constituents. Whether the difference was expressed in terms of wisdom, virtue, talents, or sheer wealth and property, they all expected and wished the elected to stand higher than those who elected them.

In the end, though, the Federalists shared the Anti-Federalist intuition that this kind of difference would result from the mere size of electoral districts (that is, through the ratio between electors and elected). The advocates of the proposed Constitution did not offer an explanation of this phenomenon any more than did their opponents. However, since the Federalists did not usually present it publicly as one of the Constitution's main merits, their inability to account for it was less of a problem for them in the debate than for the Anti-Federalists. The idea, however, occasionally appeared in Federalist speeches. Wilson, for example, declared:

And I believe the experience of all who had experience, demonstrates that the larger the district of election, the better the representation. It is only in remote corners that little demagogues arise. Nothing but

---

[69] Hamilton, "Federalist 35," p. 214, my emphasis.

real weight of character can give a man real influence over a large district. This is remarkably shown in the commonwealth of Massachusetts. The members of the House of Representatives are chosen in very small districts; and such has been the influence of party cabal, and little intrigue in them, that a great majority seem inclined to show very little disapprobation of the conduct of the insurgents in that state [the partisans of Shays].[70]

By contrast, the Governor of Massachusetts was chosen by the state's whole electorate, a rather large constituency. Clearly, Wilson went on, when it came to choosing the Governor, the voters of Massachusetts "only vibrated between the most eminent characters."[71] The allusion to the Shays rebellion of 1786 rendered fairly transparent the socio-economic dimension of what Wilson meant by "eminent characters" or "real weight of character."[72] In his speech of December 11, 1787, Wilson repeated the same argument (with only a slightly different emphasis), before arguing that large electoral districts were a protection against both petty demagogues and parochialism.[73]

Writing in "Federalist 10," Madison too establishes a connection between the size of the electorate and the selection of prominent candidates. Although he is not dealing in this passage with the electoral ratio and the size of the Chamber, but with the advantage of extended republics over small ones, he uses an argument similar to Wilson's: the more numerous the electorate, the more likely the selection of respectable characters.

> As each representative will be chosen by a greater number of citizens in the large than in the small republic, it will be more difficult for unworthy candidates to practice with success the vicious arts by which elections are too often carried; and the suffrages of the people

[70] J. Wilson, speech of December 4, 1787, in Elliot (ed.), *The Debates* . . ., Vol. II, p. 474.

[71] *Ibid.*

[72] The Shays rebellion, which broke out in Massachusetts in 1786, exercised some influence on the framing of the Constitution. It contributed to the animus against "democracy" that was expressed in Philadelphia. The small farmers of the western part of the state had revolted against the policy favorable to the seabord mercantile interests pursued by the legislature in Boston. The legislature had adopted a policy of hard currency and had decided to redeem the public debt, which had led to an increase in the tax burden. In the legislative elections following the rebellion, the forces of discontent scored great successes. On the Shays rebellion, see Pole, *Political Representation*, pp. 227–41.

[73] J. Wilson, Speech of December 11, 1787, in J. B. McMaster and F. Stone (eds.), *Pennsylvania and the Federal Constitution* (Philadelphia, 1888), p. 395.

being more free, will be more likely to center on men who possess the most attractive merit and the most diffusive and established characters.[74]

In the "Note to his speech on the right of suffrage" (an elaboration on the speech he had delivered at the Convention on August 7, 1787),[75] Madison is more explicit about the benefits he expects from large electoral districts. This note reflects on possible solutions to what he describes at the outset as the major problem raised by the right of suffrage. "Allow the right exclusively to property, and the right of persons may be oppressed. The feudal polity alone sufficiently proves it. Extend it equally to all, and the rights of property or the claims of justice may be overruled by a majority without property, or interested in measures of injustice."[76] The chief objective in matters of suffrage, therefore, is to guarantee the rights of both persons and property. Madison considers five potential solutions. The first two are rejected as unfair: a property qualification for electors in the form of a freehold or of any property; and the election of one branch of the legislature by property-holders and of the other branch by the propertyless. Madison dwells at greater length on a third possibility: reserving the right of electing one branch of the legislature to freeholders, and admitting all the citizens, including freeholders, to the right of electing the other branch (which would give a double vote to freeholders). Madison notes, however, that he is not wholly clear himself about the effects of this third solution, and believes that it could be tried. He then moves to a fourth solution, on which he has apparently more definite views:

> Should experience or public opinion require an equal and universal suffrage for each branch of the government, such as prevails generally in the US, a resource favorable to the rights of landed and other property, when its possessors become the minority, may be found in an enlargement of the election districts for one branch of the legislature, and an extension of its period of service. *Large districts are manifestly favorable to the election of persons of general respectability, and of probable attachment to the rights of property, over competitors depending on the personal solicitations practicable on a contracted theatre.* [77]

---

[74] Madison, "Federalist 10," pp. 82–3.   [75] See above, note 28.

[76] Madison, "Note to the speech on the right of suffrage" (probably 1821), in *Records*, Vol. III, p. 450.

[77] *Records*, Vol. III, p. 454. My emphasis.

Finally, should even this solution be found unacceptable, Madison sees the final bulwark of the rights of property in a combination of several elements: "the ordinary influence possessed by property and the superior information incident to its holders,"[78] "the popular sense of justice enlightened and enlarged by a diffusive education," and "the difficulty of combining and effectuating unjust purposes throughout an extensive country." The fourth and fifth solutions are obviously embodied in the Constitution.[79] Regarding the effects of large electoral districts, Madison no longer speaks (as he did in "Federalist 10") the language of virtue and wisdom; he states more bluntly that large size will work in favor of property and wealth.

It would be superficial, however, to portray Madison and the Federalist leaders in general as hypocritical and shrewd politicians, who introduced into the Constitution a surreptitious property qualification (large electoral districts), and who publicly argued, in order to gain popular approval, that the assembly would be open to anyone with merit. Conversely, it would be naive to focus exclusively on the legal side of the situation and to claim that, since there were no property requirements for representatives in the Constitution, the Federalists were champions of political equality.[80] The

[78] In *The Federalist*, Madison alludes to the deference inspired by property-holders. In an argument justifying the apportionment of seats based to some extent on slave property (the $\frac{3}{5}$ "federal ratio"), Madison explains that the *wealth* of the individual states must be taken into account *legally* because the affluent states do not *spontaneously* enjoy the benefits of superior influence conferred by wealth. The situation of the states, he argues, is different in this respect from that of individual citizens. "If the law allows an opulent citizen but a single vote in the choice of his representative, the respect and consequence which he derives from his fortunate situation very frequently guide the votes of others to objects of his choice; and through this *imperceptible channel* the rights of property are conveyed into the public representation" ("Federalist 54," p. 339; my emphasis).

[79] The status and date of this Note are not entirely clear. Madison writes at the beginning that his speech of August 7, 1787, as reported in the *Records* of the Federal Convention, does not "convey the speaker's more full and matured view of the subject." The most plausible interpretation would seem to be that the Note sets out what Madison retrospectively (in 1821) regarded as the rationale for the right of suffrage laid down in 1787, whereas at the time he had been in favor of a property qualification, as we have seen. It is difficult to date precisely the change in his opinions which he alludes to. It would seem, in the light of the arguments contained in "Federalist 10," that by the end of 1787 at the latest he had realized that large electoral districts would work in favor of property-holders. But he might have discovered this effect earlier (during the debates in Philadelphia, for example).

[80] The "naive" interpretation is manifestly contradicted by the historical documents and there is no point in discussing it.

extraordinary force of the Federalist position stemmed from the fact that when Madison or Wilson declared that the people could elect whomever they pleased, they were voicing an incontrovertible proposition. In this respect, accusing the Federalists of "deceiving the people" was simply not credible. Defenders of the Constitution were certainly stating *one* truth. But there was another truth, too, or more precisely another idea that both parties held to be true (even if they did not understand exactly why): the people would, as a rule, freely choose to elect propertied and "respectable" candidates. Both propositions (and this is the essential point) could be objectively true at the same time. The first could not then, and cannot now, be regarded as a mere ideological veil for the second.

One cannot even claim that the size of electoral districts was a way of offsetting in practice the effects of the absence of formal qualifications. The Federalists did not rely on two elements of the Constitution that were equally true (or deemed to be true), in the belief that the restrictive element (the advantage bestowed on the natural aristocracy by the size of electoral districts) would cancel the effects of the more open one (the absence of any property requirement for representatives). Such a claim presupposes that the concrete results of a formal qualification would have been strictly identical to those of large electoral districts (or perceived as such by those concerned).

It is intuitively apparent that the two provisions were not equivalent. The general principle that laws and institutions make a difference and are not merely superficial phenomena has gained wide acceptance today. Yet neither intuition nor the general principle that law is no mere "formality" is wholly adequate here. It is also necessary to explain precisely why, in the particular case of parliamentary qualifications, legal requirements would not have produced effects identical to those that both the Federalists and the Anti-Federalists expected from the size of electoral districts.

Large electoral districts were not strictly equivalent to a formal property qualification for two main reasons. First, the notion that they would give an advantage to the natural aristocracy was premised on a phenomenon that experience seemed generally to confirm: "experience demonstrates" (as Wilson put it) that in general only "respectable characters" are elected in large constituencies, or (to use the language of Brutus) this effect occurs "according to the *common* course of human affairs."[81] The connection between large districts and the election of the natural aristocracy thus appeared to obtain *most of the time*. A formal property qualification, by contrast, would have been effective *always*. If the advantage of the propertied classes is assured by a statistically proven regularity of electoral behavior, the system offers a measure of flexibility: circumstances may arise where the effect does not obtain, because an exceptional concern overrides voters' ordinary inclination toward "conspicuous" candidates. The situation is different if legislative position is reserved by law to the higher social classes, because the law is by definition rigid. Obviously, the law can be changed, either peaceably or by violent means, but the process is more complicated.

There is no justification for regarding as negligible the difference between what happens always and what occurs only most of the time. The distinction (which Aristotle developed) between these two categories is particularly relevant in politics. It is an error, and indeed a fallacy, to consider, as is often done, that the ultimate truth of a political phenomenon lies in the form it assumes most of the time. In reality, the exceptional case is important too, because what is at stake in politics varies according to circumstances, and the statistically rare case may be one with historically critical consequences. On the other hand, it is equally fallacious to confer epistemological privilege on the extreme case, that is, the one which is both rare and involves high stakes. In politics, ultimate truth is no more revealed by the exception than by the rule.[82] Crises and

---

[81] One might also recall Hamilton's remark, quoted above: "Mechanics and manufacturers will *always* be inclined, *with few exceptions*, to give their votes to merchants in preference to persons of their own professions or trades" (my emphasis). See above n. 69.

[82] The thought of Carl Schmitt is one of the most brilliant, systematic, and conscious developments of the fallacious principle that the exceptional case reveals the essence of a phenomenon. Schmitt's analyses of extreme cases are for the most part penetrating. But Schmitt unduly (albeit consciously) extends the conclusions that can be drawn from the exceptional case to the general character of the phenomenon under consideration. He writes, for example: "Precisely a philosophy of concrete life must not withdraw from the exception and the extreme case, but must be interested in it to the highest degree ... The exception is more interesting than the rule. The rule proves nothing, the exception proves everything: it confirms not only the rule but also its existence, which derives only from the exception." (*Politische Theologie: Vier Kapitel zur Lehre der Souveränität* [1922];

revolutions are certainly important; one can say that they define the ordinary in that they determine the boundaries between which ordinary situations take place. But it does not follow that they are the truth of ordinary politics and furnish the key to understanding it. In revolutions or crises some factors and mechanisms come into play that are absent from normal situations and, therefore, cannot serve our understanding of ordinary politics. The most powerful political theories are those that make room for both the ordinary and the extraordinary, while maintaining a distinction between the two and explaining them differently. Locke's thought offers a perfect illustration. Most of the time, Locke remarked, people trust the established government, particularly if they elect it; they are not easily "got out of their old forms." Only when a "long train of abuses, prevarications, and artifices, all tending the same way" unmistakably manifest an intention to betray their trust, do people rise up, "appeal to heaven," and submit their fate (quite rightly) to the verdict of battle.[83] It is one of the most notable strengths of the *Second Treatise* that neither the trust of the governed in the government nor the possibility of revolution is presented as *the* truth of politics.

Returning to the American debate, the conclusion must be that, even if large electoral districts and legal qualifications for representatives did favor candidates from the higher social classes, the two cannot be equated. The greater degree of flexibility offered by extended constituencies in exceptional cases cannot be dismissed as insignificant: it is the first reason why the size of electoral districts did not cancel the effects of the non-restrictive electoral clause in the Constitution.

Second, if the advantage of certain classes in matters of representation is written into law, abolishing it (or granting it to other classes) requires a change in the law. That means that a change in the rules has to be approved by the very people who benefit from them, since they were elected under the old rules. Such a system, therefore, amounts to subjecting the demise of a given elite to its

English trans. *Political Theology. Four Chapters on the Concept of Sovereignty*, trans. G. Schwab, Cambridge, MA: MIT Press, 1985, p. 15.)

[83] J. Locke, *Second Treatise of Government*, ch. XIX, §§ 221, 223, 242, in J. Locke, *Two Treatises of Government*, ed. P. Laslett (Cambridge: Cambridge University Press, 1960), pp. 414, 415, 427.

own approval and consent. If, by contrast, the advantage of a particular social class results only from the electoral behavior of the citizens (as with the advantage of the natural aristocracy resulting from large electoral districts), a simple change in the electorate will be sufficient to overthrow an elite or alter its composition. In this case, then, the demise of the elite in power can be achieved without its approval. This is not to say, however, that the free and deliberate decision of the electorate is sufficient to achieve such a result. For the advantage of the higher social classes in large electoral districts, though a result of the electorate's behavior, actually depends on a number of factors, only some of which are capable of being deliberately modified by voters. For instance, the electoral success of property owners in large districts no doubt owes something to the constraint of campaign expenses. It may also have to do with social norms (deference, for example). Such factors are clearly beyond the reach of the conscious and deliberate decisions of voters; the simple will of the electorate is not in itself enough to do away with the advantage of wealth. Deeper changes in socio-economic circumstances and in political culture are also necessary. Difficult though they may be, such changes do not require the approval of those already in power, whereas that approval would be required under a system of legal qualifications. And there is hardly anything more difficult than inducing an elite to acquiesce in its own diminution of power. This typically requires an inordinate amount of external and indeed violent pressure.

It may be objected that, under a system of legal qualifications, the law that must be changed in order to remove the advantage of the privileged classes is usually not ordinary but rather constitutional. This was certainly the case in the United States. Changing the legal requirements would thus not have depended simply on the approval of the representatives elected under those conditions. The argument put forward here retains its validity, however, since the legislature would have a say in the process of constitutional revision.

On this second count as well, then, legal requirements for representatives and large electoral districts do not have strictly identical effects. The difference is that with a system of large electoral districts, the advantage of wealth could be altered, or possibly even abolished, without the consent of the propertied elite. This lent itself more easily to political change than did the legal conditions that English and French founders of representative government instituted in their countries.

Thus, the geographical diversity of the American states, which prevented the Philadelphia delegates from reaching an agreement on a wealth qualification for representatives led to the invention of a system in which the distinction of the representative elite was secured in a more flexible and adaptable manner, than on the other side of the Atlantic. In America, following the phases of history and the changes in the social structure of the nation, different elites would be able to succeed one another in power without major upheavals. And occasionally, in exceptional times, voters would even be able to elect ordinary citizens.

We are now in a position to see why the American constitutional debate sheds light on representative institutions in general, and not only on American ones. This broader significance results first from the position defended by the Anti-Federalists. Their views have not been widely studied, but the history of ideas and political theory in general have been wrong to neglect this current of thought. With their unflagging insistence on the "likeness" and "closeness" that must bind representatives and represented in a popular government, the Anti-Federalists actually made an important contribution to political thought. The Anti-Federalists formulated with great clarity a plausible, consistent, and powerful conception of representation. They accepted without reservations the need for a functional differentiation between rulers and ruled. But they maintained that, if representative government were to be genuinely popular, representatives should be as close to their constituents as possible: living with them and sharing their circumstances. If these conditions were fulfilled, they argued, representatives would spontaneously feel, think, and act like the people they represented. This view of representation was clearly defeated in 1787. Thus, the American debate brings into sharp relief what representative government was *not* intended to be. From the very beginning, it was clear that in America representative government would not be based on resemblance and proximity between representatives and represented. The debate of 1787 also illuminates by contrast the conception of representation that carried the day. Representatives were to be different from those they represented and to stand above them with respect to talent, virtue, and wealth. Yet the government would be republican (or popular) because representatives would be chosen by the people, and above all because repeated elections would oblige representatives to be answerable to the people. More than in France or England, where in the eighteenth century no significant force defended representation based on social resemblance or proximity, it was in America that the combination of the principle of distinction and popular representative government emerged in exemplary form.

Moreover, beyond the constitutional problem of representation, the ideal of similarity between leaders and people proved to be a powerful mobilizing force during the following century. But it was the Anti-Federalists who had first formulated it. Viewed from a certain angle, the history of the Western world can be seen as the advance of the principle of division of labor. But every time that principle was extended to organizations involved in politics (e.g. mass parties, trade unions, citizens' groups), the ideal of likeness and closeness demonstrated its attractive force. In every organization with a political dimension, substantial energies may be mobilized by declaring that the leaders must resemble the membership, share their circumstances, and be as close to them as possible, even if practical necessities impose a differentiation of roles. The power of the ideal of resemblance derives from its ability to effect a nearly perfect reconciliation between the division of labor and the democratic principle of equality.

There is an additional element of general import in the American debate. On this side of the Atlantic, it was realized early on that the superiority of the elected over their electors could usually be achieved, even in the absence of any legal requirements, through the mere operation of the elective method. It took almost another hundred years before Europeans came to see this property of elections, or at least to rely on it in order to ensure distinction in representatives. Admittedly, the protagonists of the American debate regarded the size of electoral districts as the main factor in the selection of prominent candidates. But the Anti-Federalists recognized that, even in smaller districts, voters would sponta-

130

neously choose persons whom they regarded in one way or another as superior to themselves. When the Federal Farmer, for example, called for a larger number of representatives, it was "in order to allow professional men, merchants, traders, farmers, mechanics etc., to bring a just proportion of *their best informed men* respectively into the legislature."[84]

There was in Anti-Federalist thinking an unresolved tension between the ideal of likeness and an adherence to the elective principle (which the Federalists did not fail to exploit). In the ratification debate, however, the Anti-Federalist position was not simply inconsistent. For if the Anti-Federalists did accept a certain difference between representatives and their constituents, they were afraid that with vast electoral districts that difference would become too great; they feared that certain categories would be deprived of any representatives from their own ranks, and that in the end wealth would become the prevailing criterion of distinction. In any case, they realized that the elective principle would itself lead to the selection of what they called an "aristocracy." The Federalists undoubtedly shared that belief. The disagreement was a matter of degree: the two sides held different views on what was the proper distance between representatives and represented. Furthermore, they differed on the specific characteristics of the "aristocracy" that it was desirable to select. Reviving, without explicit reference, an ancient idea, both sides believed that election by itself carries an aristocratic effect.

[84] The Federal Farmer, Letter II, *Storing*, II, 8, 15; my emphasis.

4

A democratic aristocracy

During the nineteenth and early twentieth centuries, one trend dominated the development of representative institutions: the extension of the right to vote, which eventually culminated in universal suffrage. Another transformation also took place: wealth requirements for representatives disappeared. These two changes gave rise to the belief that representation was progressing toward popular government. Free election of representatives by all adult citizens came indeed to be almost completely identified with democracy. In this context, the hypothesis that elections might include an inegalitarian and aristocratic dimension did not even seem worthy of theoretical inquiry. More broadly speaking, the movement toward universal suffrage, without legal constraints on the social origins of candidates, constituted such a manifest advance of political equality that the possible persistence of inegalitarian or aristocratic effects appeared simply irrelevant. It seems that the aristocratic nature of elections has prompted no conceptual investigation or political debate since the beginning of the nineteenth century.[1]

The American debate of 1787 was thus the last occasion on which consideration was given to the possible presence of aristocratic features in systems based on free elections. That debate in fact marked both a turning-point and a certain advance in the understanding of what political theorists had long been saying. In the first

[1] One exception should be noted. Carl Schmitt is probably the only contemporary author in whom we find any consideration of the aristocratic nature of election. However, as we shall see, Schmitt attributes that characteristic to factors external to the elective procedure itself. His contribution, important though it is in some respects, sheds no light on the nature of election.

place, whereas philosophers from Aristotle to Rousseau had argued that election was aristocratic by comparison with lot, neither the Anti-Federalists nor the Federalists had selection by lot in mind. Both camps believed that elections select individuals who are in some way superior to those who elect them. It was in this phenomenon that they saw the aristocratic dimension of the elective method. Election appeared to them to be aristocratic not in relation to lot, but in and of itself.

Moreover, previous theorists merely argued in a general way that an elective system does not give everyone an equal chance of holding office. They did not specify whom the elective method of distribution would favor. In the American debate, by contrast, the beneficiaries of the elective system were identified. Admittedly, the nature of the superiority favored by the elective method was not defined in a clear and unequivocal manner. Election, protagonists argued, would benefit conspicuous or prominent citizens, those who practiced the most prestigious or influential professions, the most talented, or simply the wealthiest. However, the Americans departed from philosophical tradition in discerning, or seeking to discern, precisely which categories of the population would be privileged in electoral competition for office. And it was social standing and affluence that struck them as the attributes destined to play the principal role.

The American debate also spelled out what Guicciardini and Montesquieu, for example, had only hinted at, namely, that the type of aristocracy associated with election had nothing to do with any legally defined and hereditary nobility. If it is true that election favors the great, it is not the great of feudal society, but those who enjoy superior status in society, in whatever terms that superiority is defined.

Finally, the 1787 debate may have made a contribution to the theory of the aristocratic effects of election. By repeatedly emphasizing that electors would choose individuals who were more "conspicuous" or "prominent," that is, more salient and visible than others, and also those who enjoyed superior economic resources, the Anti-Federalists opened up new perspectives for an explanation of the aristocratic effects of the elective procedure.

If the age-old doctrine concerning the aristocratic nature of election and the intuitions formulated during the American debate were true, neither the extension of the franchise nor the abolition of parliamentary qualifications would be capable of obliterating two phenomena. In governments based solely on election, not all citizens would have an equal chance of holding public office. And the position of representative would be reserved for persons regarded as superior or for members of higher social classes. Representative government might in certain respects become more popular and democratic. It would nevertheless retain an aristocratic dimension, in the sense that those elected would not be similar to those electing them, even if all citizens had the right to vote. Furthermore, not everyone would have an equal chance of exercising political power, even if no one was prevented by law from running for office. We must now turn to the question of whether election does in fact possess these inegalitarian and aristocratic characteristics.

THE ARISTOCRATIC CHARACTER OF ELECTION: A PURE THEORY

We shall ask here whether there are certain elements *intrinsic* to the elective method with inegalitarian implications and leading to the elected being in some way superior to the electors. This way of framing the question is in line with the tradition of political philosophy. Aristotle, Montesquieu, and Rousseau all stated that elections were intrinsically aristocratic. They did not think that the aristocratic effect derived from the circumstances and conditions in which the elective method was employed; they believed it resulted from the very nature of election.

Let us undertake, then, a pure theoretical analysis of the elective mechanism. The hypothesis of the aristocratic nature of election could doubtless be tested empirically. For instance, the composition of elected assemblies might be compared with the composition of the respective electorates to determine whether any pattern of superiority of representatives can be found. Such a test would require a vast amount of data to be truly significant and would run into a great many technical problems, but the result would not necessarily be convincing. Even if the data supported this hypothesis, the objection might be made that such inequality is in fact due to the circumstances of the elections. And since the countries in which representative government has been in operation for a couple of centuries have always been marked by pervasive social inequalities, this objection would carry a lot of weight.

So we shall take another route. We shall attempt to deduce the inegalitarian and aristocratic effects from an abstract analysis of election. Ideally, the deduction would proceed in purely *a priori* terms in order to uncover what the act of electing logically entails. However, such a transcendental deduction of the properties of election is probably impossible. There may be no way to avoid making some assumptions based on experience, but they should be as few, simple, and uncontroversial as possible. The inegalitarian and aristocratic effects of election are to due to four factors, each of which shall be examined: the unequal treatment of candidates by voters, the distinction of candidates required by a situation of choice, the cognitive advantage conferred by salience, and the cost of disseminating information.

Unequal treatment of candidates by voters

To understand the inegalitarian character of election, we must first shift perspective. Elective governments are generally regarded as political systems in which citizens can choose the leaders they wish. Such a characterization is certainly correct, but it does not embrace every aspect of the situation; more precisely some of its implications are usually not seen.

Let us imagine a system in which not all citizens can govern at the same time, but all are equally entitled to elect those who do govern, and all are eligible for public office. In such a system, citizens are politically equal as choosers. This is the democratic side of the regime under consideration. But choosing is only one aspect of citizenship. Citizens may also desire to exercise public functions and, therefore, may also wish to be chosen. The possibility of holding office, which (as we have seen) pre-modern republicans valued above all, remains one of the components of citizenship. And in our imagined situation all citizens are at the same time choosers and potential choices. So it is also necessary to look at the way in which the system under consideration affects citizens in

135

their capacity as possible objects of choice, that is, as potential candidates.

If we look at our hypothetical situation from this angle, a different side of the system becomes visible. Running for office is not subject to any restriction, but the distribution procedure entails that candidates *may* be treated in an inegalitarian fashion. Of the candidates for public function, those who attain their goal are those individuals, identified by name, who are preferred over the rest. Positions are allocated not according to abstractly defined attributes or actions, in the light of which all are equal, but according to preferences held by the sovereign people for this or that particular individual. We generally think that equality before the law is assured if a rule attaches obtaining a benefit (or suffering a penalty) to the possession of qualities or the performance of actions defined in an abstract and anonymous way. But election considered as a way of distributing offices does not allocate public functions to anyone, whoever he or she happens to be, who presents feature X or performs action Y. When electing, voters are not required to use impartial standards to discriminate among candidates. They may decide to vote for whomever meets some general and abstract criteria (e.g. political orientation, competence, honesty), but they *may also* decide to elect someone just because they like this individual better than another. If the election is free, nothing can prevent voters from discriminating among candidates on the basis of individual characteristics. Free elections, then, cannot preclude partiality in the treatment of candidates. Indeed, the possible influence of partiality is the reverse side of the right of citizens to choose whomever they please as their representatives. Since it is the citizens who discriminate amongst themselves, no one notices that public functions are being distributed in a discretionary, non-anonymous manner, one which unavoidably opens the door to partiality. In a secret vote, the citizen does not even have to give reasons for his or her preference. In this instant, the voter is sovereign, in the old and narrow sense of the word. He could rightly adopt the motto of absolutist rulers and say: *"Sic volo, sic jubeo, stat pro ratione voluntas"* ("Thus I wish, thus I ordain, my will takes the place of reason").

The use of election carries another, slightly different, implication for candidates. Contrary to what is suggested by the parallel often

drawn between election and sports competitions, the elective procedure is not necessarily meritocratic and does not strictly guarantee
what is today conceptualized as equality of opportunity. This is not
the place to enter into the complex philosophical discussions to
which the concepts of meritocracy and equality of opportunity have
given rise over the past twenty years. There seems, however, to be a
consensus that a procedure is meritocratic and secures equality of
opportunity if the inequalities it generates in distribution of a social
good, are at least partly (some would say "wholly") the result of the
actions and choices of those who desire that good.[2] A procedure is
not described as meritocratic if the inequalities of distribution it
leads to derive exclusively from innate inequalities. A beauty
contest, for example, is surely not deemed meritocratic. On the other
hand, an academic examination is meritocratic in that, even if the
unequal performances of the candidates owe something to the
genetic lottery of talent (not to mention inequalities in social background), they are also, at least in part, the result of the candidates'
efforts, choices, and actions.

In this respect, it is instructive to compare the selection of rulers
by election and their recruitment by competitive examination
(which is how political authority was for a long time allocated in
China). Alongside lot, election, heredity, and cooptation by those
already in power, examination is another possible method of
selecting rulers. Let us consider the examination system in its pure
form, leaving aside all the external influences that usually vitiate it
in practice. If rulers are recruited through competitive examination,
candidates must meet standards that are formulated in an abstract
and general way. Moreover, those standards are publicly announced
in advance, and all candidates are aware of them. Candidates must
then apply their energies and resources (some of the latter are of
course a function of natural endowments) to meeting those standards, and they have to make a judgment as to what is the best way
of reaching that goal. The unequal distribution of posts following an
examination thus reflects, at least in part, the inequality of efforts,
actions, and judgments of the candidates.

---

[2] For a good synthetic presentation of the concept of equality of opportunity in
modern philosophy of justice, see W. Kymlicka, *Contemporary Political Philosophy.
An Introduction* (Oxford: Oxford University Press, 1990), pp. 55 ff.

This is not necessarily so under an elective system. Here the standards are not defined in an abstract manner and announced in advance. Candidates may try to guess what the voters will require. But even supposing it were possible to reconstitute, on the basis of the votes, a general and abstract definition of the desired qualities, this is something that can only be known *ex post facto*. Furthermore, there is no guarantee that, when casting their votes, electors will take even partial account of the efforts, actions, and choices of the candidates. Nothing in the elective method requires that voters be fair to candidates. Nothing can *prevent* the electorate from preferring a candidate purely on grounds of skin color or good looks. Here again, we must note that voters may not use such foolish criteria. Moreover, they will perhaps learn to their detriment the inanity of such yardsticks. And since elections are repeated, they may, over time, adopt standards of judgment that are less irrational from the point of view of their interests. But there is nothing to prevent voters from deciding, at any given moment, purely on the basis of the candidates' natural endowments, to the neglect of their actions and choices. Again, this is the corollary of freedom of choice.

It might be objected that candidates need at the very least to make themselves known and that, in this respect, election rewards the efforts and judgments made in the campaign. But that too is not strictly necessary. A person may already be known before any electoral campaigning, simply by virtue of his name or social standing, and voters may decide that these are reasons enough for preferring him to others.

In some respects, it is self-evident (though the fact is not without consequence) that elections do not ensure that all those who desire to hold office have an equal chance. It is perhaps less trivial to note that neither do they guarantee equality of opportunity among those aspiring to public functions.

The preceding argument establishes that election intrinsically opens the possibility of unequal treatment of candidates for public office, but it does not show why it tends to produce representatives who are thought to be in some way superior to those who elect them.

Distinction of candidates required by a situation of choice

To elect is to choose. Although elections have not always been organized as choices (we have seen, for example, that in England before the civil war, there was often only one candidate), and despite the fact that many authoritarian regimes organize uncontested elections, the element of choice is inherent in the concept of election in modern representative systems. In a situation of choice, voters need at least one motive for preferring one candidate over another. If candidates are indistinguishable, voters will be indifferent, and thus unable to choose in the sense of preferring one to another. To be chosen, therefore, a candidate must display at least one characteristic that is positively valued by his fellow-citizens and that the other candidates do not possess, or not to the same extent. Among the citizens aspiring to office the most capable of meeting that requirement are those who possess a quality that is both positively valued and rare, or indeed unique, in a given population: they are less likely, when all the potential candidates have decided whether to run or not, to be confronted with competitors offering the same or a superior electoral profile. A person whose quality, or combination of qualities, is widely shared among the population is likely to be faced with competitors possessing likewise that quality; he will then be indistinguishable from them. Such a person is also liable to be faced with opponents who possess, in addition to the trait he displays himself, another positively valued quality, in which case he will be defeated. Moreover, potential candidates, or the organizations that select and back candidates, are aware of this. Since running entails expenditures, at least of energy, the potential candidate, or the party selecting a candidate, have an incentive to assess what is likely to happen when he is confronted with actual opponents. Before deciding to come forward as a candidate, the person aspiring to office asks himself whether he possesses some feature that is positively valued by his fellow-citizens and is rare or unique in the population.

But a quality that is favorably judged in a given culture or environment and is not possessed by others constitutes a superiority: those who possess it are different from and superior to those who do not. Thus, an elective system leads to the self-selection and selection of candidates who are deemed superior, on one dimension or another, to the rest of the population, and hence to voters. It is no accident that the terms "election" and "elite" have the same etymology and that in a number of languages the same adjective denotes a person of distinction and a person who has been chosen.

It must be noted that the distinction requirement inherent in an elective system is entirely structural: it derives from the situation of choice in which voters are placed, and not from their psychology and attitudes. Voters can certainly desire to elect someone who shares some characteristic with them, and often do so. One could think, then, that the candidate who has the best chances of being elected is the person who shares the same quality as most voters, and hence presents the most common quality in a given population. This is not so, however, because among the large number of those who possess a widespread quality, there is also a probably a significant number of potential candidates. Admittedly, not all those sharing a given quality are likely to aspire to office, but there is no reason to suppose that only one of them does. If voters base their decisions on similarity between the candidates and themselves, they will be unable to choose from among the number of persons sharing a widespread quality. The situation of choice constrains voters to elect candidates possessing uncommon (and positively valued) characteristics, regardless of their specific preferences.

It could be objected that voters might choose the candidate whom they find to be most like themselves on a given dimension or combination of dimensions. That is a distinguishing characteristic, but not, it would seem, one that implies any superiority. However, if voters choose the candidate most like themselves on a given dimension, the quality that they value is not that which is measured along that dimension, but closeness to themselves with regard to a given trait. If they choose, for example, the candidate whose competence is most like their own, the quality that they judge favorably is not competence, but the minimal distance between their own (self-esteemed) competence and that of the candidate. For such a standard to operate successfully as a criterion of selection, the statistical distribution of traits among the population must present a particular profile: there must be only a few, and preferably one, person whose position on a given dimension is closest to those of the other members of the population. If that condition is not met, there will probably be many candidates among whom voters are indifferent. Thus, even in that case, voters are led to select a candidate who is superior to them in that he possesses a quality that they particularly value and that most of them do not possess: closeness to the others with respect to a given trait.

Of course, every individual possesses at least one trait that distinguishes him from everyone else.[3] So it might be thought that anybody wishing to hold office could put himself forward in the hope that he might convince voters to judge favorably his distinguishing quality. However, potential candidates are aware that, ultimately, electoral choice is discretionary. So it is rational for the potential candidate to treat voters' values as given, to seek to discern rather than change them, and base their decision to run on what they discern.

It could also be argued that, because of the discretionary nature of electoral choice, potential candidates cannot predict what will be judged positively by the electorate. In this case, anyone aspiring to public office would present himself in the (well-grounded) certainty that he possesses one distinctive feature, but in total uncertainty as to how voters would judge that feature. But in fact, voters' values are strongly determined by the circumstances of society and culture. And these are objective phenomena of which potential candidates are aware. For instance, it is reasonable to believe that, in a society that is frequently at war, physical strength, strategic gifts, and military skills will all stand a good chance of being judged favorably by the electorate. Potential candidates therefore know that, in a given context or culture, this or that distinctive trait will be more likely to attract favorable judgment.

It must be noted that the distinction requirement sets no limits on the programs offered by the candidates and their policy positions, it affects only the selection of persons. The candidates can propose the programs they wish, whereas they are constrained by their personality traits. Any policy position may be preferred by most voters and, thus, be adopted by a candidate seeking to win. But not anyone adopting that position is equally likely to be elected. Election is

[3] By virtue of the principle of indiscernibles first formulated by Leibniz: no two beings can be strictly identical in every respect.

indeed irreducibly (let it be stressed again) a choice of persons. Even if voters also compare what the candidates declare, the personalities of the contenders inevitably play a part. Moreover, programs and promises have a particular status in representative governments: they are not legally binding.[4] By contrast, once persons are elected, it is they who decide on public policy.

Since election involves a choice, it also includes an internal mechanism that hinders the selection of citizens who resemble others. At the heart of the elective procedure, there is a force pulling in the opposite direction from the desire for similarity between rulers and ruled.

Advantages conferred by salience in attracting attention

Election consists in choosing known individuals. To be elected, a candidate needs to attract the attention of the electorate. Cognitive psychology shows, however, that attention primarily focuses on *salient* items or individuals. Moreover, it has been established that salient stimuli have an impact on evaluative perceptions: salient stimuli elicit strong evaluative judgments.[5] If one applies these results to elections, it appears that in order to both attract attention and elicit strong positive judgments, candidates have to stand out by virtue of a positively valued characteristic. A non-salient candidate will pass unnoticed and have little chance of being elected. And a candidate that stands out on account of his uncommon negative characteristics will be rejected. Cognitive constraints produce an effect similar to that produced by the constraints of the situation of choice. In itself, election favors individuals who are salient (and therefore distinct or different) by virtue of an aspect that people

---

[4] We shall return to this point in chapter 5.

[5] The earliest studies of the effects of salience established that it influenced attributions of cause (people are more inclined to impute the cause of phenomenon X to phenomenon A, rather than to B, C, or D, if A is for whatever reason more prominent – better highlighted, better known, etc. – than B, C, or D). However, it has been shown subsequently that the effects of salience extend well beyond attributions of cause. See S. E. Taylor and S. T. Fiske, "Salience, attention, and attribution: top of the head phenomena," in L. Berkowitz (ed.), *Advances in Experimental Social Psychology*, Vol. II (New York: Academic Press, 1978); see also S. E. Taylor, J. Crocker, S. T. Fiske, M. Sprintzen, and J. D. Winkler, "The generalisation of salience effects," in *Journal of Personality and Social Psychology*, Vol. 37, 1979, pp. 257–368.

judge favorably – in other words, individuals deemed superior to others.

Salience does not, of course, result from universally determined traits. It is a contextual property. Considered universally, any trait may make a person salient. Salience depends on the environment in which a person lives and from which his or her image needs to stand out. Consequently, it is a function of the distribution of traits within the population of which the individual forms a part: an individual is salient in proportion as his particular traits are statistically rare in that population. Since such distribution varies according to time and place, the characteristics that bestow salience will also vary according to time and place. However, that does not mean that, in a given context, anyone may be salient. Salience is a relative, variable property, but in a specific situation it acts as a constraint on both voters and potential candidates.

Furthermore, in a specific situation (and if the distribution of traits in the population in question is therefore regarded as given), voters are not able meticulously to compare all the characteristics of each individual with those of each of the others. The quantity of information that they would need to process in order to reach such a result would be enormous, requiring vast expenditures of time and energy. Voters are unlikely to be willing to incur such costs, because they are aware of the infinitesimal weight their vote will carry in the end. So voters do not undertake a detailed comparison of all their fellow-citizens one by one. Instead, they operate on the basis of an overall perception, and their attention is drawn to those individuals whose image stands out from the rest.

Election campaigns undoubtedly have the effect of drawing the attention of voters to the distinguishing features of candidates they would not otherwise have noticed. And every individual wishing to be a candidate necessarily possesses at least one distinctive trait capable of being highlighted. Election campaigns were in fact instituted (among other reasons) to counteract the advantage that the elective procedure, considered in itself, confers on the particular form of eminence represented by notability. But they can never abolish that advantage entirely. Individuals who are salient in the course of their daily social relations are involved in a sort of permanent election campaign, whereas the spotlight is not directed on the distinctive traits of the other candidates until the actual campaign opens.

Cost of disseminating information

Mention of election campaigns brings us to the last inegalitarian feature of the elective procedure. The deliberate dissemination of information about candidates does, to some extent, relax the constraints of prior eminence, particularly as enjoyed by the notables. But it is expensive, which means that it favors those able to mobilize greater resources. The candidates (or at least those among them who are not notables) *need to make themselves known*. And there is every reason to suppose that the cost of such an undertaking is not negligible.

If candidates have to finance their election campaigns out of their own pockets, the advantage of the affluent classes of society assumes its most obvious and most immediate form: it is reflected directly in the social composition of the elected assembly. But that advantage does not disappear even if candidates appeal for contributions to finance their campaigns. Organizations financed by their members' dues help mitigate the effects of wealth on the selection of representatives. And in fact, that was one of the explicit objectives of the creation of mass parties in the second half of the nineteenth century.

However, such organizations do not entirely do away with the advantage of wealth: it takes more effort, more organizing, and more activism to collect a given sum through the contributions of poor citizens, than through those of citizens who are better off. It is reasonable to suppose that the political contributions made by citizens (or firms) are more or less proportionate to their income. The number of such contributions may make up for their small amounts, but it is easier to collect a smaller number of substantial contributions. Candidates are therefore more inclined to appeal to the rich than to the poor in order to finance their electoral expenses. And it is reasonable to suppose that, once elected, a candidate will devote particular attention to the interests of those who contributed financially to his election.

Inherently, then, the elective procedure favors the wealthier strata of the population. But unlike the first three inegalitarian features of election (possible unequal treatment of candidates, the dynamics of choice, and cognitive constraints), this one could be eliminated entirely by having campaigns publicly financed and electoral expenses strictly regulated. Experience seems to indicate that regulation of this sort runs into technical difficulties, but in principle it is not impossible.

It is nevertheless odd that representative governments should have waited until the final decades of the twentieth century before addressing this problem. This is probably (in part, at least) because voters themselves tend to underestimate the costs of electoral campaigns and are unwilling to allocate substantial public resources for such a purpose. Electing governments, however, is an expensive undertaking, even if the people are reluctant to admit the consequences of that fact. It is even more extraordinary that political theory has so neglected the question of electoral expenses. John Stuart Mill was one of the few exceptions, and his work was scarcely followed up on.[6] With so much attention focused on the extension of the right of suffrage (or on the Marxist critique of the "formal" character of "bourgeois democracy"), political thought failed to look into the complex aspects of election – that seemingly straightforward institution.

Definition of elective aristocracy

We can see now how the dynamics of choice and cognitive constraints usually lead to the election of representatives perceived as superior to those who elect them. However, it is a particular concept of superiority that is employed here, and it needs to be carefully defined. First, when we say that a candidate must be deemed

---

[6] Faced with the peculiar features of nineteenth-century British politics (outright bribery, with candidates buying votes and paying for voters to travel – see chapter 3), Mill doubtless had every reason to be particularly alert to the phenomenon of electoral expenses. However, his thinking went beyond corruption and the peculiarities of the British system. He wrote, for example: "Not only should not the candidate be required, he should not be permitted to incur any but a limited and trifling expense for his election." *Considerations on Representative Government* [1861], in H. B. Acton (ed.), *Utilitarianism, Liberty, Representative Government* (London: Dent & Sons, 1972), p. 308. Mill also advocated public financing of electoral expenses.

superior in order to be elected, we are not talking about a global judgment on his personality. To elect a person, voters do not have to believe that person to be better in every respect; they may despise one or even most of his character traits. The foregoing arguments merely show that voters, if they are to elect a candidate, must regard him as superior in the light of the quality or set of qualities that they consider *politically relevant*.

Second, cognitive constraints and the constraints of choice relate only to a *perceived* superiority (the situation is different, of course, concerning wealth). Candidates must stand out, but that does not mean they have to be outstanding by rational or universal criteria. They must be perceived as superior according to the dominant values of the culture. Measured against rational, universal standards, the (culturally conditioned) perception of what characterizes the best may well be mistaken and inadequate. But this is beside the point. The claim here is not that elections tend to select the "true" *aristoi*. Elected representatives only need to be *perceived* as superior; that is to say, they have to display an attribute (or set of attributes) that on the one hand is valued positively in a given context, and that on the other hand the rest of the citizens do not possess, or not in the same degree.

Two consequences follow from this. In the first place, the elective principle does not guarantee that true *political* excellence gets selected (again, if "true" means what conforms to rational, universal standards). Elections operate on the basis of a culturally relative perception of what constitutes a good ruler. If citizens believe that oratorical skills, for example, offer a good criterion of political excellence, they will make their political choice on that basis. Clearly, there is no guarantee that a gift for public speaking is a good proxy for capability to govern. The recurrent nature of elections certainly introduces a measure of objectivity: voters may discover from experience that the criteria they employed at the previous election led to a government which turned out to be extremely bad or incompetent, and they can alter those criteria at the next election. Repetition makes elections a learning process in which voters can discover the objective political value of their criteria for selection. Nevertheless, the fact remains that on each occasion they choose what they perceive to be a relevant political superiority, their current perception being also based on earlier experience.

Second, nothing in the nature of the elective method guarantees that it will result in the selection of elites in the general (as opposed to purely political) sense that Pareto gave to the term. Although Pareto's formulations are not wholly unambiguous on this point, his concept of elite seems to imply universal criteria. In his *Treatise of General Sociology*, the term "elite" denotes those who have the highest ranking in "capacity" in their sphere of activity.

> Let us assume, then, that in every branch of human activity each individual is assigned an index which stands as a sign of his capacity, very much the way grades are given in examinations in the various subjects taught in schools ... To the man who has made his millions – honestly or dishonestly as the case may be – we will assign 10. To the man who has earned his thousands we will assign 6 ... Let us then form a class of those who have the highest indices in their branch of activity, and to that class give the name of elite.[7]

Pareto is very careful to strip his concept of elite of any moral dimension. He explains, for example, that a clever thief who is successful in what he undertakes will receive a high index and will consequently belong to an elite, whereas a petty thief who fails to elude the police will get a low ranking. Moral considerations aside, however, Pareto's elites are apparently defined by universal criteria. The ranking or grading that defines who belongs to an elite is made, in the passage quoted above, by the social scientist himself ("To the man who has made his millions ... *we* will assign 10. To the man who has earned his thousands *we* will assign 6"), who is by definition an outside observer. Therefore what defines an elite is not what a given society perceives as the embodiment of success or excellence in each field of activity, but what the social scientist views as such.[8] If the term "elite" is taken in Pareto's sense, then, the

---

[7] Vilfredo Pareto, *Traité de Sociologie Générale* [1916], ch. XI, §§ 2027–31, in *Oeuvres Complètes*, publiées sous la direction de G. Busino (Genève: Droz, 1968, 16 vols.), Vol. XII, pp. 1296–7. English translations: *Compendium of General Sociology*, ch. 8, ed. E. Abbott (Minneapolis: University of Minnesota Press, 1980), pp. 272–3, or *A Treatise on General Sociology*, trans. A. Bongiorno and A. Livingston, four volumes bound as two (New York: Dover Publications, 1935), Vol. II, pp. 1422–3.

[8] The purely objective or universal character of what defines an elite is not entirely clear in the body of Pareto's writings. It appears to be deduced in the main from the definition given in the *Treatise on General Sociology*. In an earlier work,

constraints of cognition and choice mentioned above do not prove that the elective method inherently favors elites. Voters choose what they perceive as an instance of superiority, but in every sphere their culturally determined standards may be mistaken when compared with criteria of the type employed by Pareto. To return to the example of skill in public speaking, voters may not only be mistaken in thinking that such a characteristic indicates political talents; they may also consider someone a good public speaker who would not be so judged by the social scientist or by the expert in rhetoric. The crucial distinction in the arguments put forward here is not between moral value and success in activity, however immoral (in fact, there is every reason to believe that voters do bring moral criteria to bear); it is between perceived superiority and superiority defined by universal standards. The elective principle leads naturally to the selection of the former but not of the latter.

Finally, it should be pointed out that the attributes which, in a given context, produce the perception of superiority do in all likelihood have objective existence. Since the problem for voters is to find criteria that enable them to distinguish between the candidates, they most probably use easily *discernible* traits to make their choice. If the presence or absence of those traits were open to doubt, the traits would be useless in the process of selection, and they would not have been adopted in the first place. In other words, although voters may very well be mistaken in their belief that oratorical talents are a good proxy for political skills, and may also be mistaken in their conception of what a good orator is, they are unlikely to err in their perception that, with respect to public speaking, candidate X possesses some characteristic that others do not. This last element is of critical importance, because it means that, to get elected, candidates must *actually* possess some attribute that distinguishes them from their fellow-citizens. The superiority of

however, Pareto had defined elites as follows: "These classes represent an elite, an aristocracy (in the etymological sense of *aristos* = the best). So long as the social equilibrium is stable, the majority of the individuals composing these classes appear highly endowed with certain qualities – good or bad as may be – which guarantee power" V. Pareto, *Les Systèmes Socialistes* [1902–3], in *Oeuvres Complètes*, Vol. V, p. 8. English translation: *Sociological Writings*, selected and introduced by S. E. Finer, trans. D. Mirfin (New York: Praeger, 1966), p. 131. If elites are defined by the qualities that "guarantee power" in a particular society, the objective or universal character of the definition disappears.

candidates (the positive evaluation of their distinguishing attributes) is merely perceived or subjective, but the difference between them has to be objective. In other words, election selects perceived superiorities and actual differences.

Given this particular definition of superiority, one may wonder whether it is still justified to speak of the "aristocratic" nature of election. The term is indeed conventional and might be replaced by any other ("elitist," for example), so long as we keep in mind the precise phenomenon that it denotes: the selection of representatives different from and perceived as superior to those who elect them. The adjective "aristocratic" is used here largely for historical reasons.

The arguments put forward above offer, at least in part, an explanation of the phenomenon that the Athenian democrats, Aristotle, Guicciardini, Harrington, Montesquieu, and Rousseau had in mind when they claimed that election was inherently aristocratic. The American Anti-Federalists also used the term "aristocratic" to denote the lack of similarity between electors and elected, which is another reason for retaining it. But the only essential point in the argument developed here is that, for reasons that can be discovered and understood, election cannot, by its very nature, result in the selection of representatives who resemble their constituents.

THE TWO FACES OF ELECTION: THE BENEFITS OF AMBIGUITY

However, just as elections undoubtedly have inegalitarian and aristocratic aspects, so too are their egalitarian and democratic aspects undeniable, so long as all citizens have the right to vote and are all legally eligible for office. Under a system of universal suffrage, elections give each citizen an equal say in the choice of representatives. In this respect, the humblest and poorest carry the same weight as the wealthiest and most distinguished. More importantly, they all equally share the power of dismissing those who govern at the end of their term. No one can deny the existence of this double power of selection and rejection, and it is sheer sophistry to dismiss it as negligible. The fundamental fact about elections is that they are *simultaneously* and indissolubly egalitarian and inegalitarian, aristocratic and democratic. The aristocratic dimension deserves particular attention today because it tends to be forgotten or attributed to the wrong causes. This is why, in what precedes, the emphasis has been placed on that aspect. But this by no means implies that the egalitarian or democratic side of election is any less important or real than its inegalitarian and aristocratic side. We spontaneously tend to look for the ultimate truth of a political phenomenon in a single trait or property. However, there is no reason to suppose that an institution presents only one decisive property. On the contrary, most political institutions simultaneously generate a number of effects, often very different from one another. Such is the case with election. Like Janus, election has two faces.

Among modern political theorists, Carl Schmitt seems to be the only author who notes the dual nature of election. Schmitt writes:

> In comparison with lot, designation by election is an aristocratic method, as Plato and Aristotle rightly say. But in comparison with appointment by a higher authority or indeed with hereditary succession, this method may appear democratic. In election both potentialities lie [*In der Wahl liegen beide Möglichkeiten*]; it can have the aristocratic sense of elevating the superior and the leader or the democratic sense of appointing an agent, proxy, or servant; compared to the elected, the electors can appear either as subordinates or as superiors; election can serve the principle of representation as well as the principle of identity ... One must discern which sense is given to election in the concrete situation [*in der Wirklichkeit*]. If election is to form the basis of true representation, it is the instrument of an aristocratic principle; if it merely signifies the selection of a dependent delegate [*eines abhängigen Beauftragten*], it may be regarded as a specifically democratic method.[9]

This passage can only be understood in the light of Schmitt's distinction between identity and representation, the two principles which can form the political content of a constitution ("election can serve the principle of representation as well as that of identity"). Schmitt describes these principles as two opposite conceptual poles between which every actual constitution falls. Any constitution, Schmitt argues, presupposes a certain conception of the unity of the people. To be considered capable of agency, a people must be seen as unified in one way or another. Identity and representation are the two extreme conceptions of what may make a people a unified agent.

[9] C. Schmitt, *Verfassungslehre*, § 19 (Munich: Dunker & Humblot, 1928), p. 257.

The principle of identity rests on the notion that the people "may be capable of acting politically by the mere fact of its immediate existence – by virtue of a powerful and conscious similarity [*Glei-chartigkeit*], as a result of clear natural boundaries, or for some other reason. It is then politically unified and has real power by virtue of its direct identity with itself."[10] When a group of individuals has a strong sense of being similar in a way that is particularly important, that group thereby becomes a community capable of political action. Their unity is spontaneous; it is not imposed upon them from outside. In such a case, since the members of the community perceive themselves as being fundamentally similar, they set up institutions that treat all members in a similar fashion. Above all, though, because they see one another as sharing essentially the same nature, they tend to abolish, as far as possible, any difference between rulers and ruled. In this sense, according to Schmitt, the principle of identity forms the basis for democracy, and it has found its most profound expression in Rousseau. "Democracy," Schmitt writes, "is the identity of the dominant and the dominated [*Herrscher und Beherrschten*], the ruler and the ruled, of those who command and those who obey."[11] In its purest form, democracy is not compatible with representation. However, democracy does not necessarily exclude a functional differentiation between rulers and ruled. What it does exclude is:

> that within the democratic state the distinction between dominating and being dominated, ruling and being ruled, is based upon, or gives rise to, a qualitative difference. In democracy, domination and government cannot be based on inequality, and hence not on any superiority of those who dominate or govern, nor on the fact that the rulers are in some way qualitatively better than the ruled.[12]

Rulers may hold a particular role or position different from that occupied by the ruled, but that position can never be the reflection of their superior nature. If they are authorized to rule, it is only because they express the will of the people and have received a mandate from them.

"The opposite principle [that of representation] stems from the idea that the political unity of the people as such can never be

[10] Schmitt, *Verfassungslehre*, § 16, p. 205.
[11] *Ibid.*, § 17, p. 235. [12] *Ibid.*

present in its real identity and must therefore always be represented by particular persons."[13] The person of the representative makes present in a certain sense that which is not actually present (in this case, the political unity of the people). The body of the people becomes unified solely through the medium of a person or institution external to it. One can think here of Hobbes's Leviathan, which bestows (from above) political unity and agency upon what is concretely at first no more than a disbanded multitude. Understood in this way, the principle of representation has a variety of implications, according to Schmitt. Here we need note only that the representative, who by definition is external to the people, is independent from them and cannot be bound by their will.[14]

Schmitt sensed, then, the dual nature of elections. Strangely, however, he did not realize that, on his own definition of democracy – a political system based on identity between rulers and ruled – elections inherently entail a non-democratic element in that they cannot produce similarity or likeness between rulers and ruled. Rather, his account relates the duality of elections to the legal and constitutional form of the relationship between electors and elected. Election, he argues, *can* be a democratic method if those elected are regarded as "agents, proxies, or servants," that is, if they are treated as "dependent delegates." This, however, implies that elections are aristocratic if representatives are independent in the sense that constitutional theory gives to the the term – that is to say, if they are not bound by instructions or imperative mandates. The term used in this passage ("*abhängigen Beauftragten*") belongs to the standard vocabulary of constitutional theory. For Schmitt, election is potentially *either* democratic *or* aristocratic ("*In der Wahl liegen beide Möglichkeiten*"). One or the other is actualized by the constitutional provisions regulating the relationship between constituents and representatives in the particular concrete case ("*in der Wirklichkeit*"). In other words, Schmitt does not see that elections *actually* have both an aristocratic and a democratic component, irrespective of the constitutional relationship between elected and electors. Even if representatives are not bound by mandates, elections are democratic in that they give each citizen an equal say in the selection and

[13] Schmitt, *Verfassungslehre*, § 16, p. 205.   [14] *Ibid.*, p. 212.

dismissal of representatives. Conversely, even if representatives are bound by mandates or instructions, elections have an aristocratic character in that representatives cannot be similar to their constituents. They cannot be a people in miniature, spontaneously thinking, feeling, and acting like the people at large. And this is probably why the most democratically minded among the partisans of representative government advocated the practice of mandates and instructions. They wanted representatives to be constrained by legal provisions to counteract the effects of their inevitable dissimilarity.

Nevertheless, Schmitt's theory remains crucial to the understanding of elections in so far as it characterizes the fundamental principle of democracy as identity or resemblance between rulers and ruled. Schmitt perceives with great acumen that one of the most powerful appeals of democracy lies in the idea of similarity between rulers and ruled, even though he does not realize that the very nature of election impedes such similarity.

The specific form of the aristocratic component of election probably accounts for much of the exceptional success of this method for selecting rulers. In the allocation of public offices, election favors individuals or groups endowed with distinctive traits that are positively valued. However, elections present first the notable property that, except for the influence of wealth, the method does not predetermine *which* traits confer advantage in the competition for office. Even assuming that people are aware of the aristocratic effect, anyone may hope to benefit from it one day as a result of changes, either in the distribution of traits among the population, or in the relevant culture and value judgments, or both.

Moreover, in a particular context (i.e. taking as fixed the distribution of traits among the population and the value judgments that it makes), the simultaneous presence of elitist and egalitarian components helps secure a broad and stable consensus in support of the use of the elective method. In any society or culture, there are usually groups distinguished by their wealth or by some favorably judged trait not possessed by other groups. Such elites generally exercise an influence disproportionate to their numbers. Their support is, therefore, particularly important for the establishment and stability of institutions. Because the elective method tends *de facto* to reserve representative functions for those elites, it is particularly likely to get their support and approval, once such elites have grasped the aristocratic nature of the procedure. The advantages of wealth, as we have seen, can be mitigated or even abolished. But even if the effect of wealth is entirely canceled, the elective procedure still favors groups in possession of a favorably judged distinctive characteristic. One distinctive trait or another will inevitably be utilized in political choice, since cognitive constraints and the constraints of choice cannot be removed.

The unavoidable constraint of distinction further allows for some flexibility and leaves a margin of uncertainty, even within the limits of a given culture. In a specific cultural context not anyone can hope that his distinctive quality will be judged favorably, but nor does the culture unequivocally determine a single quality that people view positively. Therefore, various elites may hope to have their distinctive trait judged favorably or may at least attempt to achieve that result. The elective method is thus capable of simultaneously attracting support from a number of different elites.

Finally, even those who, in a given context, do not see themselves as possessing any favorably judged distinctive trait, cannot fail to realize (or can at least always be brought to realize) that they have a voice equal to that of everyone else in the selection and dismissal of rulers. They may also become aware that it is they who have the power to arbitrate between various elites in the competition for public office. Thus, because of its dual nature, election also gives to such ordinary citizens powerful motives for supporting its use.

The combination of election and universal suffrage even constitutes what might be called a point of argumentative equilibrium. Imagine a situation in which ordinary citizens (as defined above), realizing that elections reserve political office to persons superior to themselves, demand a new method of selection, one that ensures greater equality in the allocation of offices or a greater degree of similarity between rulers and ruled. The partisans of the existing elective system can argue that if, under conditions of universal suffrage and in the absence of legal parliamentary qualifications, the electorate decides to elect mainly elites, the responsibility lies with the voters, ordinary citizens included. Ordinary citizens are unlikely to insist that the power of selecting rulers be given to an authority other than the people. Similarly, if a particular elite calls for a distribution procedure that gives it a larger share of posts than it obtains under an elective system, a counterargument is readily available. It can be retorted that having an outside authority arbitrate the competition for office among the various elites is the most prudent arrangement, because none of them could award itself a larger share of posts (or impose a procedure leading to that result) without some risk of provoking the opposition of the others. As Guicciardini was probably among the first to point out, letting those who do not have access to office arbitrate between competing elites is an acceptable solution from the standpoint of those elites themselves, because it avoids open conflict between them. So in both cases of protest against the elective system, a powerful argument can be mobilized to restore the initial situation.

This brings us back to the idea of the mixed constitution. The mixed constitution was defined as a mix of monarchical, aristocratic (or oligarchic), and democratic elements, the combination of which was seen as the cause of its astonishing stability.[15] Leaving aside the monarchical dimension, election could, by analogy, be termed a mixed institution.

It should be stressed that the two dimensions of election (aristocratic and democratic) are objectively true and both carry significant consequences. Well-intended but perhaps naive democrats, when not simply unaware of the aristocratic aspect, are always looking for new arguments to prove that only the egalitarian dimension counts. But there will always be an empirical study to show that representatives belong primarily to certain distinguished strata of the population, and that this influences their decisions, thereby giving the lie to whatever novel argument has been advanced by pious democrats. Conversely, partisans of realism and demystification, whether they welcome or deplore the fact, will never succeed in demonstrating convincingly that the egalitarian aspect is pure delusion. No doubt the debate will go on.

Not only are the two dimensions equally real; they are inseparable. Unlike the mixed constitution, which was a complex structure comprising a number of elements, election by the people is a *simple* operation that cannot be split into its component parts.[16] Its two

[15] See chapter 2.
[16] Recall that, in the mixed-constitution models, each of the three dimensions was

properties are so tightly interwoven that they cannot possibly be separated from each other. Neither the elites nor the ordinary citizens are in a position to retain the property that they regard favorably, while getting rid of the other, because neither dimension is embodied by a distinct institution. Moreover, the egalitarian and inegalitarian properties being the two sides of a single, indissoluble operation, the elective procedure may be perceived either as wholly democratic or as wholly aristocratic, depending on which way it is looked at.

In a passage of the *Politics* that can be interpreted in a number of ways, Aristotle wrote:

> In a constitution that is well mixed, both of the elements [the democratic and oligarchical elements], and neither of them, should seem to be present [*dei d'en tē politeia tē memigmenē kalōs amphotera dokein einai kai mēdeteron*]. It should be preserved by its own means and not by external aid, and by its own means not merely because a majority wants its preservation (for that could be the case even with a poor constitution), but because no single part of the city would wish to have a different constitution.[17]

One possible interpretation of this complex passage is that a mixed constitution is "well mixed" if it can be perceived as simultaneously democratic and oligarchic, or neither the one nor the other, because then both democrats and oligarchs will be able to see in it what they are looking for, and thus equally support the constitution.

Election is perhaps one of those institutions in which the mixture is so complete that elites and ordinary citizens alike can find what they want. The ambiguity of election may be one key to its exceptional stability.

ELECTION AND THE PRINCIPLES OF MODERN NATURAL RIGHT

As we have seen, the triumph of election as a method of selecting rulers owes much, historically, to the modern conception of natural

---

embodied in a distinct organ: consuls (or the king in the English system, which was also seen as a model of a mixed government) embodied the monarchic element, the Senate (or House of Lords) the aristocratic element, and the assemblies (or the House of Commons) the democratic element.

[17] Aristotle, *Politics*, IV, 9, 1294b 35–40.

right which developed from writers such as Grotius, Hobbes, Pufendorf, Locke, and Rousseau. However, when compared with the principles of modern natural right, the aristocratic nature of election, as defined and set out here, seems to raise two related problems.

The modern conception of natural right rests on the idea that all human beings share an essential element of equality, whether it is termed free will, reason, or consciousness. Modern natural right theory acknowledges that many inequalities of strength, ability, virtue, or wealth separate human beings, but it holds that none of these inequalities gives by itself to those who are superior in one respect or another the right to rule over others.[18] Because of the fundamental equality of all human beings, the right to rule can only come from the *free consent* of those over whom power is exercised. But if the intrinsic properties of election are such that the ruled are able to choose their rulers only from certain categories of the population, can they still be said to be giving their consent freely? Moreover, if it is true that election necessarily leads to the selection of individuals who are in some way superior, does it not follow that under an elective system it is their superior qualities that give some people power over others?

In response to the first problem, it must be noted that the constraints of distinction and salience do not in fact abolish voters' freedom. They merely imply that voters are only able to choose individuals who (1) possess a distinctive trait, that (2) is judged favorably, and (3) provides a criterion of political selection. However, as has been pointed out, only the first element (the existence of a distinctive trait) is an objective fact, determined by the

---

[18] This is where the crucial difference lies between the ancient conception of justice (as found in Aristotle, for example) and the modern conception of natural right. For Aristotle, certain characteristics give by themselves or by nature to those who possess them a title to govern and to impose their will on others, even if in a city it is neither prudent nor entirely justified to reserve positions of power exclusively to those in possession of such characteristics. Certain people have a particular title to govern others, says Aristotle, because they realize or come closer than others to the excellence and flourishing of human nature. The fundamental divergence separating Aristotle from Grotius, Hobbes, Pufendorf, or Locke concerns the question of what it is that confers such a title to govern and impose one's will on others. Modern natural right theorists maintain that no particular quality gives a person the right to govern others. That right must of necessity be conferred externally, through the consent of those others.

statistical distribution of qualities within a given population. The other two elements (positive evaluation of the trait in question and its use as a criterion for selection) are decided by the electorate. So voters are free to choose among persons presenting qualities that are sufficiently rare to be noticeable. Their freedom is limited but not abolished. Not just anyone can be selected in a particular context (unlike with lot), but, within the limits traced by that objective context, any individual may appear superior to others in one respect or another. He may then be chosen in an elective system, so long as the others judge that person's distinctive feature positively and make it their criterion of selection. Since the elective method sets no objective limits on what may be judged favorably and serve as such a criterion, voters retain a broad measure of freedom.

The response to the second problem has to do with a different consideration. Saying that, in an elective system, only those who are objectively different and perceived as superior can reach positions of power, is not the same as saying that *objectively superior* individuals alone can reach power. In the latter case, individuals would owe their position of power to their superiority. In the former, what brings them to power is the *perception* of their superiority or, to put it another way, the *judgment* other people pass on their distinctive characteristics. In an elective system, although an individual may be objectively outstanding in every respect, he will not be elected if his qualities are not perceived as superiorities by his fellow-citizens. Thus, power is not conferred by distinctive traits themselves, but by the agreement of others about what traits constitute superiority.

Thus the aristocratic nature of election *can* be compatible with the fundamental principles of modern political right. This compatibility, however, is actually achieved only if one crucial condition is met: voters must be free to determine which qualities they value positively and to choose from among those qualities the one they regard as the proper criterion for political selection. A distinction needs to be made between the purely formal constraints of objective difference and of perceived superiority on the one hand, and the specific contents of the distinctive traits and of the standards of judgment on the other. Formal constraints are compatible with the principles of modern right on the condition that the particular content of the superiority is a matter of free choice. It is not against the principles of modern natural right that representatives belong mainly to certain categories of the population, so long as (and this is the essential condition) those categories are not objectively predetermined, but are freely chosen by the electorate.

Clearly, this freedom of choice regarding the content of the superiority is only imperfectly realized in contemporary representative governments. Nor was it ever actually achieved in the past. In this respect, the argument defended here does not amount to a justification of the status quo; rather, it points to the direction of the changes that would be required in representative governments in order to bring election into line with the normative principles that presided over its establishment.

The first and most important of those changes concerns the role of economic resources in elections. While the constraints of distinction and salience do not contravene the norms of modern political right, there is no doubt the constraint of wealth does. The reason is not, however, that there is something about wealth that makes it particularly unworthy to serve as a criterion for selecting rulers. It is rather that, if the advantage enjoyed by wealthy candidates (or the wealthy classes which candidates are inclined to address principally in their appeals for funds) derives from the cost of disseminating information, then superiority in wealth confers power *by itself*, and not because voters choose it as the proper criterion of selection. One can imagine a situation in which voters particularly value wealth and freely decide to adopt it as their selection criterion. They may believe that the rich are more likely to be good rulers than the poor, because, for example, there is often a correlation between wealth and education. In that case, wealth being freely chosen as the appropriate superiority, the principles of modern right are not violated. So the first change required is the elimination of the effect of wealth on election. A ceiling on electoral expenses, a strict enforcement of that ceiling, and a public financing of electoral campaigns are the most obvious means of progressing towards this goal. However, recent experience seems to show that such arrangements are not sufficient. They also present a number of technical difficulties, and no representative government appears, not even in our own day, to have solved this problem in a satisfactory manner. But even if the skewing effect of wealth is hard to eliminate completely, the general direction of the changes required is fairly clear.

A second change would be needed, but its practical implications are far less clear. The elective method, as we have seen, is in itself open to changes in the distinctive traits that can serve as selection criteria. History shows that such changes have indeed taken place over the last two centuries. Different types of elites have succeeded one another in power.[19] In light of the exigencies of natural right, this openness to change is one of the merits of election. It is a necessary condition if citizens are to be able to choose freely the kind of superiority they wish to select. However, openness to change is not in this case sufficient to secure freedom of choice. Such variation, as seen in the types of elites selected in the last 200 years, appears to have resulted mainly from social, economic, and technological developments. But freedom of choice is not secured if the specific content of the superiority is determined solely by external factors and circumstances. The distinctive traits of those who are elected ought, as far as possible, to result from a conscious and deliberate choice of the electorate.

One must note, however, that even if such changes were effected, one thing would still be ruled out by the elective procedure, namely that representatives be similar to their constituents. Elected representatives must of necessity have a positively valued trait that distinguishes them from, and makes them superior to, those who elect them. The democratic ideal of similarity between rulers and ruled has demonstrated, since the end of the eighteenth century, such a powerful appeal that it may not be unimportant to show that it is incompatible in principle with the elective procedure, however amended.

In an elective system the only possible question concerns the type of superiority that is to govern. But when asked "Who are the *aristoi* that should govern?" the democrat turns to the people and lets them decide.

[19] We shall return to this point in chapter 6.

5

The verdict of the people

A number of twentieth-century authors have put forward theories of democracy that have been categorized (mostly by their critics) as elitist.[1] The first and most influential of these was advanced by Joseph Schumpeter. Such theories employ the term democracy to denote political systems of the type in place in Britain, the United States, or France – that is to say, governments we refer to here as representative.

These theories have been termed elitist not because they stress the qualitative superiority of representatives over those they represent (in the sense defined in the previous chapter), but because they highlight another difference, presented as essential, between representative government and government by the people. It has been pointed out, not without justification, that the epithet "elitist" ill-befits such theories, that it mistakenly connects them to the explicitly elitist conceptions of Gaetano Mosca or Vilfredo Pareto, for example, and finally that the term has more to do with political polemics than with scholarly analysis.[2] It is true (to take only the forerunner of such theories) that Schumpeter does not use the

---

[1] See, for example, P. Bachrach, *The Theory of Democratic Elitism: A Critique* (Boston: Little Brown, 1967). Bachrach groups together under the title "democratic elitism" the theories of democracy proposed by Joseph Schumpeter in *Capitalism, Socialism, and Democracy* [1942], 3rd edn (New York: Harper & Row, 1957), Robert Dahl in *A Preface to Democratic Theory* (Chicago: University of Chicago Press, 1956), or Giovanni Sartori in *Democratic Theory* (Detroit, MI: Wayne State University Press, 1962).

[2] It is particularly this point that Giovanni Sartori makes in his more recent *The Theory of Democracy Revisited*, 2 vols. (Chatham: Chatham House Publishers, 1987), Vol. I, p. 157.

concept of elites. He is not interested in the characteristics of representatives and makes no reference to Mosca or Pareto. One can understand, nonetheless, why many authors have characterized Schumpeter's definition of democracy as elitist.

Schumpeter stresses that, in contrast to what is assumed by the "classical" conception of democracy, the empirical reality of representative democracies is not that the electorate makes decisions on public affairs. Elections, Schumpeter argues, do not express any popular will concerning policies. In a representative democracy, he claims, the people do not govern indirectly "by choosing individuals who will assemble to put their will into action."[3] The people merely select, from among a number of competitors, those who will make political decisions. Thus, in an often-quoted formulation, Schumpeter proposes to define democracy (or representative government) as "that institutional arrangement for arriving at political decisions, in which individuals acquire the power to decide by means of a competitive struggle for the people's vote."[4] In such a conception, representatives are not agents charged with implementing the popular will expressed in elections. Schumpeter's definition makes representative democracy something other than indirect government by the people. It has been termed elitist for that reason, elitist being here opposed to democratic. Supporters of government by the people see as undemocratic a conception that reduces representative democracy to a competition for votes.

Questions of terminology aside, the debate between Schumpeter and his critics draws attention to a real problem: do representative institutions establish any kind of link between the decisions of those who govern and the electorate's policy preferences? We have seen that the founders of representative government did not intend to create a system in which the popular will would govern, but neither did they desire that the decisions of representatives would have no connection with what voters want. Madison, as we have seen, described republican or representative government as a system that would "refine and enlarge the public views by passing them through the medium of a chosen body of citizens" ("Federalist 10"). A link of some sort was thus posited or presupposed between the

[3] Schumpeter, *Capitalism, Socialism, and Democracy*, p. 250.
[4] *Ibid.*, p. 269.

preferences of the people and the decisions of their representatives. However, the terms employed by Madison are only metaphors. Suggestive as these images are, their precise meaning remains unclear.

So we must look at the institutional arrangements that, in representative government, determine how public decisions are arrived at and how they relate to what the electorate wants.

PARTIAL INDEPENDENCE OF REPRESENTATIVES

It is a fact that the institutional mechanisms of representative government allow representatives a certain independence from their constituents' preferences. Representative systems do not authorize (indeed explicitly prohibit) two practices that would deprive representatives of any kind of independence: imperative mandates and discretionary revocability of representatives (recall). None of the representative governments established since the end of the eighteenth century has authorized imperative mandates or granted a legally binding status to the instructions given by the electorate. Neither has any of them durably applied permanent revocability of representatives.

The idea gained acceptance in eighteenth-century England that Members of Parliament represented the nation as a whole rather than their particular constituency. Voters of each electoral district were hence not authorized to give them "instructions."[5] In the early nineteenth century, the Radicals attempted to reintroduce a practice analogous to that of instructions by requiring candidates to make "pledges"; indeed after the First Reform Act (1832), they demanded that deputies be legally required to respect these promises. The Radicals' primary aim, however, was to shorten the length of parliamentary terms (which the Septennial Act of 1716 had set at seven years). It seems that pledges were merely, in their eyes, a "makeshift" and an expedient, failing a shorter parliamentary term.[6] It should be noted, moreover, that Bentham expressly rejected the

[5] See J. R. Pole, *The Gift of Government. Political Responsibility from the English Restoration to the American Independence* (Athens: University of Georgia Press, 1983), p. 103.

[6] "Pledges are a makeshift, in the absence of shorter parliaments," wrote a Radical pamphleteer, D. Wakefield ("Pledges defended: a letter to the Lambeth electors"

practice of instructions: voters should only be allowed to influence their representatives by their right not to reelect them.[7] In any case, electoral pledges were never made legally binding in England.

In America, the practice of instructions was extensive, both during the colonial period and the first decade of independence.[8] Some states, especially in New England, even included the right of instruction in their constitutions. When the First Congress (elected under the 1787 Constitution) discussed the constitutional amendments that became the Bill of Rights, some members proposed that the First Amendment (which guarantees freedom of religion and speech) include also the right to instruct representatives. The proposal was discussed at some length but was eventually rejected.[9] American voters would remain free to give instructions, but these would have no legally binding force.

In France, deputies to the Estates General, including those summoned in 1789, were bearers of instructions (called *cahiers de doléances*). One of the first decisions of the French revolutionaries (July 1789) was to prohibit imperative mandates. This decision was never challenged, either during the revolution or afterwards. In 1793–4, a segment of the *"Sans-Culotte"* movement pressed to have elected officials made revocable at any point during their term by local electoral assemblies. The constitution voted by the Assembly in 1793 contained such a provision, but the constitution was never implemented.

Almost a century later, the Paris Commune (1871) established a system of permanent revocability for members of the Council. In fact Marx saw the practice as one of the most important and promising political inventions of the Commune. After pointing out that members of the Commune Council, elected by universal suffrage, were "responsible and revocable at any time" (*verantwor-*

[1832]), quoted in N. Gash, *Politics in the Age of Peel* [1953] (New York: Norton Library, 1971), p. 30.

7   J. Bentham, *Constitutional Code* [1822–34], ed. F. Rosen and J. H. Burns (Oxford: Clarendon Press, 1983), Vol. I, p. 26.

8   See J. P. Reid, *The Concept of Representation in the Age of the American Revolution* (Chicago: University of Chicago Press, 1989), pp. 100–2.

9   See Debate in House of Representatives (August 15, 1789) (*Annals of Congress. The Debates and Proceedings in the Congress of the United States*, Vol. I), reproduced in P. B. Kurland and R. Lerner (eds.), *The Founders' Constitution*, 5 vols. (Chicago: University of Chicago Press, 1987), Vol. I, pp. 413–18.

tlich und jederzeit absetzbar),[10] Marx, in a passage reminiscent of Rousseau's famous chapter on representation, praised the system: "Rather than decide once every three or six years which member of the ruling class should 'represent' and trample on [*ver- und zertreten soll*] the people in Parliament, universal suffrage should serve the people constituted in communes as universal suffrage serves any other employer in search of workers, inspectors, and accountants for his business. And it is a well-known fact that companies, like individuals, when it comes to real business, usually know how to put each man in his place and, if once they make a mistake, are able to rectify it promptly."[11] However, the practice much vaunted by Marx was as short-lived as the Commune itself.

In addition to the aristocratic effects of election, another difference thus appears between representative government and democracy understood as government of the people by the people. This difference too was clearly perceived in the late eighteenth century by those who, like Rousseau, rejected representation. Delegation of governmental functions, necessitated by the size of modern states, might have been rendered compatible with the principle of government by the people. This could have been achieved by establishing a legal obligation for representatives to carry out the instructions of their constituents. In his *Considerations on the Government of Poland*, Rousseau accepted a form of representation for practical reasons. Drawing the logical consequences of his principles, he then recommended the practice of imperative mandates.[12] It is not only the

[10] Marx, *Der Bürgerkrieg in Frankreich* [1871], in Karl Marx and Friedrich Engels, *Werke*, 36 vols. (Berlin: Dietz Verlag, 1957–67), Vol. XVII, p. 339. English trans. *The Civil War in France*, in K. Marx and F. Engels, *Collected Works* (New York: International Publishers, 1986), Vol. XXII, p. 331. It must be noted that the English translation is inaccurate. It reads as follows: the members of the Council were "responsible and revocable at short terms." The German "*jederzeit*" does not mean "at short terms," but "at any time." The difference is not insignificant.

[11] Marx, *Der Bürgerkrieg in Frankreich*, p. 340. English trans. *The Civil War in France*, p. 333. Here again, the English translation is incorrect. The first sentence of the passage cited here is rendered as: "Instead of deciding every three or six years which member of the ruling class was to misrepresent the people in Parliament." To render the two German verbs associated by Marx in the same phrase (*vertreten* [represent] and *zertreten* [trample on]) by one single verb (misrepresent) is not only inaccurate, it entirely fails to convey the radical criticism of representation implied by Marx's formulation. The same error can be found in another English translation: *The Civil War in France*, in *Marx-Engels Reader*, ed. R. Tucker (New York: W. W. Norton, 1972), p. 633.

[12] J.-J. Rousseau, *Considérations sur le Gouvernement de Pologne* [1772], in J.-J. Rous-

delegation of government to a limited number of citizens that differentiates representation from government by the people, nor even the qualitative superiority of representatives over those they represent; the difference between the two systems also results from the partial independence of representatives.

Institutions or practices which give the people complete control over representatives have thus been proposed and occasionally established. Like the use of lot, such institutions were not strictly impracticable.[13] The point could of course be made that, in governments whose sphere of activity has gone beyond the general and relatively stable rules necessary for collective life, and in which public authorities need to make a large number of concrete decisions and to adjust to changing circumstances, a system of imperative mandates becomes unworkable. Instructions presuppose that the electorate knows in advance the issues government will confront.[14] However, this argument does not apply to permanent revocability of representatives. Being subject to recall leaves representatives with the freedom of action that is required to face unpredictable situations. But at the same time, permanent revocability guarantees congruence between the preferences of the electorate and the decisions of those in power, since voters can immediately punish and dismiss a representative whose decisions they disagree with. Though a practicable system, revocability was never established in any lasting fashion, presumably on grounds of principle rather than for purely practical reasons. Furthermore, whatever the reason why imperative mandates and permanent revocability were rejected, that initial decision, never successfully challenged afterwards, points to a fundamental difference between representative government and a system that guarantees complete congruence between the preferences of the governed and the decisions of the elected.

seau, *Oeuvres Complètes,* Vol. III (Paris: Gallimard, 1964), p. 980. English trans. *Considerations on the Government of Poland,* in J.-J. Rousseau, *Political Writings,* trans. F. Watkins (Madison: University of Wisconsin Press, 1986), pp. 193–4.

[13] It is noteworthy that Weber counts as characteristics of direct democracy the following practices and institutions: permanent revocability of public authorities, rotation in office, selection of public officials by lot, and imperative mandates. See Max Weber, *Economy and Society* [1921], ed. G. Roth and C. Wittich, 2 vols. (Berkeley: University of California Press, 1978), Vol. I, part 1, ch. 3, § 19, p. 289.

[14] This argument is put forward by Max Weber in particular. See *Economy and Society,* Vol. II, ch. 14, sec. 2, § 5, p. 1128.

Promises or programs might be put forward, but representatives have, without exception, retained the freedom to decide whether to fulfill them. Representatives undoubtedly have an incentive to keep their promises. Keeping promises is a deep-rooted social norm, and breaking them carries a stigma that can lead to difficulties in being reelected. Representatives remain, however, free to sacrifice the prospect of their reelection if, in exceptional circumstances, other considerations appear to them more important than their own careers. More importantly, they can hope that, when they stand for reelection, they will be able to convince voters that they had good reasons for their actions, even though that meant betraying their promises. Since the link between the will of the electorate and the behavior of elected representatives is not rigorously guaranteed, the latter always retain a certain amount of discretion. Those who insist that in representative democracy the people govern through their representatives must at least acknowledge that this does not mean that representatives have to implement the wishes of the electorate.

FREEDOM OF PUBLIC OPINION

Since the end of the eighteenth century, representation has been accompanied by the freedom of the governed at all times to form and express political opinions outside the control of the government. The link between representative government and the freedom of public political opinion was established straightaway in the United States, gradually in Britain, and after a complicated process in France.

Freedom of public political opinion requires two elements. In order that the governed may form their own opinions on political matters, it is necessary that they have access to political information, and this requires that governmental decisions are made public. If those in government make decisions in secret, the governed have only inadequate means of forming opinions on political matters. Making parliamentary debates public knowledge became accepted in Britain in the late eighteenth century (prior to which, the secrecy of debates was considered a prerogative of Parliament, essential for protecting against royal interference).[15] In the United States, the

[15] See Pole, *The Gift of Government*, pp. 87–116.

deliberations of both the Continental Congress and the Philadelphia Convention were kept secret. The first Senate elected under the Constitution initially decided that its proceedings should be secret, but the practice was discarded four years later.[16] In France, the Estates-General of 1789 opted from the outset for the principle of openness and, thereafter, the debates of all the revolutionary assemblies took place in the presence of the public. Pressure (not to mention threats) from the galleries notoriously influenced the debates of the successive revolutionary assemblies. The French and American examples suggest that although a certain amount of openness of political acts is required to keep citizens informed, it is not necessary at each stage of the decision process. It is reasonable to think that the American public as a whole had a better opportunity of forming opinions about its Constitution (between the end of the Philadelphia Convention and the ratification debates) than the French public ever had with respect to the various revolutionary constitutions.

The second requisite for freedom of public opinion is freedom to express political opinions at any time, not just when voting in elections. However, the relationship between freedom of opinion and the representative character of government is not obvious. It might seem that representative governments established freedom of opinion because their founders adhered to the liberal principle that a part of individuals' lives should be free from the influence of collectively made decisions, even those made by elected representatives. One might indeed argue, following the distinction popularized by Isaiah Berlin, that freedom of opinion belongs to the category of "negative liberties" that protect the individual from the encroachment of government. Thus understood, freedom of opinion does not have an intrinsic connection with the representative character of government, because representation is concerned with giving citizens control over government, and therefore, with securing a "positive liberty." On this interpretation, then, representative government has been associated with freedom of opinion merely *de facto*, just because the partisans of representation happened to be at the same time partisans of the freedom of conscience.

---

[16] See Pole, *The Gift of Government*, pp. 117–40.

There is no doubt that freedom of opinion was established in the wake of religious freedom, which protects the sphere of inner beliefs against state intervention. However, there is also an important intrinsic connection between freedom of opinion and the political role of the citizen in representative government.

This is particularly clear in the First Amendment to the US Constitution and in the debates over its adoption. The First Amendment stipulates that: "Congress shall make no law respecting an establishment of religion, or prohibiting the free exercise thereof; or abridging the freedom of speech, or of the press; or the right of the people peaceably to assemble, and to petition the government for a redress of grievances." Religious freedom and freedom of political expression are thus closely associated. One should also note that this formulation links individual and collective expressions of opinion: freedom of religion, which may apply to individuals, is joined with the rights of assembly and petition, which are collective expressions. The collective character of an expression affects its political weight: authorities can, without great risk, ignore the dispersed expression of individual opinions, but they cannot as easily disregard crowds in the streets, however peaceable, or petitions with thousands of signatures. Finally, by combining in the same clause both the freedom of assembly and the freedom to "petition the *government for a redress of grievances,*" the First Amendment clearly reveals its political dimension: it is concerned with protecting not only the collective expressions of opinion in general, but also those specifically addressed to the authorities with the intent of obtaining something from them. Because the First Amendment guarantees freedom to petition the government at the same time that it guarantees freedom of religion, it establishes not merely a "negative freedom" of the individual, but also a way for citizens positively to act upon the government.

Moreover, the debate that led to the adoption of the First Amendment shows that its political implications were clearly on the minds of its framers. The mere fact that the questions of instructions and imperative mandates were discussed on this occasion demonstrates that the participants perceived a link between freedom of speech and representation. But various speeches, those by Madison in particular, make even clearer the political significance of the First Amendment.

Those who had proposed and supported the addition of the "right of instruction" had claimed that in a republican government the people must have the right to make their will prevail. Madison declared himself against including the right of instruction in the amendment, responding that this principle was true "in certain respects" but "not in others":

> In the sense in which it is true, we have asserted the right sufficiently in what we have done [i.e. in formulating the amendment as proposed and as it was eventually adopted]; if we mean nothing more than this, that the people have a right to express and communicate their sentiments and wishes, we have provided for it already. The right of freedom of speech is secured; the liberty of the press is expressly declared to be beyond the reach of this government; the people may therefore publicly address their representatives, may privately advise them, or declare their sentiments by petition to the whole body; in all these ways they may communicate their wills.[17]

Freedom of opinion, understood in its political dimension, thus appears as a *counterpart* to the absence of the right of instruction. Freedom of public opinion is a democratic feature of representative systems, in that it provides a means whereby the voice of the people can reach those who govern, whereas the independence of the representatives is clearly a non-democratic feature of representative systems. Representatives are not required to act on the wishes of the people, but neither can they ignore them: freedom of public opinion ensures that such wishes can be expressed and be brought to the attention of those who govern. It is the representatives who make the final decisions, but a framework is created in which the will of the people is one of the considerations in their decision process.

Public expression of opinion is the key element here. It has the effect not only of bringing popular opinions to the attention of those who govern, but also of connecting the governed among themselves. Indeed this horizontal dimension of communication affects the vertical relationship between the governed and the government: the more the people are aware of each other's opinions, the stronger the incentive for those who govern to take those opinions into account. When a number of individuals find themselves expressing similar

[17] Madison, "Address to the Chamber of Representatives," August 15, 1789 (*Annals of Congress. The Debates and Proceedings in the Congress of the United States*, Vol. I), quoted in Kurland and Lerner (eds.), *The Founders' Constitution*, p. 415.

views, each realizes that he is not alone in holding a particular opinion. People who express the same opinion become aware of the similarity of their views, and this gives them capacities for action that would have not been available had they kept that opinion to themselves. The less isolated people feel, the more they realize their potential strength, and the more capable they are to organize themselves and exercise pressure on the government. Awareness of a similarity of views may not always result in organization and action, but it is usually a necessary condition. Moreover, public expression of an opinion generates momentum. People who silently harbor an opinion that is voiced aloud by others become more self-confident when they discover that they are not alone in thinking that way, and thus they become more inclined to express that opinion.

In fact, one of the oldest maxims of despotism is to prevent subjects from communicating among themselves. Although dictators often seek to know the political opinions of all their subjects severally and to form an aggregate picture, they take great care to keep such information to themselves.[18] By contrast, one of the distinguishing features of representative government is the possibility for the governed themselves to become aware of each other's views at any time, independent of the authorities.

The expression of a shared political opinion seldom brings together all of the governed or even a majority of them. The electorate as a whole rarely expresses itself outside elections, though this can happen. Most of the time, then, the expression of public opinion remains partial in the sense that it is only the point of view of a particular group, however large. Opinion polls, which in recent decades have been added to the older forms of the expression of public opinion, are no exception to the rule. Polls, too, remain partial expressions of the popular will. This is not because only a small number of citizens are interviewed (representative sampling, properly used, ensures that the distribution of opinions is approximately the same in the sample as in the population at large), but because the questions are drawn up by particular people, namely the polling organizations and their clients. The entire population

---

[18] We know, for example, that some governments of the formerly Communist countries occasionally carried out opinion polls, even taking advice from Western experts in the field. The results of such polls were never published, of course.

expresses opinions, but only on subjects that have been chosen by a particular group in the society. Moreover, respondents cannot express any opinion they wish, they must choose from among a predetermined set of alternatives. It is true that in an election citizens can also only choose from among a set of alternatives that they have not determined themselves (the candidates). In an election, however, the terms of the choice eventually offered to voters are the product of a process that is open to all (or all who wish to be candidates), whereas in a poll the alternatives from among which respondents have to choose remain under the exclusive control of the polling organization and its client.

Similarly, the expression of a shared political opinion rarely stems from the spontaneous initiative of all those who express it (although this too can happen). Usually, the initiative comes from an even smaller group of citizens who solicit the expression of the same opinion by a larger group. For instance, a small number of militants organize a demonstration and call for others to participate, or a few high-profile personalities start a petition and appeal for signatures. A measure of voluntariness nevertheless remains in the expression of those who agree to voice the opinion in question. They could have stayed away from the demonstration, or they could have refused to sign the petition; there was no penalty for such refusals. More importantly, expression of the opinion was neither compelled nor solicited by the government. Here again, polls do not depart from the rule. Granted, polling organizations and their clients do not invite the interviewees to express one view rather than another among those that are on offer, but they take the initiative of asking some questions rather than others and of formulating those questions in what they regard as the most appropriate manner. Opinion polls, therefore, do not provide wholly spontaneous opinions any more than do demonstrations or petitions.

A resurgence of the ideal (or ideology) of direct democracy accompanied the rise and growth of opinion polls. Owing to polls, it was said, it would at last be possible to find out what people truly and spontaneously believe or want, without any adulterating mediation.[19] Critics retorted that opinion polls are no more than a way

---

[19] A notable example of this rudimentary view can be found in George Gallup and Saul F. Rae, *The Pulse of Democracy* (New York: Simon & Schuster, 1940).

of manipulating opinion, precisely because they impose questions that might be quite foreign to people's concerns and to which people respond in order to please the interviewer or to avoid appearing ignorant.[20] One is tempted to say that the practice deserves neither so much credit nor so much blame. Opinion polls, like demonstrations and petitions, do not deliver the pure, undistorted opinion of the public. Although the medium of expression as well as the social identity of the mediators and of those who express opinions vary between opinion polls, demonstrations, and petitions, in all cases the opinions are solicited rather than spontaneous. Conversely, once the illusion is dispelled that opinion polls reveal what the people spontaneously think or are concerned with, there is no reason to regard polls as any more manipulative than calls to demonstrate or sign petitions.

So whether it takes the form of demonstrations, petitions, or polls, expression of public opinion is usually partial and initiated by small groups. However, from the point of view of those in power, even such limited expressions are worth taking into account in the decision-making process: an opinion voiced at one point by a particular group may become widespread, the group may be sufficiently organized and influential for its opinion to be difficult to ignore, or a series of polls may reveal a trend that foreshadows the result of a forthcoming election. Those in government have to estimate these various probabilities and decide in consequence what importance they want to give to this or that opinion.

Apart from situations in which the people seriously threaten public order and constrain those in government by a sheer contest of force, the only binding will of the citizens is that expressed in a vote. Independently of elections, however, the governed always have the possibility to voice a collective opinion that differs from that of the representatives. One generally terms as public opinion this collective voice of the people which, without binding power, can always manifest itself beyond the control of those in government.[21]

---

[20] See for example, Pierre Bourdieu, "L'opinion publique n'existe pas" [1972], in his *Questions de Sociologie* (Paris: Editions de Minuit, 1980), pp. 222–34; Pierre Bourdieu, "Questions de politique," in *Actes de la Recherche en Sciences Sociales*, Sept. 17, 1977.

[21] The term is a matter of convention. A number of discussions prompted by the notion of public opinion in recent years turn out to be no more than terminological

Freedom of public opinion distinguishes representative government from what has been called "absolute representation," whose most notable formulation can be found in Hobbes. For him, a group of individuals constitute a political entity only when they have authorized a representative or assembly to act on their behalf and to whom they place themselves in subjection. Prior to designating the representative and independently of his person, the people have no unity; they are a *multitudo dissoluta*, a disbanded multitude. The people acquire political agency and capability of self-expression only through the person of the representative. Once authorized, however, the representative entirely replaces the represented. They have no other voice than his.[22] It is precisely this total substitution that freedom of public opinion precludes. The populace can always manifest itself as a political entity having a (usually incomplete) unity independent of the representative. When individuals as a group give instructions to their representatives, when a crowd gathers in the street, when petitions are delivered, or when polls point to a clear trend, the people reveal themselves as a political entity capable of speaking apart from those who govern. Freedom of public opinion keeps open the possibility that the represented might at any time make their own voices heard. Representative government is, thus, a system in which the representatives can never say with complete confidence and certainty "We the people."

Both popular self-government and absolute representation result in the abolition of the gap between those who govern and those

---

disputes, even if the details of the arguments put forward are often of real interest. Studying historically the various meanings with which the term has been invested since its invention in the eighteenth century (from Rousseau, the Physiocrats, and Necker, through Bentham, Tocqueville, Mill, and Tarde, to Schmitt, Habermas, and Noëlle-Neumann) is an entirely justified pursuit, but one that would fill a whole volume. Having done some research on the subject, I feel that the definition I adopt is in keeping with the element shared by the various meanings that have been (simultaneously or successively) attached to the term "public opinion." However, in the context of the argument developed here, that definition may be regarded as stipulative. The argument concerns the existence and the influence, in representative government, of opinions that the governed can express at any time beyond the control of government. The term employed to denote the phenomenon constituted by those opinions is, strictly speaking, of no consequence.

[22] See Hobbes, *Leviathan* [1651], ed. C. B. Macpherson (Harmondsworth, UK: Penguin, 1968), p. 220 (ch. 16), and ch. 18. The absolute nature of representation in Hobbes is analysed in a penetrating manner in H. Pitkin, *The Concept of Representation* (Berkeley: University of California Press, 1967), pp. 15–27.

who are governed, the former because it turns the governed into the governors, the latter because it substitutes representatives for those who are represented. Representative government on the other hand, preserves that gap.

THE REPEATED CHARACTER OF ELECTIONS

The most important feature of representative systems that allows voters to influence the decisions of their representatives is the recurring character of elections. Indeed, repeated elections provide one of the key incentives for those in government to take account of public opinion. Representatives no doubt have many reasons for doing so, but the most powerful is that shifts in public opinion may prefigure the results of the forthcoming election.

Representative government is based not only on the election of those who govern, but on their being elected at regular intervals. This second characteristic is often overlooked or tends to be taken for granted. It is surprising that Schumpeter scarcely mentions the periodic nature of elections in his theory of democracy. Although, as we saw, Schumpeter presents his definition of democracy as closer to observable reality than is the "classical conception," his definition does not include the empirical fact that electoral competition is repeated. Having formulated his conception, Schumpeter adds, it is true, that it "implicitly" recognizes the people's power to dismiss rulers.[23] However, the principle that the electorate chooses its government by means of a competitive electoral process, in no way logically implies that the electorate can also regularly remove the government from office. Admittedly, since the late eighteenth century the two principles have always been associated in practice, but this does not warrant the claim that the second is somehow contained in the first.

Indeed, it is quite possible to conceive of a situation in which the position of ruler might be conferred by the will of the ruled following a competitive process, but in a definitive fashion – for instance, by election for life. Such a system is not only a logical possibility; it has actually been proposed. At the Philadelphia

---

[23] Schumpeter, *Capitalism, Socialism, and Democracy*, p. 269.

Convention, Hamilton suggested that the President be elected for life.[24] One must conclude from this that the principle of election for life was deliberately rejected, and for specific reasons, by the founders of representative government. Furthermore, it is immediately apparent that a system of election for life possesses one important property: it leaves voters with no effective means of influencing the actions of their rulers, once elected. The cardinals elect the Pope, but this does not make him any less independent of them in his actions. By contrast, if governments are regularly subjected to election, they can be changed if their performance has not proved satisfactory to voters. And since it is reasonable to suppose that the prestige and benefits attached to the position of ruler usually make them desire to be reelected, it seems that they have reason to take into consideration the wishes of the electorate in their decisions.

The principle of regularly renewed popular consent distinguishes representative government from modes of government deemed legitimate by Grotius, Hobbes, or Pufendorf. For them, popular consent, once given, is sufficient for the establishment of a legitimate government, either in the case of a sovereign having the right to appoint his successor or in the case of a dynasty. According to these authors, the people can *once and for all* transfer to some entity its right to govern itself, and such transfer is a valid and sufficient source of legitimacy, as long as it is freely consented to.[25] Among modern natural right theorists, only Locke mentions the need to renew popular consent by the regular election of Parliament. Representative government cannot be understood without mentioning the role of time.

Voters' preferences about future policies can exert only limited influence on public decisions, because, as noted earlier, when voters

---

[24] Hamilton, speech of June 18, 1787, in M. Farrand (ed.), *The Records of the Federal Convention of 1787*, 4 vols. (New Haven, CT: Yale University Press, 1966), Vol. I, pp. 289–92.

[25] Grotius, Hobbes, and Pufendorf all emphasize that, by consenting to establish a government, the people transfer their right to govern themselves in perpetuity. The establishment of government is, thus, similar to alienation of property: a person is said to alienate a property when he sells it, thereby losing any right to it for ever. In a system of regular elections by contrast, the people transfer the right to govern only temporarily. In this sense, election at regular intervals should be seen as the mark of the inalienable nature of the sovereignty of the people.

elect a candidate with the aim of seeing his program implemented, they have no guarantee that the candidate will not break his electoral promises. On the other hand, by requiring those who are elected to answer on a regular basis to those who elect them, the representative system gives voters the effective ability to dismiss rulers whose policies fail to meet with their approval. Citizens do not necessarily use their vote to express preferences about public policy; they may also elect (or not elect) on the basis of the character of candidates.[26] But at least they are able, should they wish, to use their vote to express preferences about the policies that were pursued or are proposed.

In a situation in which representatives are subject to reelection, each new election allows voters to express two types of preferences regarding public policy. People may use their vote to express rejection and to stop the incumbents from pursuing the current policy, or they may use their vote to bring about the implementation of a proposed policy. Obviously, these two types of preferences may be combined in varying proportions. However, as a result of the absence of imperative mandates the two types of preferences are not equally effective. By not reelecting the incumbents, voters do indeed prevent them from continuing a rejected policy, but by electing a candidate because he proposes a particular policy they are not necessarily bringing about the adoption of that policy. In representative government negation is more powerful than affirmation: the former constrains those in power, while the latter remains an aspiration.

One may wonder, however, what degree of control the electorate can really exercise through the ability to dismiss rulers. Since citizens are unable to compel those they elect to pursue a particular policy, they cannot, by unseating representatives whose policy in a given area they reject, ensure that the action of the new representatives will be any different from that of their predecessors. Imagine a situation in which a government (or administration) is dismissed because unemployment increased during its term in office, and challengers win the election by promising to restore full employment. Once in power, however, they decide not to keep their

---

[26] On this point, see the arguments set out in chapter 4.

promises, either because these were no more than electoral rhetoric to begin with, or because, on assuming office, they discover new information that convinces them that a policy of full employment is unfeasible. The members of the new government, knowing that unemployment brought about the defeat of their predecessors, have reason to believe that it might also bring about their own defeat at the next election. However, to obviate that eventuality, they may decide to give voters cause for satisfaction in other areas, for example, by combating crime more vigorously than had been done before. The conclusion could be drawn, then, that the ability to dismiss rulers whose policy they reject does not really permit voters to orient the course of public policy.

One intuitively senses that repeated elections give the governed a certain control over the conduct of public affairs, but why this should be so is not obvious, given the absence of imperative mandates and of binding electoral promises. Theories of democracy, such as Robert Dahl's, which stress the importance of repeated elections and argue that this recurring character makes governments "responsive" or "accountable" to voters do not succeed in showing the precise mechanism through which voters' repeated expression affects public decisions.

The central mechanism whereby voters influence governmental decisions results from the incentives that representative systems create for those in office: representatives who are subject to reelection have an incentive to *anticipate* the future judgment of the electorate on the policies they pursue. The prospect of possible dismissal exercises an effect on the actions of the government at every point of its term. Representatives pursuing the goal of re-election have an incentive to ensure that their present decisions do not provoke a future rejection by the electorate. They must, therefore, try to predict the reactions that those decisions will generate and include that prediction in their deliberations. To put it another way, at any point in time it is in the interest of the government to take into account in its *present* decisions the future judgment of voters on those decisions. That is the channel through which the will of the governed enters into the calculations of those in power. In the above-mentioned example of a new government fighting crime instead of trying, as promised, to reduce unemployment, consideration of the popular will plays a part in the calculations. What actually happens is that those in power proceed on the assumption that, come the next election, voters will reverse their previous order of preferences and give greater weight to considerations of law and order than they did before. Since those acceding to power know that their chance of reelection depends on that assumption being correct, they have a powerful motive for not forming it lightly.

It is because Schumpeter failed to note the central importance of anticipation in the decision-making of representatives that he wrongly believed that representative democracy could be reduced to the competitive selection of decision-makers and that he could dismiss as myth the idea of voters influencing the content of public decisions.

But if the central mechanism whereby voters can influence public policy is anticipation by those in government, one key implication follows. What those in government must anticipate in order to avoid being voted out of office is a judgment of their policies that, at the time it is expressed, will relate to the past. Voters thus influence public decisions through the *retrospective* judgment that representatives anticipate voters will make. This is not to say that, as a matter of fact, voters generally make their electoral decisions on the basis of retrospective considerations, though some empirical studies do point to the importance of the retrospective dimension in actual electoral behavior.[27] The argument is rather that, in view of the institutional structure and the incentives it creates for representatives, it is by voting in a retrospective manner that voters are most likely to influence the decisions of those who govern. Voters may not behave in this way, of course, but in that case they are conferring greater freedom of action on their representatives. In other words, in a representative system, if citizens wish to influence the course of public decisions, they *should* vote on the basis of retrospective considerations.[28]

[27] The classic empirical study of retrospective voting is that of M. Fiorina, *Retrospective Voting in American National Elections* (New Haven, CT: Yale University Press, 1981).

[28] It has been shown, by means of a formal model, that retrospective voting does indeed enable citizens to control their representatives; see J. Ferejohn, "Incumbent performance and electoral control," in *Public Choice*, Vol. 50, 1986, pp. 5–25. In Ferejohn's model, voter control through retrospective voting presupposes two conditions: (1) the electorate must vote exclusively on the basis of retrospective

The question occurs whether it is plausible that people vote on the basis of retrospective considerations when the election of representatives is by definition an act whose consequences lie in the future. Why should the electorate behave like a god, dealing out rewards and punishments? When citizens vote, they inevitably have their eyes on the future. However, they do in fact have good reasons for using the candidates' records as criteria of decision in an act that bears on the future. They know (or at least it would be reasonable for them to know) that electoral pledges are not binding and that those who are elected often fail to keep them. So it may, from their standpoint, be reasonable to take no notice of the candidates' programs in the belief that their records offer a better way of predicting future conduct than do their words. Furthermore, even assuming that voters choose to pay some attention to the candidates' promises, they know, or should know, that the credibility of those promises is an open question. It is not reasonable on their part to suppose that candidates will necessarily honor their commitments. But one of the only means available to assess how much trust is to be placed in candidates' commitments is the way in which those candidates have conducted themselves in the past. On both counts, therefore, it may be reasonable for voters to use the past behavior of candidates as criteria in decisions bearing on the future.

Of course, the ability of voters to form a retrospective judgment and the effectiveness of that judgment presuppose institutional conditions that do not always obtain in existing representative governments, or that obtain only to varying degrees. Three conditions are particularly important. First, voters must be able clearly to assign responsibility. In this regard, coalition governments, or institutional arrangements that favor coalition governments (proportional representation, for instance), impair retrospective judgment. Under a coalition government, when the electorate

considerations; and (2) in evaluating a representative's performance, voters must take into account aggregate social or economic data (e.g. the overall increase in unemployment during the representative's term) rather than their personal situation (e.g. the fact that they lost their jobs during that period). Ferejohn sums up the second precondition by saying that, to exert effective control over their representative, voters must be "sociotropic" rather than purely individualist. It must also be noted that in this model there is only one representative (or party) that voters need to reelect or not. Apparently, dealing mathematically with a situation in which the incumbent is in competition with other candidates involves major difficulties.

disapproves of a particular policy, the members of the coalition are able to shift responsibility for the unpopular decisions on to each other. If a policy is the outcome of intricate negotiations among a number of partners, it is extremely difficult for voters to assign blame when that policy provokes their rejection. Second, voters should be able to drive from power those they consider responsible for a policy they reject. Here again, proportional representation gets in the way of such retrospective sanctioning.[29] Finally, if incumbents have access to resources that are not available to their opponents (e.g. using government employees to help disseminate electoral messages), the mechanism of retrospective sanctions is impaired because it becomes structurally more difficult for voters not to reelect a representative than to reelect him.

The fact remains, however, that given the institutional structure of representative government and the desire of those in office to retain power, it is the retrospective judgment delivered by the electorate that counts in the deliberations of the decision-makers. If representatives assume that voters will make up their minds at the next election solely on the basis of the programs put forward at that time, they have complete freedom of action. They are able, in the present, to pursue whatever policies they wish, telling themselves that there will be plenty of time, in the next election campaign, to propose a program that is sufficiently attractive for the electorate to return them to power.

Attention should also be drawn to another key property of the mechanism of retrospective sanction. The arrangement leaves most of the *initiative* to those in government. Granted, representatives are not absolutely free to make any decision they wish, since they must act in such a way as not to provoke rejection by the voters at the end of their term. Nevertheless, representatives have a much wider margin of freedom than they would if they had to implement the prospective choices of the electorate. They may, for example, embark on a policy entirely on their own authority and even

---

[29] On these points, see G. Bingham Powell, "Constitutional design and citizen electoral control," in *Journal of Theoretical Politics*, Vol. 1, 1989, pp. 107–30; G. Bingham Powell, "Holding governments accountable: how constitutional arrangements and party systems affect clarity of responsibility for policy in contemporary democracies," paper delivered at the 1990 meeting of the American Political Science Association (manuscript).

contrary to the wishes of the people, if they anticipate that, once implemented, that policy will not provoke rejection. They can thus reveal to the electorate that a policy of which voters had no idea or that they did not want at the time of its adoption may in fact be one they find satisfactory.

Imagine an economic crisis marked by both high unemployment and a large public deficit. If those coming to power determine that the crisis is essentially due to low investment by firms, they may decide to raise taxes (something voters, presumably, will not appreciate) in order to reduce the budget deficit and the need for government to borrow on the capital market. If their diagnosis is correct, interest rates will go down, firms will be able to finance their investments more cheaply, and they will begin to hire once again. Those in government may think that, at the next election, the electorate will take account of their reduction of unemployment.

Many policies appear in a different light depending on whether it is their immediate or long-term effects that are considered, or even whether they are looked at before or after their application.[30] Since retrospective appraisal of policies occurs only at elections and not immediately after each initiative, most of the time voters have to pronounce not only on the initiative itself, but on the actual decision and on the effects that it has had time to produce. Except for decisions made on the eve of an election, voters are thus placed in the position of evaluating public decisions in light of their consequences. If the people governed itself, in order to make rational decisions it would need to anticipate their consequences; in representative government, the effort of anticipation required of the people is less great, the consequences of public decisions having

---

[30] A notable example of the second category of policies mentioned here is analysed by R. Fernandez and D. Rodrik in "Resistance to reform: status quo bias in the presence of individual specific uncertainty," in *American Economic Review*, Vol. 81, No. 5, 1991 (December), pp. 1146–55. The article studies a policy that, once implemented, will bring a small benefit to a very large number of individuals while imposing a high cost on a very small number. However, people do not know in advance whether they will be among the beneficiaries or among the losers. In such conditions, the expected utility of the policy in question is negative for a very large number of people. So there would never be a majority in favor of its adoption *ex ante*. However, once the policy has been implemented, and the uncertainty regarding the identity of the winners and losers has been removed, it will have the approval of the very large number who will have gained. There will thus be an *ex post* majority to uphold it.

already manifested themselves, at least in part, at the time when the electorate delivers its verdict.

The institutional structure of representative government thus gives a quite specific shape to the relationship between the elected and the electorate, one that is different from what both common sense and democratic ideology imagine. It confers influence over the course of public policy to citizens passing retrospective judgment on the actions of their representatives and the consequences of those actions, not to citizens expressing *ex ante* their wishes regarding actions to be undertaken. In representative government, the electorate judges *ex post facto* the initiatives taken in a relatively autonomous manner by those it has placed in power. Through their retrospective judgment, the people enjoy genuinely sovereign power. Come election time, when all has been said for and against the incumbents' policy, the people render their verdict. Against this verdict, whether right or wrong, there is no appeal; that is the democratic aspect of election. However, every election is also – and inseparably – a choice regarding the future, since it is about appointing those who will govern tomorrow. In this, its prospective aspect, election is not democratic, because the governed are unable to compel those who govern to implement the policy for which they elected them.

Again, therefore, in a different form this time and in the conduct of public policy, we find the same combination, within a single action, of democratic and non-democratic dimensions, as we found to characterize election considered as a procedure for selecting individuals. But here there is the additional paradox that it is by considering the past that voters are best able to influence the future.

TRIAL BY DISCUSSION

It has become common today to consider that representative government was originally viewed and justified as "government by discussion." The analyses of Carl Schmitt appear to have played a key role in the diffusion of this interpretation.[31] It is worth noting, however,

---

[31] See in particular C. Schmitt, *Die Geistesgeschichtliche Lage des heutigen Parlamentarismus* [1923], [1926]. English translation: *The Crisis of Parliamentary Democracy*, trans. E. Kennedy (Cambridge, MA: MIT Press, 1988), pp. 3–8 (Preface to the 2nd

that the texts cited by Schmitt in support of his view date principally from the nineteenth century, when representative government was no longer an innovation. He cites much less frequently writings or speeches of the seventeenth and eighteenth centuries, the period when the principles of representative government were first formulated and put into place.[32] The virtues of discussion are certainly praised by Montesquieu, Madison, Siéyès, or Burke, but as a theme it occupies a much smaller space than in Guizot, Bentham, or, later, John Stuart Mill. Discussion is not even mentioned in Locke's *Second Treatise on Government*. And neither the American Founding Fathers nor the French Constituents of 1789–91 defined representative government as "government by discussion." Furthermore, the formula of "government by discussion" is quite confused. It does not indicate exactly what place discussion is supposed to occupy in government. Is it thought to direct all stages of the decision-making process or only certain ones? Does the phrase mean that, in representative government, as in the "perpetual conversation" dear to the German Romantics, everything is the subject of unending discussion?

Even if discussion does not figure as prominently in the formulations of the inventors of representative government as it does in nineteenth-century reflections, there is no doubt that, from the origins of representative government, the idea of representation was associated with discussion. This found expression in an arrangement, adopted in Britain, the United States, and France, whereby representatives enjoy complete freedom of speech within the walls of the assembly. The link between representation and discussion can be understood only by introducing the intermediary notion of assembly. Representative government has always been conceived and justified as a political system in which an assembly plays a decisive role. One might imagine, as Schmitt rightly points out, that representation could be the privilege of a single individual, ap-

edn), and pp. 33–7, 48–50; or C. Schmitt, *Verfassungslehre* (Munich: Duncker & Humblot, 1928), §24, pp. 315–16.

[32] Schmitt relies principally on the texts by Guizot collected in his *Histoire des origines du gouvernement représentatif* (Brussels, 1851); see Schmitt, *The Crisis of Parliamentary Democracy*, pp. 34–5. On the role of discussion and of the "sovereignty of reason" in Guizot, see Pierre Rosanvallon, *Le Moment Guizot* (Paris: Gallimard, 1985), pp. 55–63, 87–94. Schmitt also quotes Burke, Bentham, and James Bryce.

pointed and authorized by the people.[33] It is nonetheless undeniably true that representative government was neither proposed nor established as a regime in which power was entrusted to a single individual chosen by the people, but as one in which a collective authority occupied a central position. Schmitt and many authors after him, however, go beyond noting the link between the representative idea and the role of the assembly; they interpret the preeminent place accorded to the assembly as the consequence of a prior and more fundamental belief in the virtues of debate by a collective authority and in the principle of government by truth (*veritas non auctoritas facit legem*).[34] According to this interpretation, the structure of beliefs justifying representative government defined as government by an assembly would have been as follows: truth must "make the law," debate is the most appropriate means of determining truth, and therefore the central political authority must be a place of debate, that is, a Parliament.

In reality, the arguments of the inventors and first advocates of representative government do not follow this pattern. In Locke, Montesquieu (in his analysis of the English system), Burke, Madison, and Siéyès, the collective nature of the representative authority is never deduced from a prior argument concerning the benefits of debate. In all these authors, the fact that representation requires an assembly is put forth as self-evident. Actually, the association between representation and assembly was not a creation *ex nihilo* of modern political thought, but a legacy of history. Modern parliaments have taken shape through a process of transfor-

---

[33] "If for practical and technical reasons the representatives of the people can decide instead of the people themselves, then certainly a single trusted representative could also decide in the name of the people. Without ceasing to be democratic, the argumentation would justify an antiparliamentary Caesarism" (Schmitt, *The Crisis of Parliamentary Democracy*, p. 34).

[34] Schmitt, *The Crisis of Parliamentary Democracy*, pp. 35, 43. This idea is developed at length by Jürgen Habermas in *The Structural Transformation of the Public Sphere* [1962] (Cambridge, MA: MIT Press, 1989). Schmitt draws a parallel between the value placed on debate by advocates of parliamentarism and the merits of the market as extolled by liberals: "It is exactly the same: That the truth can be found through an unrestrained clash of opinion and that competition will produce harmony" (*The Crisis of Parliamentary Democracy*, p. 35). The idea that truth emerges from discussion is in fact quite common, and Western philosophical tradition, starting with Plato and Aristotle, has given many elaborate versions of it. It is not justified to consider it a belief specific to liberal thought taken in its narrowest sense.

mation (gradual in England, rather more abrupt in France), or imitation (in the American colonies) of representative bodies begun in feudal society, the "assemblies of estates." The first advocates of modern representative assemblies insisted that they differed from previous institutions, but that very insistence showed an awareness of the links between the old and new. The collective nature of the representative authority was one such element of continuity. In writings and speeches by the founders of modern representation, discussion appears as a characteristic of assemblies that is inevitable and in a certain way natural.

Moreover, the idea of representative government has from the start been linked to an acceptance of social diversity. Representation was first proposed as a technique that permitted the establishment of a government emanating from the people in large, diverse nations. Madison and Siéyès asserted repeatedly that direct democracy was made possible in ancient republics by the homogeneity and small size of the body politic. They stressed that these conditions no longer obtain in a modern world characterized by the division of labor, the progress of commerce, and the diversification of interests. (Inversely, the most notable opponent of representation, Rousseau, condemned "commercial society," the progress of the arts and sciences, and praised small, homogeneous communities enjoying unadulterated unity.) In the eighteenth century, it was generally considered that representative assemblies ought, within limits, to reflect that diversity. Even among authors such as Siéyès or Burke, who emphasized most insistently that the role of the assembly was to produce unity, it was assumed that representatives, elected by diverse localities and populations, imparted a certain heterogeneity to the assembly.[35] The representative body was thus always seen as both collective and diverse in character.

---

[35] The most significant of Burke's writings in this connection is his famous "Speech to the Electors of Bristol," in which he declares: "If government were a matter of will upon any side, yours, without question, ought to be superior. But government and legislation are matters of reason and judgment, and not of inclination; and what sort of reason is that in which the determination precedes the discussion, in which one set of men deliberate and another decide, and where those who form the conclusion are perhaps three hundred miles distant from those who hear the arguments? ... Parliament is not a *congress* of ambassadors from different and hostile interests, which interests each must maintain, as an agent and advocate, against other agents and advocates; but Parliament is a *deliberative* assembly of *one*

It is the collective and diverse character of the representative organ, and not any prior or independently established belief in the virtues of debate, that explains the role conferred on discussion. In a collective entity whose members, elected by diverse populations, are initially likely to hold different points of view, the problem is to produce agreement, a convergence of wills. However, as we have seen, at the root of their political conceptions, the founders of representative government posited the equality of wills: no intrinsic superiority gives certain individuals the right to impose their will on others. Thus, in an assembly where a convergence of wills must be achieved despite diverse starting positions, if neither the most powerful, nor the most competent, nor the wealthiest are entitled to impose their will, all participants must seek to win the consent of others through debate and persuasion. The obviousness of this solution, given the principle of equality of wills, explains why it is rarely the subject of explicit argument among the founders, and why discussion is presented as the natural way for representative assemblies to proceed. Equality of wills, the root of the elective procedure for appointing rulers, likewise makes discussion the legitimate form of interaction among them.

The idea of discussion and of its function that prevailed among the earliest advocates of representation is expressed with particular clarity in Siéyès's *Vues sur les moyens d'exécution dont les représentants de la France pourront disposer en 1789*, a pamphlet that can be considered one of the founding texts of modern representative government. The passage that Siéyès devoted to debate clarifies several crucial points, and is worth quoting at some length. It must first be noted that Siéyès introduces his reflections on debate *after* he has established the necessity of representative government, and he does so to respond to objections made "against large assemblies and against freedom of speech." He thus assumes, without further justification, that representation requires an assembly and that the role of an assembly is to debate.

---

nation, with *one* interest, that of the whole – where not local purposes, not local prejudices, ought to guide, but the general good, resulting from the general reason of the whole." E. Burke, "Speech to the Electors of Bristol" [1774], in R. J. S. Hoffmann and P. Levack (eds.), *Burke's Politics, Selected Writings and Speeches* (New York: A. A. Knopf, 1949), p. 115; original emphasis.

First, one disapproves of the complication and slowness that affairs appear to take in large deliberating assemblies. This is because in France one is accustomed to arbitrary decisions that are made secretly, deep in ministerial offices. A question treated in public by a large number of people with separate opinions, all of whom can exercise the right of discussion with more or less prolixity, and who allow themselves to vent their ideas with a warmth and brilliance foreign to the tone of society, is something that must naturally frighten our good citizens, as a concert of noisy instruments would most certainly tire the weak ear of those ill in a hospital. It is difficult to imagine that a reasonable opinion could arise from such a free and agitated debate. It is tempting to desire that someone greatly superior to everyone else should be called forth to make all these people agree who otherwise would spend all their time quarrelling.[36]

For Siéyès, then, discussion provides the solution for two related problems. Disagreement will inevitably reign at the outset in an assembly, but on the other hand, representative government rejects the simple and tempting solution advocated by its critics: that it should terminate such discord through the intervention of one will that is superior to the others. Later in the text, Siéyès continues:

In all the deliberations, there is something like a problem to be solved, which is to know in a given case, that which general interest prescribes. When the debate begins, one cannot at all judge the direction that it will take to arrive surely at this discovery. *Without doubt the general interest is nothing if it is not the interest of someone: it is that particular interest that is common to the greatest number of voters. From this comes the necessity of the competition of opinions.*[37] That which seems to be a mixture, a confusion capable of obscuring everything, is an indispensable preliminary step to light. One must let all these particular interests press against one another, compete against one another, struggle to seize the question, and push it, each one according to its strength, towards the goal that it proposes. In this test, useful and detrimental ideas are separated; the latter fall, the former continue to move, to balance themselves until, modified and

---

[36] E. Siéyès, *Vues sur les moyens d'exécution dont les représentants de la France pourront disposer en 1789* (Paris: unnamed publisher, 1789), p. 92.

[37] The importance of these sentences (the emphasis is mine) cannot be overestimated. They demonstrate that for Siéyès, (1) parliamentary debate does not constitute a disinterested activity, oriented solely by the search for the truth, but a process that aims to identify the interest common to the greatest number, and (2) the general interest, unlike Rousseau's "general will," does not transcend particular interests and is not of a different nature than them.

purified by their reciprocal effects, they finally melt into a single opinion.[38]

For the founders of representative government, debate thus performs the specific task of producing agreement and consent; it does not in itself constitute a principle of decision-making. What turns a proposition into a public decision is not discussion but consent. It must be added that this consent is the consent of a majority, not universal consent, and even less an expression of some truth.[39] As Locke had already observed, the essential function of the principle of majority rule is to make decision possible. Locke wrote:

> For that which acts any community, being only the consent of the individuals of it, and it being necessary to that which is one body to move one way; it is necessary the body should move that way whither the greater force carries it, which is the *consent of the majority*: or else it is impossible it should continue act or continue one body, one *community* ...[40]

It is worth noting that this key text of Locke does not base the principle of majority rule on the qualities or virtues of the majority, (e.g. its aptitude for expressing what is true and just), but on the stark fact that decisions need to be made and actions taken. Debate, on the other hand, cannot meet that need; it does not provide a decision-making principle. On a given subject, discussion ceases when agreement has been reached by all participants and no one has any further objections, but by itself discussion contains no limiting principle. The consent of the majority, by contrast, does provide a principle of decision-making, because it is compatible

---

[38] Siéyès, *Vues sur les moyens* ... , pp. 93–4.

[39] The statement (in the text just quoted) that, at the end of the debate, opinions "finally melt into a single opinion," might suggest that Siéyès makes unanimity the principle of decision-making. This is not the case, as an earlier passage from the same pamphlet shows: "But for the future, requiring that the common will always be this precise sum of all wills would be equivalent to renouncing the possibility of forming a common will, it would be dissolving the social union. It is thus absolutely necessary to resolve to recognise all the characters of the common will in an accepted plurality" (Siéyès, *Vues sur les moyens* ... , p. 18). In his reflections on debate, his principal aim is different, so he does not go to the trouble of repeating the argument.

[40] J. Locke, *Second Treatise of Government*, ch. 7, § 96, in J. Locke, *Two Treatises of Government*, ed. P. Laslett (Cambridge: Cambridge University Press, 1988), pp. 331–2; original emphasis. The arguments of Locke and Siéyès on this question are obviously very close. Locke's formulations are perhaps a little more incisive, which is why they are cited here.

with the temporal limitations to which all action, and particularly all political action, is subject. One can at any time count heads and determine which proposition has obtained the broadest consent. Academic debates can be governed exclusively by the principle of discussion because, unlike political debates, they are not subject to any time limit. The founders of representative government certainly did not confuse a parliament with a learned society.

The principle of representative government must therefore be formulated as follows: no proposal can acquire the force of public decision unless it has obtained the consent of the majority after having been subjected to trial by discussion. It is the consent of the majority, and not debate, that makes the law. The principle presents a notable feature: in no way does it regulate the origin of the proposals or projects to be discussed. There is nothing in the principle to prevent a member of the debating authority from conceiving and formulating a legislative proposal outside the assembly and the context of discussion. Nothing in the principle implies either that only members of the assembly are entitled to formulate propositions. Thus, the principle of representative government does not determine the origin of the proposals to be discussed by the assembly; they may come from anywhere. It is of no importance whether a bill originates within the assembly, whether an individual conceived it in the isolation of his study, or whether it has been prepared by persons outside the assembly. One can only say that, in so far as formulators of such bills know in advance that their proposals will be debated, they have an incentive to anticipate various arguments that their bills may elicit, and to take them into account when conceiving and formulating propositions. Some members of the assembly may form their proposals during the course of a debate, because the arguments give them new ideas, but this is not a necessary implication of the principle. A proposition may also be amended in the course of the discussion, in which case the final decision incorporates elements that originated in the debate. But that, too, is not necessarily implied by the principle of debate: a proposal may eventually win the consent of the majority and thus become a decision in the same form in which it was originally brought before the assembly.

The fact that the decision is made by a collective body at the end of a debate guarantees only one thing: that all legislative proposals have to undergo the *trial* of discussion. Debate acts as a screen or filter, whatever the origin of the bills may be. But this is enough to secure an essential effect on decision-making: no measure can be adopted unless a majority deems it *justified* after argumentative scrutiny. Representative government is not a system in which everything must originate in debate, but in which everything has to be justified in debate.

Such a fervent advocate of discussion as John Stuart Mill considered that, in matters of legislation (not to mention administration), Parliament was not a suitable place for the conception and formulation of proposals. He suggested that propositions of laws be drafted by a commission of experts appointed by the Crown and then brought before Parliament only for discussion and approval. He even went so far as to deny Parliament the right to amend the commission's propositions in the course of discussion. Mill wrote: "[The bill] once framed, however, Parliament should have no power to alter the measure, but only to pass or reject it; or, if partially disapproved of, remit it back to the Commission for reconsideration."[41] According to Mill, the principal function of the debating body should be to grant or withhold "the final seal of national assent" after a public exchange of arguments, not to conceive and formulate legislative measures.[42] As Mill emphasized, the principle of representative government is not violated if bills are in fact prepared, with or without discussion, by persons outside the assembly and not even elected by it. This explains why representative government proved compatible with the development and increasing role of bureaucracy. It is of no importance that proposed laws are mainly drafted by bureaucrats or non-elected experts, as long as none of these propositions becomes law without being debated by the elected collective authority.

To define representative government simply as government by discussion is thus insufficient. It obscures the fact that it is the function of persuasive discussion neither to make decisions, nor

---

[41] J. S. Mill, *Considerations on Representative Government* [1861], ch. V, in J. S. Mill, *Utilitarianism, On Liberty, and Considerations on Representative Government*, ed. H. B. Acton (London: Dent & Sons, 1972), p. 237.

[42] Mill, *Considerations on Representative Government*, p. 240.

necessarily to generate proposals for decision, but only to produce consent in a situation in which no individual will is entitled to impose itself on others. Once again, we see here the critical role of passing judgment: proposals are not necessarily initiated by the debating body, but no proposal is passed unless it has been submitted to its judgment.

Thus, analysis of the system of decision-making shows that, in contrast to what both common sense and democratic ideology affirm, representative democracy is not an indirect form of government by the people. Such analysis, however, also makes apparent a positive characteristic of representative democracy, namely the central role granted to the judgment of the community. The electorate as a whole is made judge of the policies implemented by its representatives: the electorate's retrospective appraisal of the relatively independent initiatives of those in government influences the conduct of public affairs. The role of the debating body is also primarily that of judge, in the sense that all proposals must be submitted for its approval, even though they do not all originate from within. For different reasons in each case, it is thus the concept of passing judgment that best describes the role assigned to the community, whether to the people itself or to its representatives. Representative democracy is not a system in which the community governs itself, but a system in which public policies and decisions are made subject to the verdict of the people.

6

Metamorphoses of representative government

It is sometimes claimed that, in Western countries, political representation is experiencing a crisis. For many years, representation appeared to be founded on a powerful and stable relationship of trust between voters and political parties, with the vast majority of voters identifying themselves with, and remaining loyal to, a particular party. Today, however, more and more people change the way they vote from one election to the next, and opinion surveys show an increasing number of those who refuse to identify with any existing party. Differences between the parties once appeared to be a reflection of social cleavages. In our day, by contrast, one gets the impression that it is the parties imposing cleavages on society, cleavages that observers deplore as "artificial." Each party used to propose to the electorate a detailed program of measures which it promised to implement if returned to power. Today, the electoral strategies of candidates and parties are based instead on the construction of vague images, prominently featuring the personality of the leaders. Finally, those moving in political circles today are distinguished from the rest of the population by their occupation, culture, and way of life. The public scene is increasingly dominated by media specialists, polling experts, and journalists, in which it is hard to see a typical reflection of society. Politicians generally attain power because of their media talents, not because they resemble their constituents socially or are close to them. The gap between government and society, between representatives and represented, appears to be widening.

Over the last two centuries, representative government has undergone significant changes, notably during the second half of the nineteenth century. The most obvious of these, the one on which most histories of representative government concentrate, concerns voting rights: property and culture have ceased to be represented and suffrage has been extended. This change took place along with another: the rise of mass-based parties. Modern representative government was established without organized political parties. Most of the founders of representative government even regarded division into parties or "factions" as a threat to the system they were establishing.[1] From the second half of the nineteenth century, however, political parties organizing the expression of the electorate came to be viewed as a constitutive element of representative government. Moreover, as we have seen, the founding fathers had banned imperative mandates and the practice of "instructing" representatives, and they clearly had a deep distrust of electoral pledges, even of a non-binding nature. Mass parties, by contrast, made the political platform one of the main instruments of electoral competition.

The rise of mass parties and political programs seemed to transform *representation* itself understood as a link between two terms – that is to say, both the qualitative relationship between representatives and represented (in the sense defined in chapter 4), and the relationship between the wishes of the governed and the decisions of the governors. First, rather than being drawn from the elites of talent and wealth, as the founding fathers had wished, representative personnel seemed to consist principally of ordinary citizens who had reached the top of their parties by dint of militant activity and devotion to a cause. Moreover, since representatives, once elected, remained under the control of party managers and activists, as a result of the party's internal discipline, the autonomy pre-

---

[1] It is sometimes thought that, whereas the English and the Americans were always more favorably disposed to political parties, hostility toward "factions" was more prevalent in the French political culture of the late eighteenth century. This claim is inaccurate. Virtually all of the Anglo-American political thinkers of the same period were opposed to party system. (See Richard Hofstadter, *The Idea of a Party System. The Rise of Legitimate Opposition in the United States 1780–1840* (Berkeley: University of California Press, 1969), esp. ch. 1. Edmund Burke's praise for parties was an exception; moreover, Burke did not have in mind parties analogous to those which came to dominate the political scene from the second half of the nineteenth century.

viously enjoyed by representatives during their term appeared to be violated. And political platforms seemed to further restrict the freedom of action of representatives.

This is why a number of late nineteenth-century observers interpreted the new role played by parties and platforms as evidence of a crisis of representation.[2] The model of representative government was then identified as "parliamentarianism" or "liberal parliamentarianism." The English system as it had functioned prior to 1870, was regarded as the most perfected form of representative government.[3] At the beginning of the twentieth century reflections on a "crisis of parliamentarianism" multiplied.[4] It gradually became apparent, however, that if mass parties had indeed brought about the demise of "parliamentarianism," representative government had not been destroyed in the process; its constitutive principles, including the partial autonomy of representatives, were still in effect.

Observers then came to realize that a new and viable form of representation had emerged. This was not conceptualized as unequivocally as parliamentarianism had been, but its identification as an internally consistent and relatively stable phenomenon was signaled by the coining of new terms: "party government" among Anglo-American theorists, *"Parteiendemokratie"* among German authors. Each of these terms aimed at gathering under a single heading the characteristics which distinguished the new form of representative government from parliamentarianism.

Even though some writers initially deplored the demise of parliamentarianism, the new form of representation was eventually hailed as progress. It was definitely accepted as an advance toward democracy, not only because of the expanded electorate but also because of the new ways in which representatives were linked to the electorate. Parties brought representatives closer to the grassroots,

---

[2] See Moisey Ostrogorsky, *La Démocratie et l'organisation des partis politiques*, 2 vols. (Paris: Calmann-Lévy, 1903), *passim*, esp. Vol. I, p. 568.

[3] Both the Birmingham Caucus and the National Liberal Federation, generally regarded as the first mass based political organizations, were founded around 1870.

[4] To mention only examples among the most significant and influential, see Carl Schmitt, *Die geistesgeschichtliche Lage des heutigen Parlamentarismus* [1923], English translation: *The Crisis of Parliamentary Democracy* (Cambridge, MA: MIT Press, 1988), and Gerhard Leibholz, *Das Wesen der Repräsentation* [1929] (Berlin: Walter de Gruyter, 1966).

making possible the nomination of candidates whose social position, way of life, and concerns were close to those of the rank and file. These changes were interpreted as progress towards greater democratic identity and resemblance between governors and governed.[5] Moreover, since election platforms enabled voters to choose the direction of the government, and since, furthermore, party organizations exercised continuous control over their members in Parliament, it was felt that "party democracy" enhanced the role of the popular will in the conduct of public affairs.[6] When it became clear that mass parties had not undermined representative institutions, the changes that at first had seemed to threaten representation were reinterpreted as rendering it more democratic. Representative government seemed to be moving toward an identity of representatives and the represented, and toward popular rule. Ceasing to dwell on how far the system had traveled, commentators looked rather towards the future. Representative government may not have been democratic from the beginning, but now it seemed that it would increasingly become so. Democracy was on the horizon. This progress towards democracy was interpreted as an extension of Whig history, or in a Tocquevillian mode, as a step in the irresistible advance of equality and popular government only imperfectly implemented by liberal parliamentarianism.

A curious symmetry thus emerges between the present situation and that of the late nineteenth and early twentieth centuries. Now, as then, the idea is gaining currency that representation is in a state of crisis. This parallel prompts the hypothesis that we are witnessing today perhaps less a crisis of political representation than a crisis of a particular form of representation, namely the one established in the wake of mass parties. Is it possible that the various developments affecting representation today signal the emergence of a third form of representative government, one that possesses as much internal coherence as parliamentarianism and party democracy?

It is even more curious that today's alleged crisis of representation is commonly ascribed to the erosion of the very features that

---

[5] See chapters 3 and 4 on the significance of these notions of democratic identity and resemblance.

[6] The term "party democracy" is mine; it is coined as a combination of the English "party government" and the German "*Parteiendemokratie.*"

differentiated party democracy from parliamentarianism. These were the features that seemed to bring representative government closer to popular rule, namely the identification of voters with particular parties and their representatives in Parliament, and the choice of representatives on the basis of platforms. It was believed that the type of representation constitutive of representative government at its origins had been forever superseded. The role of mass parties and platforms seemed to be the consequence of extended rights of suffrage, and since it did not appear likely that universal suffrage would be challenged in the future, it was felt that the nature of representation had been irreversibly altered. Current developments suggest that such a prognosis may have been incorrect. The changes wrought by party democracy were perhaps less fundamental than was supposed. We must, then, take a closer look at the turn associated with party democracy and compare it with the changes occurring today. The history of representative government presents perhaps a sequence of three forms separated by two breaks.

In this chapter, we shall examine the metamorphoses of representative government in the light of the four principles identified in previous chapters: election of representatives at regular intervals, the partial independence of representatives, freedom of public opinion, and the making of decisions after trial by discussion. At no time have those principles ceased to apply. So let us analyse and compare the successive ways in which they were implemented.

One thing needs to be made clear, however, with regard to the fourth principle (trial by discussion). Studying the successive forms of public discussion throughout the history of representative government does pose a problem not encountered in the case of the first three principles. The election of representatives at regular intervals, the relative freedom of action that they enjoy, or the free expression of political opinions are easily identified and defined. The notion of discussion is more elusive, the phenomena it denotes harder to pin down. The problem is further complicated by the fact (already noted) that the earliest advocates of representative government did little to develop the notion, even if they did make use of it. In their reflections on debate within the assembly, they did not appear to speak of just any type of verbal exchange. Siéyès and Burke, for example, expected discussion to facilitate agreement and produce "insights" through the exchange of "arguments" and "reasons." But that merely shifts the problem to the notions of insights, arguments, and reasons, which lend themselves to a variety of interpretations. So if we want to study the changes public discussion has gone through, we cannot avoid providing a definition.

In the following pages, then, "discussion" will be understood as meaning a type of communication in which at least one of the parties (a) seeks to bring about a change in the other party's position, and (b) does so using propositions that are impersonal or relate to the long-term future.

The first characteristic denotes the element of persuasion that political discussion must include if it is to perform its essential function of generating consent, particularly the consent of a majority. Only persuasive discourse seeking to change the opinion of others is in fact capable of eliciting the consent of a majority where, at the outset, there is nothing but a large number of divergent opinions. This first characteristic distinguishes discussion from types of verbal communication in which interlocutors do not seek to persuade each other – for example, when individuals exchange information or, as lawyers in a courtroom, appear to reply to each other, while in fact attempting to persuade a third party.

The second characteristic (the use of impersonal or long-term propositions) corresponds to the rational, argumentative dimension of discussion. This distinguishes discussion from what one might call haggling, in which the participants seek to change each other's positions through rewards or threats affecting each other's immediate personal interests.[7] For example, we call it haggling, not discussion, when one party seeks to change the other's mind by offering money, goods, or services in exchange.

The distinction between haggling and discussion enables us to clarify the rational nature of discussion without recourse to the exacting category of "disinterested discussion."[8] To capture the

---

[7] I use the term "haggling," despite its shortcomings, to distinguish what is meant here from the notion of "bargaining," as it has been elaborated in "bargaining theory." The standard concept of bargaining implies the use of threats and rewards, but it does not make reference either to their individual nature or to their immediacy. On the distinction between discussion and bargaining, see, for example, J. Elster, "Argumenter et négocier dans deux assemblées constituantes," in *Revue Française de Science Politique*, Vol. 44, No. 2, April 1994, pp. 187–256.

[8] In a sense, any kind of sensible, comprehensible communication necessarily

argumentative dimension of discussion deemed integral to representative government, one might be tempted to reserve the term "discussion" for wholly disinterested exchanges in which interlocutors seek to persuade each other to adopt a position purely on the grounds that it is true or conforms to moral norms. "Disinterested discussion" is doubtless an apt and fruitful concept from a general philosophic point of view, but in politics it constitutes only an extreme situation. To seek to make it a central category in an analysis of representative government would be an *angélisme*.

The notion of haggling is more useful for purposes of political analysis because it distinguishes among forms of interested communication, which provide the staple of politics. There is a difference between haggling, in which one party promises another that, should he adopt a certain position, a reward or penalty will incur, and discussion in which one party also appeals to the other's self-interest, but in this case, by showing him that, should he adopt a position, some advantage or harm will result for the group to which he belongs, or to himself personally but over the long run.

Haggling uses propositions addressing the other party as an individual, and as he is at the moment he is addressed. Discussion, on the other hand, uses impersonal and general propositions concerning classes of individuals, or propositions bearing on the long term.[9] In order to formulate such propositions, the speaker

involves reason. But when the founders of representative government thought about the type of exchange to which that system should assign a crucial role, they obviously had in mind a kind of communication that appealed to reason in a preeminent way. It is the nature of this preeminent use of reason that needs to be defined and made operative in order to study the successive forms of discussion in representative government.

[9] The characteristics of generality and long-term relevance may of course be combined. Political actors often seek to persuade by highlighting the benefits that classes or groups will enjoy in the long term. In the description of discussion given here (the use of impersonal propositions *or* ones that relate to the long term), the "or" is not exclusive; it merely reflects the fact that it is possible to use propositions that relate to classes but not in the long term. For instance, it might be argued that, if a certain decision is made a class will obtain an immediate benefit. In haggling, on the other hand, the characteristics of individuality and immediacy seem more rarely separated. When someone is personally offered a reward to make a political decision, the offer nearly always relates to the present or near future. This is because it is only with great difficulty that long-term rewards can be made the object of offers in the strict sense of the term (see below). This accounts for the lack of symmetry between the definition of haggling (using propositions that are personal *and* bear on the short term) and that of discussion (using general *or* long-term propositions).

must engage in classification and abstraction. He must associate people according to traits he deems relevant, instead of viewing them as concrete individuals. Or he must form an idea of their lasting identity, beyond their immediate transient characteristics. Symmetrically, the person to whom the speech is addressed has to make a mental detour in order to conceive what he stands to gain; he needs to see himself not as a concrete, named individual (which is his immediate perception of himself) but as a member of a class. Or, he must detach himself from his present identity to form an idea of his future identity. It follows that this type of communication requires both parties to detach themselves from the singular and the immediate in order to attain the general and durable. This calls for reason.

Moreover, in haggling, the proposition that indicates to the other party that he will obtain some benefit has the specific linguistic status of an offer, or a threat. The actualization of its content (benefit or loss) is certain, as soon as the proposition has been uttered, or at least this actualization depends solely on the will of whoever formulated the proposition. The same cannot be true (barring exceptional circumstances) when the propositions announcing a gain or loss for the other party are general and impersonal, or bear on the long term. Usually a person cannot offer a reward (or make a threat) to whole classes, since to do so, he would have to have at his disposal an inordinate amount of resources – the more substantial, indeed, the larger the class he makes the offer or the threat to. In this case, then, the proposition announcing the gain or loss at least partially assumes the character of a prediction, the realization of which does not depend solely on the will of the person uttering the proposition but also on external factors, such as the cooperation of a large number of other people or, more generally, social and economic forces. The same reasoning applies to propositions announcing a long-term benefit for the other party: the more distant the point in time to which such propositions refer, the more they constitute predictions, since the passage of time increases the probability of intervening events. And clearly, this predictive quality is even stronger if the propositions concern both classes and the longer term.

But to make predictions without exposing oneself to being refuted by the facts, one has a strong incentive to analyse the world and understand the way it works. One is pushed to know, for one cannot merely will. In this sense too, then, communication that uses general or long-term propositions calls for the use of reason. Reason being this time distinguished from volition, rather than from immediate perception. The predictive dimension inherent in the communication that announces general or long-term benefits gives rise to its persistent character. The speaker multiplies arguments to show that the benefit will materialize, because he cannot simply *offer* that benefit. When a person is offered a good in exchange for something, either that person accepts the offer and the communication ends, or that person rejects it and a different offer has to be made. One does not pile up arguments to get the other's agreement. The two sides haggle until they agree on a price; they do not "argue."

The personal offering of money, goods, or services in exchange for political action is widespread, as the familiar phenomena of corruption and patronage attest. So, the concept of haggling introduced here is not simply an intellectual construct designed to contrast the notion of discussion. The definition of discussion as communication aimed at bringing about a change of mind through the use of impersonal or long-term propositions is only of an ideal-type. It can sometimes be difficult to determine whether a situation falls on one side or the other of the definitional boundary. For example, information is occasionally provided with the intention of changing the other party's opinion, and it will then be hard to tell whether the situation is one of persuasive communication or not. Similarly, it may sometimes be difficult to decide whether a proposition is impersonal or not. On which side of the line between haggling and discussion are we to place the situation where one person seeks to persuade another by offering rewards for the other's relatives or friends? Applying the distinction between short term and long term can also, on occasion, give rise to similar problems. Nevertheless, the concept of discussion retains a certain utility, making it possible to classify concrete situations according to how closely they approximate it.

The definition set out here does purport to capture an eternal and universal essence of discussion. The claim is not even that it is always appropriate to use the word "discussion" as defined here. The definition that has been proposed is largely stipulative (in particular, it would be possible to draw the boundaries differently). But this is not an obstacle, given the objective here, which is to study the transformation of the phenomena covered by our definition.

In the following pages, three ideal-types of representative government will be constructed and compared: parliamentarianism, party democracy, and a third type that, for reasons that analysis will bring out, I shall call "audience" democracy.[10] These ideal-types are deliberately schematic; they are not meant to provide an exhaustive description of every form of representative government but to allow comparison between the forms assumed by the four key principles of representation in each case. The three ideal-types do not cover all the possible forms of political representation or even all the forms it has actually taken. These ideal-types will be examined only in the light of the kind of *representation* – that is to say, the kind of relationship between representatives and represented – they contain. The extent of the franchise and the size of the population represented will deliberately be left out. At a given point in time and in a given country, the various forms of political representation that are analysed here may coexist and fuse into one another, but, depending on the time and place, one form or another predominates.

PARLIAMENTARIANISM

Election of representatives

Election was devised as a means of placing in government persons who enjoyed the confidence of their fellow citizens. At the origins of representative government this confidence derived from particular circumstances: the successful candidates were individuals who inspired the trust of their constituents as a result of their network of local connections, their social prominence, or by the deference they provoked.

In parliamentarianism, the relation of trust has an essentially

---

[10] See the figure on p. 235 below.

personal character. It is through individuality that the candidate inspires confidence, and not through his connections with other representatives or with political organizations. The representative has a direct relationship with constituents; he is elected by people with whom he comes into frequent contact. Besides, election appears to be the reflection and expression of non-political interaction. This trust stems from the fact that representatives belong to the same social community as their electors, whether that community is defined geographically (constituency, town or city, county) or in terms of more general "interests" (what Burke called the "great interests of the realm": landed, commercial, manufacturing etc.). Relations of local proximity or membership in one of these great interests are the spontaneous result of social ties and interactions. They are not generated by political competition. Rather they constitute preexisting resources that politicians mobilize in their struggle for political power. At the same time, representatives have achieved prominence in the community by virtue of their character, wealth, or occupation. Election selects a particular type of elite: the *notables*. Representative government began as the rule of the notable.

Partial autonomy of representatives

Each elected representative is free to vote according to his conscience and personal judgment. It is not part of his role to transmit a political will already formed outside the walls of Parliament. He is not the spokesman of his electors, but their "trustee." This is the concept of the representative formulated by Burke in his famous "Speech to the Electors of Bristol." On this point his speech reflects the most widely accepted view of his time.[11] And the idea continued to prevail throughout the first half of the nineteenth century. The period from the First Reform Bill (1832) to the Second (1867) has

---

[11] See Edmund Burke, "Speech to the Electors of Bristol" [1774], in R. J. S. Hoffmann and P. Lavack (eds.), *Burke's Politics, Selected Writings and Speeches*, (New York: A. A. Knopf, 1949), pp. 114–16. On the fact that Burke's formulations reflected the generally accepted view of the role of the representative, see J. R. Pole, *Political Representation in England and the Origins of the American Republic* (Berkeley: University of California Press, 1966), p. 441 but also pp. 412, 419, 432. Blackstone supports a similar point of view in *Commentaries on the Laws of England* [1765–9], Bk. I, ch. 2, (facsimile of the 1st edn, 4 vols., Chicago: University of Chicago Press, 1979), Vol. I, p. 155.

even been called "the golden age of the private MP (Member of Parliament)," in other words the representative whose vote is dictated by his private convictions, and not by any commitments made outside Parliament.[12] One may view the House of Commons from the end of the Napoleonic Wars to the Second Reform Bill as the archetype of parliamentarianism. The political independence of the individual representative is due in part to his owing his seat to non-political factors such as his local standing.

Freedom of public opinion

The first half of the nineteenth century saw a proliferation of extra-parliamentary movements (e.g. Chartism, Catholic rights, Parliamentary reform, Corn Law repeal), which organized demonstrations, petitions, and press campaigns.[13] However, the cleavages reflected by these movements cut across party lines. The expression of public opinion differed from the election of representatives not only in its constitutional status – only the latter had legally binding consequences – but also in its aims. Some issues, such as freedom of religion, the reform of Parliament, and free trade, were neither raised during election campaigns nor settled by election results. They were brought to the fore rather by *ad hoc* organizations and settled through external pressure on Parliament. Differences might exist between representative and representative, but the splits that divided Parliament did not coincide with those dividing the country on these issues.

The difference in aims which separates the election of representatives from the expression of public opinion was due not only to the restricted franchise, but also to the character of parliamentarianism. For if elections select individuals on the basis of the personal confidence they inspire, the opinions of the citizenry on political issues and policies must find another outlet. The electorate do not always have such opinions; this may occur only in situations of crisis. Such a possibility is nonetheless implied by the principle of freedom of public opinion. And the structure of parliamentarianism

[12] See S. Beer, *British Modern Politics: Parties and Pressure Groups in the Collectivist Age* [1965] (London: Faber & Faber, 1982), pp. 37–40.
[13] See Beer, *British Modern Politics*, pp. 43–8.

entails that if the people do hold such opinions, they must be expressed outside elections.

Thus, in this form of representative government, freedom of public opinion gives rise to the possibility of a gap opening up between public opinion and Parliament. One could say, to use a spatial metaphor, that the possibility exists of a horizontal split between the higher will (that of Parliament as a whole) and the lower will (that which is expressed in the streets, in petitions, and in the columns of the press). The underlying structure of this configuration is revealed most dramatically when the voice of the crowd outside the Parliament expresses concerns shared by no one inside it. The most perceptive observers have noted that the possibility of such a confrontation between Parliament and the voice of the people, however threatening it may be to public order, is essential to parliamentarianism. In analysing the functioning of English parliamentarianism before the formation of mass-based parties Ostrogorsky wrote:

> Outside elections, where it formally holds court, public opinion is supposed to provide members of parliament and their leaders with a steady source of inspiration and at the same time to exercise continuous control over them. By manifesting itself independently of any constitutional avenue, this dual power imposes itself and carries the day ... However, for this power of opinion (which is of an eminently elusive and fluctuating nature) to make itself felt, it must be completely free to emerge *in its various irregular forms and go straight to the doors of parliament.*[14]

But when the crowd is physically present in the streets, confronting Parliament, the risk of disorder and violence increases. This form of representative government is characterized by the fact that freedom of public opinion appears inseparable from a certain risk to public order.

Trial by discussion

Since representatives are not bound by the wishes of those who elect them, Parliament can be a deliberating body in the fullest sense – that is to say, a place where individuals *form* their wills through

[14] Ostrogorsky, *La Démocratie*, Vol. I, p. 573 (my emphasis).

discussion and where the consent of a majority is reached through the exchange of arguments. A discussion can produce agreement among participants with divergent opinions at the outset only if they are in a position to change their minds during the course of exchange. In circumstances where such a change is not possible, discussion cannot serve to build the consent of a majority. And it makes no difference whether participants exchange verbal remarks or not: there is no genuine discussion taking place. The possibility of participants changing their minds is a necessary (even if not sufficient) condition of persuasive discussion. It is precisely in order to enable meaningful deliberation within Parliament that, in parliamentarianism, representatives are not bound by the wishes of their constituents. In England during the first half of the nineteenth century, the dominant belief was that MPs ought to vote according the conclusions they arrived at through parliamentary debate, not according to decisions made beforehand outside Parliament. Even if practice did not always conform to this model, such at least was the principle subscribed to by most candidates and members of Parliament. In any case, the freedom of the elected representative can be seen in the continually changing cleavages and groupings among representatives.[15]

PARTY DEMOCRACY

Election of representatives

The enlarged electorate resulting from the extension of the suffrage is precluded from a personal relationship with its representatives. Citizens no longer vote for someone they know personally, but for someone who bears the colors of a party. Political parties, with their bureaucracies and networks of party workers, were established in order to mobilize the enlarged electorate.

When mass parties were formed, it was believed that they would bring the "common man" into office. The rise of such parties, it seemed, signaled not only the "demise of the notable," but also the end of the elitism that had characterized parliamentarianism. In

[15] This feature of parliamentarianism still survives today in the United States Congress.

countries where mass parties reflected class divisions, it was
expected that through the socialist or social democratic party the
working class would henceforth be represented in Parliament by its
own members, ordinary workers. Robert Michels's analysis of the
German Social Democratic Party, however, soon belied these
expectations.[16]

Michels exposed (and bitterly denounced) the gap between
leaders and rank and file in a paradigmatic mass and class party. He
demonstrated that, while the leaders and deputies of the party may
have a working-class background, they lead in effect a petty
bourgeois rather than a proletarian life. Michels argued not only
that the leaders and deputies of the working-class party *became*
different once they had reached their positions of power, but also
that they originally *were* different. The party, according to Michels,
furnishes an opportunity "to the most intelligent members [of the
working class] to secure a rise in the social scale," and elevates
"some of the most capable and best informed" proletarians.[17] At the
dawn of the capitalist era, these "more intelligent and more ambitious" workers would have become small entrepreneurs, whereas
now they become party bureaucrats.[18] The party is thus dominated
by "de-proletarianized" elites, markedly distinct from the working
class. These elites, however, rise to power on the basis of specific
qualities and talents, namely activism and organizational skill.

Michels's analysis deserves particular attention on two counts.
First, the vehemence with which he denounces as undemocratic,
"aristocratic," or "oligarchic" the difference in status and living
conditions between the party's grassroots and its leaders testifies to
the enduring attractiveness of the ideal of resemblance and closeness between rulers and ruled, more than a century after the
argument between the American Federalists and Anti-Federalists. In
the early years of the twentieth century, democracy was still being
identified with a form of power in which leaders should resemble
those they lead in their circumstances and characteristics, even
though collective action requires functional differentiation between

---

[16] Robert Michels, *Political Parties: A Sociological Study of the Oligarchical Tendencies of
Modern Democracy* [1911], trans. E. & C. Paul (New York: Free Press, 1962); see esp.
part IV, "Social analysis of leadership."
[17] Michels, *Political Parties*, pp. 263–4.   [18] *Ibid.*, pp. 258–9.

them. Furthermore, Michels's attachment to the ideal of resemblance was not an isolated case. The attractiveness of that ideal may also be seen in a document that, half a century earlier, had played a crucial role in French politics. The "Manifesto of the Sixty" (*Manifeste des Soixante*), published by a group of Parisian workers in 1864, criticized the view of representation then prevalent in Republican circles. The "Sixty" complained that there were no working-class candidates. The Republicans had assured workers of their sympathy and promised to defend their interests, but the Sixty replied that they wanted to be represented in Parliament "by workers like themselves." [19]

Second (returning to Michels), his study demonstrates that, when representative government comes to be dominated by mass parties, its elitist character does not disappear; rather a new type of elite arises. The distinctive qualities of the representatives are no longer local standing and social prominence, but activism and organizational skill. Admittedly, voters do not elect their representatives directly on this basis, these qualities get selected by the party machine. But in voting for candidates put forth by the party, electors consent to, and ratify the use of such criteria. Party democracy is the rule of the *activist* and the *party bureaucrat*.

In party democracy, the people vote for a party rather than for a person. This is evidenced by the notable phenomenon of electoral stability. Out of a long succession of party candidates, voters continue to choose those of the same party. Not only do individuals tend to vote constantly for the same party, but party preferences are handed down from generation to generation: children vote as their parents did, and the inhabitants of a geographic area vote for the same party over decades. André Siegfried, one of the first to document electoral stability, spoke of "climates of opinion" peculiar to certain places. Electoral stability, a major discovery of political science at the turn of the century, has been corroborated by count-

---

[19] P. Rosanvallon, *La question syndicale* (Paris: Calmann-Lévy, 1988), p. 204. Proudhon published a lengthy commentary on the manifesto in a work entitled *De la capacité politique des classes ouvrières* [1873] (Paris: Marcel Rivière, 1942). The text of the manifesto is given as an appendix to that edition of Proudhon's book. According to Rosanvallon, the manifesto "marked a turning-point in French political and social culture, and must be considered one of the most important political texts in nineteenth-century France" (*La question syndicale*, p. 204).

less studies up to the 1970s.[20] However, electoral stability removes one of the bases of parliamentarianism: an election is no longer the choice of a person whom the voters personally know and trust. In some quarters the disintegration of this personal link was interpreted as a sign of a crisis in political representation.

Electoral stability results to a large extent from the determination of political preferences by socio-economic factors. In party democracy electoral cleavages reflect *class divisions*. Although the influence of socio-economic factors can be found in all democratic countries during the first half of the twentieth century, it is especially noticeable in countries where one of the major parties was formed as and regarded to be the political expression of the working class. Socialist or social democratic parties are generally considered the archetype of the mass-based party that has become a linchpin of representative democracy since the late nineteenth century.[21] Thus, it is in countries where social democratic parties are strong that one finds, in its purest form, the type of representation that is generated by stable party loyalties reflecting class divisions.[22]

For decades in Germany, England, Austria, and Sweden, voting was a means of expressing a class identity. For most socialist or social democratic voters, the vote they cast was not a matter of choice, but of social identity and destiny.[23] Voters placed their trust in the candidates presented by "the party" because they saw them as members of the community to which they felt they belonged themselves. Society seemed to be divided by fundamental cultural and economic differences into a small number of camps, usually into just two: a conservative camp, which was generally united by

---

[20] To mention only a few prominent works in that area, see: A. Siegfried, *Tableau politique de la France de l'Ouest sous la III République* (Paris: Armand Colin, 1913); B. Berelson, P. Lazarsfeld, and W. McPhee, *Voting* (Chicago: University of Chicago Press, 1954); A. Campbell, P. E. Converse, W. E. Miller, and D. E. Stokes, *The American Voter* (New York: Wiley, 1964).

[21] This is particularly true since Michels's study of the German Social Democratic Party.

[22] The Communist parties in certain democratic countries (France and Italy, for instance) in a sense fall into the same model. However, their place in the operation of representative democracy being more complex and problematic, the form of representation induced appears less clearly in their case.

[23] The analyses of Alessandro Pizzorno on voting as an expression of identity are particularly relevant to party democracy. See A. Pizzorno, "On the rationality of democratic choice," *Telos*, Vol. 63, Spring 1985, pp. 41–69.

religion and traditional values, and a socialist camp, defined by the socio-economic position of its members.[24] A voter would find himself bound by all his interests and all his beliefs to the same camp. Each camp was a community, united from top to bottom by powerful links of identification.

In such a situation, representation becomes primarily a reflection of the social structure. Originally only one component of representation, reflection of social diversity, comes to predominate in this form of representative government. However, the social forces that express themselves through elections are in *conflict* with one another. As in parliamentarianism, elections reflect a social reality that is prior to politics. But whereas the local communities or the "great interests" which expressed themselves in the case of parliamentarianism were not necessarily in conflict, here social conflict assumes critical importance. While the inventors of representation had considered the plural character of representative bodies as one of their virtues, they had never imagined that this pluralism might become the reflection of a fundamental and lasting social conflict. This metamorphosis of representation resulted from industrialization and the conflict it engendered.

In this form of representation, a sense of membership and social identity determines electoral attitudes much more than adherence to party platforms. The mass parties formed at the end of the nineteenth century certainly proposed detailed platforms and campaigned on them. In this regard, they were markedly different from the parties that existed before. However, the greater part of the electorate had no detailed idea of the measures proposed. Even when voters knew of the existence of such platforms, what they retained was primarily vague and attention-grabbing slogans emphasized in the electoral campaign. Albeit for quite different reasons, the supporters of mass parties did not know much more about the precise policies advocated by those for whom they voted than did electors in parliamentarianism, when they chose a person in whom they placed their trust. Knowledge of the policies to be pursued was no doubt greater than under parliamentarianism; the existence of platforms certainly made this possible. Nevertheless, in

---

[24] In Austria, the term "camp mentality" (*Lagermentalität*) was used to characterize the political culture of the country between the two world wars.

party democracy the confidence of voters is not awarded principally because of the measures proposed, but flows instead from a feeling of belonging and a sense of identification. Platforms have another effect and serve another purpose: they help mobilize the enthusiasm and energy of activists and party bureaucrats who do know about them. In party democracy, as in parliamentarianism, election remains an expression of trust rather than a choice of specific political measures. It is only the object of that trust that is different: it is no longer a person, but an organization – the party.

Partial autonomy of representatives

The representative, deputy, or Member of Parliament is no longer free to vote according to his own conscience and judgment: he is bound by the party to which he owes his election. As Karl Kautsky, for example, one of the German Social Democratic Party's most prestigious leaders, wrote: "The Social Democrat deputy as such is not a free individual – however harsh this may sound – but simply the delegate (*Beauftragte*) of his party."[25] The member of the working class sitting in Parliament is a mere spokesman for his party. This view translates into effective practices employed in all countries where social democracy is strong: strict voting discipline within Parliament, and control by the party apparatus over the deputies. Hans Kelsen, whose political writings express in exemplary fashion the principles of party democracy, proposed various measures aimed at giving parties effective control over their elected representatives: that representatives be forced to resign should they leave the party, and that parties be able to dismiss representatives.[26]

---

[25] Karl Kautsky, *Der Parlamentarismus, die Volksgesetzgebung und die Sozialdemokratie* (Stuttgart: Dietz Verlag, 1893), p. 111. On the subject of the Marxist critique of representation and its acceptance in a reoriented form by the leaders of the social democratic parties, see A. Bergounioux and B. Manin, *La social-démocratie ou le compromis* (Paris: Presses Universitaires de France, 1979), chs. I and III.

[26] H. Kelsen, *Vom Wesen und Wert der Demokratie* [1929] (Aalen: Scientia Verlag, 1981), pp. 42–3. According to Kelsen, "it is illusion or hypocrisy to maintain that democracy is possible without political parties," and "democracy is necessarily and inevitably party government [*Parteienstaat*]" (*ibid.*, p. 20). Kelsen was considered to be close to the Austrian Socialist Party. He played an important part in drafting the Constitution of the First Republic, particularly with regard to the creation of the constitutional court. He was appointed a life member of that court but had to leave Austria following anti-Semitic campaigns. His political and legal

Parliament then becomes an instrument that measures and registers the relative forces of clashing social interests. It is worth noting, moreover, that, with the exception of Britain, the countries where social democracy is powerful (Germany, Austria, Sweden) usually practice proportional representation, that is, an electoral system which has the effect of reflecting the precise state of the balance of forces within the electorate. Kelsen considers proportional representation to be necessary "in order for the effective situation of interests to be reflected" in the composition of Parliament.[27] However, in a society in which the central political authority reflects, with minimal distortion, the balance of forces between opposing interests, each of which is solidly unified, there is a risk of violent confrontation.[28] Since individual voters are attached to a particular camp by all their interests and beliefs, if one camp carries the day, the opposing camp are subject to total defeat extending into every area of their existence: they may, therefore, prefer to resort to arms. Electoral stability even increases this risk; the minority has little hope of seeing the situation reversed in the near future. In one sense, party democracy thus maximizes the risk of open confrontation. But the very raising of the stakes also creates an incentive for the parties to avoid that outcome. Furthermore, since the balance of social forces is directly reflected in election results, neither protagonist can be under any illusion as to the enemy's strength. In general, the more political actors are unaware of the resistance they will meet (they usually tend to underestimate it), the more inclined they will be to make risky moves. Party democracy brings political forces face to face, both with each other and with the prospect of civil war.

In order to avoid the risk of violent confrontation, the majority camp has only one solution: to strike a compromise with the minority, that is, to refrain from subjecting it unreservedly to its will. Party democracy is a viable form of government only if the

thought exercised a wide influence over social democratic leaders, both in Austria and Germany. Kautsky frequently refers to him.

[27] Kelsen, *Vom Wesen und Wert*, p. 61.

[28] Note that, for Kelsen, polarization into two "camps" is a necessary condition if democracy is to function. The central opposition dissolves the oppositions within each camp and is thus an integrating factor (*Vom Wesen und Wert*, p. 56). However, Kelsen sees polarization as characteristic of politics; for him, it results from the principle of majority rule.

opposing interests deliberately accept the principle of political compromise, since there is nothing to temper their opposition in the social sphere. Kelsen makes the principle of compromise the keystone of his theory of democracy, though he fails to explain what motivates protagonists to reach compromises.[29] Historically, social democratic parties came to power and managed to remain in power only after they had accepted the principle of compromise. They generally signaled such acceptance in symbolic fashion by adopting a strategy of coalition when they first acceded to government. By forming a coalition, a party puts itself deliberately in a position of not being able to carry out all its plans. It chooses from the outset to leave room for a will other than its own.[30] Moreover, proportional representation encourages strategies of coalition by rarely producing an overall majority in Parliament.

But if party democracy is based on compromise, parties have to be at liberty not to implement all their plans once in office. In order to be able to reach compromises or form coalitions, parties must reserve room to maneuver after the election. Such freedom of action is facilitated by the fact that, when voting, people express their trust in a party and leave things to it. To be sure, a party is to some extent bound by its platform, since it had publicly committed itself to a certain policy. Moreover, party activists have been mobilized around it. Thus, the party leadership has some incentive to act in accordance with the general orientation of the platform. Nonetheless if the party is to arrive at a compromise with the opposition or with its allies (likewise publicly committed to platforms), the party leadership must remain the sole judge of the *extent* to which the program will be implemented. It must retain the freedom not to carry out *all* the measures promised in the manifesto.

This explains why, despite the importance that programs assume in this context, party democracy does not *de facto* (let alone *de jure*) abolish the partial independence of those in power from voters'

---

[29] See Kelsen, *Vom Wesen und Wert*, pp. 53–68. Kelsen's texts on the subject often give the impression that compromise results from the goodwill of the protagonists.

[30] On social democracy, the principle of deliberate compromise, and coalition strategy, see B. Manin, "Démocratie, pluralisme, libéralisme," in A. Bergounioux and B. Manin, *Le régime social-démocrate* (Paris: Presses Universitaires de France, 1989), pp. 23–55.

wishes.[31] It is not, in this sense, the indirect form of popular government. In the original form of parliamentarianism, it is the individual representative who enjoys freedom of judgment and decision-making. Here, although this freedom of the individual representative no longer exists, the partial independence of those who govern has undergone a shift within the institutional structure of representative government, becoming the prerogative of the group formed by the representatives (i.e. the parliamentary party) and the party leadership. It also takes a different form: it no longer signifies freedom pure and simple for representatives to act as they see fit, but the freedom to decide how far to go in putting into practice a prearranged plan, to choose, within the parameters of that plan, what can and should be achieved.

This room for maneuver within set limits also appears in the relationship between the party itself and its parliamentary expression. It is worth noting, for example, that, to regulate the relationship between the annual party conference and the parliamentary party, in 1907 the British Labour Party adopted the following motion: "That resolutions instructing the Parliamentary Party as to their actions in the House of Commons be taken as the opinions of the Conference, on the understanding that the time and method of giving effect to these instructions be left to the party in the House, in conjunction with the National Executive." In the words of Keir Hardie, a member of the party leadership, the resolution amounted to giving the parliamentary party and the party leadership the power to decide "which questions should have *priority*."[32] In light of the fact that the party would not remain in office for ever, this power of setting priorities within a predetermined framework conferred a far from negligible autonomy on the party leadership.

---

[31] In spite of his emphasis on the principle of compromise, Kelsen does not mention that political parties who campaigned on different platforms must necessarily retain some discretion if a compromise is to be reached between majority and opposition or among the members of a coalition. This is because his concept of compromise is insufficiently precise. Kelsen fails to see that compromise implies a gap between the originally formulated intention and the action eventually undertaken.

[32] These two quotations are reproduced from Beer, *British Modern Politics*, p. 118 (my emphasis).

Freedom of public opinion

In party democracy, parties organize both the electoral competition and the expression of public opinion (demonstrations, petitions, press campaigns). All expressions of public opinion are structured along partisan cleavages. The various associations and the press are associated with one of the parties. The existence of a partisan press is particularly important. Well-informed citizens, those most interested in politics and opinion leaders, get their information from a politically oriented press; they are little exposed to opposing views, which reinforces the stability of political opinions. Since the parties dominate both the electoral scene and the articulation of political opinions outside the vote, cleavages of public opinion coincide with electoral cleavages. The election of representatives and the expression of public opinion no longer differ in their aims, as they did in parliamentarianism, but only in their constitutional status. Ostrogorsky characterized mass parties as "integral associations": a person who supports a party "completely gives himself over to it" – that is to say, he adopts all the party's positions, whatever the subject.[33] In his analysis of the Weimar Republic, Schmitt described the consequences of this tendency towards integrality. He noted that:

> The extension [of politics] to every sphere of human life, removal of the separations and neutralizations of different domains such as religion, economics, and culture, in a word ... the tendency towards "totalization" is to a large extent realized for a segment of the citizenry by networks of social organizations. The result is that, while we certainly do not have a total state, we do have partisan social institutions that tend toward totalization and organize their troops from the youngest age, each of them ... offering a "complete cultural program."[34]

Since, within each camp, all means of expression are directly or indirectly controlled by the party leadership, ordinary citizens cannot speak for themselves. They have no voice other than that of the party and its affiliated organizations, which also finds expression in Parliament. Such a situation would seem to violate the

[33] See Ostrogorsky, *La Démocratie*, Vol. II, p. 621.
[34] Carl Schmitt, *Der Hüter der Verfassung* (Tübingen: J. C. B. Mohr, 1931), pp. 83–4.

principle of representative government that public opinion can express itself outside the control of those who govern.

Schmitt's formulations, however, help clarify why this is not the case. Each camp certainly speaks with a single voice; its parliamentary and extra-parliamentary voices exactly coincide, but there is more than one camp, and they do not all participate in government. The governing authority is no longer, as in parliamentarianism, the entire Parliament; it is the majority party or a coalition. Party democracy is the age of *party* government. This means, however, that there is something that the party in power does not control, namely the opposition party and its voice. Thus, an opinion different from that of the governors can freely express itself, even though, in opposition and majority alike, ordinary citizens cannot articulate opinions outside the control of the leaders. In party democracy, the freedom of public opinion takes the form of the freedom of opposition. In contrast with parliamentarianism, the freedom of opinion is thus displaced. One could say, to return to the spatial metaphor used earlier, that the vertical gap between the majority and the opposition takes the place of the horizontal gap between the Parliament and those outside it.

One may observe, of course, that the Weimar Republic is not a model of viable government. But the regime fell because the parties upholding the constitution failed to agree on a compromise. If compromises can be reached, a political order based on solidly unified camps may be viable. Post-Second World War Austria provides the purest example of such a representative government.

Trial by discussion

Plenary sessions of Parliament are no longer a forum of deliberative discussion. Strict voting discipline reigns within each camp. Moreover, representatives cannot change their minds as a result of the exchange of parliamentary debate, once the position of the party has been decided. Finally, voting alignments within parliament are virtually identical on all questions. This suggests that, on each occasion, representatives do not vote in light of the arguments exchanged in Parliament, but as a result of decisions formed elsewhere. As a rule, each parliamentary group votes according to its attitude towards the government: the majority camp systematically supports the initiatives of the government and the minority opposes them.

This break from parliamentarianism was the subject of numerous studies around the turn of the twentieth century. It has generally been interpreted as signifying the end of government by discussion. In reality, discussion was shifting towards other forums. It is true that, once the party's position has been fixed, the representatives can no longer change their minds. It is also true that party decisions are made before parliamentary debates. But in the intra-party exchanges that precede parliamentary debates, participants truly deliberate. The party leadership and Members in Parliament debate among themselves what collective position should be adopted. And in that debate, the participants are able to change their minds as a result of the exchange of arguments. True deliberative discussion can thus take place within each camp. Indeed, the history of social democratic parties shows that intense discussion within the party leadership and Members in Parliament does precede debates in Parliament, and that positions change during the course of such discussion. To be sure, this kind of discussion does not involve the views of other parties, but party democracy also encourages discussion between the leaders of the various parties. Party democracy, it was noted earlier, rests on the principle of compromise both between the majority and the minority and between the members of a coalition. Elections do not determine what policy is to be pursued; they determine the relative forces of the various parties, each with its own platform. The relation of forces between the parties does not indicate the particular questions on which a compromise can be achieved, nor does it mark with precision how the difference is to be split. The precise content of the compromise, therefore, is a matter of negotiation between the parties and their leaders. Prior to such negotiations, positions are not fixed; the participants may change their minds as a result of their exchanges. Finally, social democratic parties have often institutionalized a process of consultation and negotiation between organized interests, such as labor unions and employers' associations. This phenomenon, termed "neo-corporatism" has received much attention in political science

217

recently.[35] Neo-corporatist institutions, whose objective is to facilitate compromise between opposing social interests, also provide forums for discussion. The terms of the compromise are not fixed prior to the confrontation; they emerge as its result.

The importance of discussion in party democracy has often been underestimated, because the critical place of compromise in this form of government has not been adequately recognized. It was believed that the representatives of the different camps were strictly bound by detailed, established programs – in which case, indeed, no change in position and therefore no deliberative discussion could have taken place. In reality, however, when party democracy is a stable form of government, it does not function through the rigid implementation of political programs.

"AUDIENCE" DEMOCRACY

Election of representatives

In recent years, a notable shift has occurred in the analysis of election results. Before the 1970s, most electoral studies came to the conclusion that political preferences could be explained by the social, economic, and cultural characteristics of the voters. A number of recent works on the subject demonstrate that this is no longer the case. Election results vary significantly from one election to the next even when the socio-economic and cultural backgrounds of the voters remain unchanged.[36]

---

[35] This term can be misleading if one does not realize that "neo-corporatism" is based on the recognition of a fundamental conflict between organized interests, whereas traditional corporatism assumed a functional complementarity – and therefore harmony – between the social forces. The difference is not merely abstract or ideological: in neo-corporatist arrangements, one of the principal instruments of social conflict, the right to strike, remains untouched, whereas traditional corporatism prohibits strikes. See Manin, "Démocratie, pluralisme, libéralisme," pp. 51–5.

[36] One of the first writers to stress that political preferences were largely a response to the electoral choice offered to voters, quite independently from the socio-economic and cultural characteristics of the electorate, was V. O. Key; see esp. his *Public Opinion and American Democracy* (New York: Knopf, 1963), and *The Responsible Electorate* (Cambridge, MA: Belknap Press of Harvard University Press, 1966). In the 1970s this idea was taken up and developed in a number of studies. See, for example (to mention only two of the more influential works), G. Pomper, *Voters' Choice* (New York: Dodd, Mead, 1975), or N. H. Nie, S. Verba, and J. R.

The personalization of electoral choice

The individuality of candidates appears to be one of the essential factors in these variations: people vote differently from one election to another, depending on the particular persons competing for their vote. Voters tend increasingly to vote for a person and no longer for a party or a platform. This phenomenon marks a departure from what was considered normal voting behavior under representative democracy, creating the impression of a crisis in representation. As we have seen, however, the predominant role of party labels in elections is characteristic only of a particular type of representation, namely party democracy. It is equally possible to regard the current transformation as a return to a feature of parliamentarianism: the personal nature of the representative relationship.

Although the growing importance of personal factors can also be seen in the relationship between each representative and his constituency, it is most perceptible at the national level, in the relationship between the executive and the electorate.[37] Analysts have long observed that there is a tendency towards the personalization of power in democratic countries. In countries with direct election of the chief executive, presidential elections tend to become the main elections, shaping the whole of political life. In countries where the chief executive is also the leader of the majority in Parliament, legislative campaigns and elections center on the person of the leader. Parties still play a central role. They provide critical resources such as networks of contacts and influences, fundraising capacities, and the volunteer work of activists. But they tend to become instruments in the service of a leader. In opposition to parliamentarianism, the head of the government rather than the Member of Parliament is seen as the representative *par excellence*. As in parliamentarianism, however, the link between the represen-

Petrocik, *The Changing American Voter* (Cambridge, MA: Harvard University Press, 1976). Recent French studies also stress the determining role of the terms of choice offered to the electorate. See in particular, A. Lancelot, "L'orientation du comportement politique," in J. Leca and M. Grawitz (eds.), *Traité de science politique*, Vol. III (Paris: Presses Universitaires de France, 1985); D. Gaxie (ed.), *Explication du vote* (Paris: Presses de la Fondation Nationale des Sciences Politiques, 1985).

[37] On the role of personality in congressional elections, see B. Cain, J. Ferejohn, and M. Fiorina, *The Personal Vote, Constituency Service and Electoral Independence* (Cambridge, MA: Harvard University Press, 1987).

tative thus defined and his electors has an essentially personal character.

The present situation seems to have two causes. First, the channels of political communication affect the nature of the representative relationship: through radio and television, candidates can, once again, communicate directly with their constituents without the mediation of a party network. The age of political activists and party men is over. Moreover, television confers particular salience and vividness to the individuality of the candidates. In a sense, it resurrects the face-to-face character of the representative link that marked the first form of representative government. Mass media, however, favor certain personal qualities: successful candidates are not local notables, but what we call "media figures," persons who have a better command of the techniques of media communication than others. What we are witnessing today is not a departure from the principles of representative government, but a change in the type of elites that are selected. Elections continue to elevate to office individuals who possess distinctive features; they retain the elitist character they have always had. However, a new elite of experts in communication has replaced the political activist and the party bureaucrat. Audience democracy is the rule of the *media expert*.

Secondly, the growing role of personalities at the expense of platforms is a response to the new conditions under which elected officials exercise their power. The scope of governmental activity has increased substantially over the last hundred years. No longer does government simply regulate the general framework of social existence; today, it intervenes in a whole series of areas (particularly in the economic sphere), making concrete decisions. It is more difficult for candidates to make detailed promises: such platforms would become unwieldy and unreadable. More importantly, since the Second World War the environment in which governments operate has become much more complex. As a consequence of the growing economic interdependence, the environment that each government confronts is the result of decisions made by an ever-increasing number of actors. This means, in turn, that the problems which politicians have to confront once in office become less and less predictable. When standing for office, politicians know they will have to face the unforeseen; so they are not inclined to tie their hands by committing themselves to a detailed platform.

The nature and environment of modern governmental activity thus increasingly call for discretionary power, whose formal structure may be compared to the old notion of "prerogative" power. Locke defined prerogative as the power to take decisions in the absence of preexisting laws. The necessity for such a power is justified in the *Second Treatise* by the fact that the government may have to confront the unforeseen, whereas laws are fixed rules promulgated in advance.[38] By analogy, one may say that contemporary governments need discretionary power in relation to political platforms, for it is increasingly difficult to foresee all the events to which governments have to respond. If a certain form of discretionary power is required by present circumstances, it is rational for candidates to put forth their personal qualities and aptitude for making good decisions rather than to tie their hands by specific promises. Voters too know that the government must deal with unpredictable events. From their point of view, then, the personal *trust* that the candidate inspires is a more adequate basis of selection than the evaluation of plans for future actions. Trust, so important in the origins of representative government, again takes a central role.[39]

Thus contemporary voters must grant their representatives a measure of discretion in relation to platforms. This has actually always been the case, once the decision had been made to prohibit imperative mandates. The present situation only makes more visible a permanent feature of political representation. But discretionary power does not mean irresponsible power. Contemporary voters continue to retain the ultimate power they have always had in representative governments, namely, the power to dismiss the representatives whose record they find unsatisfactory. The age of voting on the candidates' platforms is probably over, but the age of voting on the incumbents' record may be beginning.

[38] "Many things there are, which the law can by no means provide for, and those must necessarily be left to the discretion of him, that has the executive power in his hands, to be ordered by him, as the public good and advantage shall require" (Locke, *Second Treatise of Government*, ch. XIV, § 159; see also the whole of ch. XIV).

[39] On the notion of trust and its continued relevance as regards political action from Locke to the present day, see John Dunn, *Interpreting Political Responsibility* (Oxford: Polity Press, 1991), esp. the essay "Trust and political agency."

The role of electoral choice in general

Aside from the individuality of the candidates, present-day electoral studies emphasize that voting behavior varies according to the terms of the electoral choice. For example, citizens vote for different parties in presidential, legislative, and local elections. This suggests that voting decisions are made on the basis of perceptions of what is at stake in a particular election, rather than as a result of socio-economic and cultural characteristics. Similarly, voters' decisions seem to be sensitive to issues raised in electoral campaigns. Election results vary significantly, even over short periods of time, depending on which issues figure most prominently in the campaigns.[40] Voters seem to *respond* (to particular terms offered at each election), rather than just *express* (their social or cultural identities). In this regard, the present situation marks a departure from the formation of political preferences in party democracy. Today, the reactive dimension of voting predominates.

An election always involves an element of division and differentiation among voters. On the one hand, an election necessarily aims at separating those who support a candidate from those who do not. Moreover, individuals mobilize and unite more effectively when they have adversaries and perceive differences between themselves and others. A candidate, then, must not only define himself, but also his adversaries. He not only presents himself, he presents a difference. In all forms of representative government politicians need differences that they can draw upon to mobilize supporters. The social cleavages, which outside the elections divide the mass of the citizens, are an essential resource.

In societies where one division is both lasting and especially salient, politicians know prior to the election which cleavage to exploit. They can frame differentiating principles on the basis of that knowledge. In such situations, then, the terms of choice offered by politicians appear as a transposition of a preexisting cleavage. This

---

[40] See, for example, Nie, Verba, and Petrocik, *The Changing American Voter*, pp. 319, 349: "A simple but important theme runs through much of this book: the public *responds to the political stimuli offered it*. The political behavior of the electorate is not determined solely by psychological and social forces, but also by the issues of the day and by the way in which candidates present those issues" (p. 319, emphasis mine).

is the essential dynamic of party democracy. But in a number of Western societies the situation today is different. No socio-economic or cultural cleavage is evidently more important and stable than others. To be sure, citizens do not constitute a homogeneous mass that can be divided in any manner by the choices they are offered, but the social and cultural lines of cleavage are numerous, cross-cutting, and rapidly changing. Such an electorate is *capable* of a number of splits. Politicians have to decide which of these potential splits will be more effective and advantageous to them. They may activate one or another. Thus, those who articulate the terms of choice have a degree of autonomy in the selection of the cleavage they want to exploit.

In such a situation, the *initiative* of the terms of electoral choice belongs to the politician and not to the electorate, which explains why voting decisions appear primarily today as reactive. In fact, in all forms of representative government the vote constitutes, in part, a reaction of the electorate faced with the terms proposed. However, when these terms themselves are a reflection of a social reality independent of the politicians' actions, the electorate appears as the origin of the terms to which it responds in elections. The reactive character of voting is eclipsed by its expressive dimension. When, on the contrary, the terms of choice result in large part from the relatively independent actions of politicians, the vote is still an expression of the electorate, but its reactive dimension becomes more important and more visible. Thus, the electorate appears, above all, as an *audience* which responds to the terms that have been presented on the political stage. Hence, this form of representative government is called here "audience democracy."

Politicians, however, have only a measure of autonomy in their selection of dividing issues: they cannot invent in total freedom lines of cleavage. Not any division is possible because social, economic, and cultural differences within the electorate exist prior to the candidates' decisions. Furthermore, politicians cannot even choose among existing divisions as they please. They know that each possible division is not equally useful: if a candidate promotes a cleavage line that does not effectively mobilize the voters, or one that eventually works against him, he will lose the election. Politicians may take the initiative in proposing one principle of division rather than another, but the election brings its own sanction to their autonomous initiatives. Candidates do not know in advance which principle of cleavage would be most effective, but it is in their interest to seek it. In comparison to party democracy, the autonomy of the politicians increases, but at the same time they have constantly to identify the appropriate divisions to exploit. Since, however, the politically most effective cleavages are those which correspond to the preoccupations of the electorate, the process tends to bring about a *convergence* between the terms of electoral choice and divisions in the public. In party democracy, by contrast, there can be an immediate correspondence between the two sets, because politicians know in advance, and with reasonable certainty, what is the fundamental cleavage of the electorate. In audience democracy, convergence establishes itself over time through a process of trial and error: the candidate takes the initiative of proposing a line of division either during an election campaign, or – with less risk – on the basis of opinion polls. The audience then responds to the proposed line of division, and finally the politician corrects or maintains the initial proposition, depending on the public's response.

It may be observed, moreover, that the final choice offered to the voters is not the result of a conscious or deliberate plan. Each candidate proposes the issue or term which he thinks will divide the electorate in the most effective and beneficial manner. But the choice that is finally presented and the cleavage it activates are the result of the combination of the terms offered by each candidate. The final configuration of the choice is the product of a plurality of uncoordinated actions.

As the now common use of the expression "the electoral market" demonstrates, the economic metaphor of the market has come to dominate the study of elections. Every metaphor is by definition partly unsuited to the object to which it is applied. The metaphor of the market, however, presents particular difficulties – or rather it gives rise to the possibility of a crucial misunderstanding. It is certainly justifiable to describe politicians as entrepreneurs in competition with one another to win votes and maximize their benefits – the material and symbolic rewards of power. But to characterize voters as consumers is much less appropriate. A consumer who enters the economic market knows what he wants: his preferences are independent of the products offered. Economic theory presupposes that consumer preferences are exogenous. In politics, however, such a presupposition is unrealistic and contrary to experience. When a citizen enters what may be called the political market, his preferences are usually not already formed; they develop through listening to public debates. In politics demand is not exogenous; in general, preferences do not exist prior to the action of politicians.[41]

It has not been sufficiently appreciated that the author generally regarded as the founder of economic theories of democracy, Joseph Schumpeter, himself recognizes that in politics, there is no such thing as a demand independent of supply. Schumpeter insists that in the domain of "national and international affairs," it is unjustified to suppose that individuals have well-defined volitions independent of the politicians' proposals. Such volitions exist on subjects of immediate importance to the individual and of which he has direct knowledge: "the things that directly concern himself, his family, his township or ward, his class, his church, trade union or any other group of which he is an active member."[42] Within this "narrower field" the direct experience of reality permits the formation of defined and independent preferences. However, "when we move still farther away from the private concerns of the family and the business into regions of national and international affairs that lack a direct and unmistakable link with those private concerns," the sense of reality weakens.[43] Schumpeter writes as follows:

> This reduced sense of reality accounts not only for a reduced sense of responsibility but also for *the absence of effective volition*. One has one's phrases, of course, and one's wishes and daydreams and grumbles; especially, one has one's likes and dislikes. *But ordinarily they do not amount to what we call a will* – the psychic counterpart of purposeful responsible action.[44]

It is remarkable that in this passage Schumpeter denies not only the

---

[41] For a more detailed argumentation on this point see B. Manin, "On legitimacy and political deliberation," *Political Theory*, Vol. 15, No. 3, (August 1987), pp. 338–68.

[42] Joseph Schumpeter, *Capitalism, Socialism and Democracy* [1942], 3rd edn (New York: Harper & Row, 1975), p. 258.

[43] Schumpeter, *Capitalism, Socialism and Democracy*, p. 261.

[44] *Ibid.* Emphasis mine.

responsible or rational character of individual will beyond the narrow circle of private concerns, but also the very existence of volition. Later Schumpeter observes that voters do not have a political will independent of the influence of the politicians. "What we are confronted with in the analysis of political processes is largely not a genuine but a manufactured will." [45]

If exogenous demand does not really exist in politics, the analogy between electoral choice and the market becomes particularly problematic, obscuring one of the fundamental characteristics of the political sphere. Even the action of those who set the terms of choice cannot be conceptualized as supply, if what it faces is not a demand in the sense used by economic theory. The only valid element in the metaphor of the market is the notion that the initiation of the terms of choice belongs to actors who are distinct and relatively independent of those who finally make the choice. Thus, the metaphor of stage and audience is more adequate, even if imperfect, to represent this reality. It expresses nothing more than the ideas of distinction and independence between those who propose the terms of choice and those who make the choice. Such is, at any rate, the sense it has here.

What we see emerging today is a new form of representation. Representatives are persons who take the initiative in proposing a line of division. They seek to identify cleavages within the electorate, and to bring some of them to the public stage. They bring to public awareness this or that social division, drawing attention to a split in society that was not previously apparent. Representatives are thus no longer spokesmen; the personalization of electoral choice has, to some extent, made them trustees. But they are also *actors* seeking out and exposing cleavages.

Partial autonomy of representatives

It is generally recognized that today's representatives are elected on the basis of "image," both the personal image of the candidate and that of the organization or party to which he belongs. The term "image," however, may give rise to confusion. It is often employed

---

[45] Schumpeter, *Capitalism, Socialism and Democracy*, p. 263.

in contrast to "substance" to denote vague and superficial perceptions devoid of political content. Voting on the basis of image is
contrasted with voting on the basis of detailed political proposals,
usually as a prelude to deploring the way in which the former is
gaining ground over the latter. Such a conception of political image
fosters the sense of a crisis in representation. In fact, opinion surveys
show that the images formed by voters are not free of political
content. It is true, to take only one example, that in the 1981 French
election won by the Socialists, the electorate did not have clear ideas
and preferences about the economic policy proposed by the Socialists (nationalizations, pump-priming of internal demand). French
voters did not put the Socialists in power on the basis of a specific
economic platform. Nonetheless, it has been demonstrated that the
Socialist victory was in large part the result of a perception which,
however vague, did include a certain content: the idea that the
economic crisis was a consequence of the policy pursued by the
incumbents, and that it was possible to reestablish economic growth
and full employment.[46]

An electoral campaign, it should be noted, is an *adversarial* process;
it pits several images against each other. Taken in isolation, each
image may indeed mean almost anything. But the error is precisely
to consider each of them in isolation. Voters are presented with a
variety of competing images. Even though each of them is fairly
vague, they are not totally indeterminate or without boundaries,
because an electoral campaign creates a *system of differences*: there is
at least one thing that the image of a candidate cannot designate, and
that is the image of his competitor. An electoral campaign may be
compared to a language as characterized by the founder of linguis-
tics, Ferdinand de Saussure: the meaning of each term is a result of
the coexistence of several terms distinguished from one another.

These images are, in fact, highly simplified and schematic mental
representations. The importance of these schematic representations
is, of course, due to the fact that large numbers of voters are not
sufficiently competent to grasp the technical details of the proposed
measures and the reasons that justify them. But the use of simplified

[46] See Elie Cohen, "Les Socialistes et l'économie: de l'âge des mythes au déminage,"
in Gérard Grunberg and Elisabeth Dupoirier (eds.), *La drôle de défaite de la Gauche*
(Paris: Presses Universitaires de France, 1986), pp. 78–80.

representations is also a method for solving the problem of information costs. It has long been noted that one of the major problems confronting the citizen of large democracies is the disproportion between the costs of political information and the influence he can hope to exercise on the election outcome. In party democracy, that problem does not really arise because voters' decisions are driven by a sense of class identity. One could argue also that party identification is the solution to the problem of information costs under party democracy. But in any case, when social identity or party identification lose their importance as determinants of the vote, there is a need for alternative shortcuts in the costly search for political information.

Since representatives are elected on the basis of these schematic images, they have some freedom of action once elected. What led to their election is a relatively vague commitment, which necessarily lends itself to several interpretations. In what has been called here "audience democracy," the partial independence of the representatives, which has always characterized representation, is reinforced by the fact that electoral promises take the form of relatively hazy images.

Freedom of public opinion

The crucial fact is that, in audience democracy, the channels of public communication (newspapers, television etc.) are for the most part politically neutral, that is, non-partisan. This does not of course mean that those channels of information give an undistorted reflection of reality. They introduce their own distortions and prejudices. They may even have political preferences, but they are not *structurally* linked to parties that compete for votes. Technological and economic reasons have led to a decline of the partisan press. Today, political parties usually do not own papers with wide circulation. Moreover, radio and television are established on a non-partisan basis. The rise of popular, non-partisan media has an important consequence: whatever their partisan preferences, individuals receive the same information on a given subject as everyone else. Individuals, of course, still form divergent opinions on political subjects, but the perception of the subject itself tends to be independent of individual partisan leanings. This does not mean that the subjects or the facts – as distinct from judgments – are perceived in an objective manner without distortion by the medium, but simply that they are perceived in a relatively uniform manner across the spectrum of political preferences. By contrast, when the press is largely in the hands of political parties (as in party democracy), one's source of information is selected according to one's partisan leanings; the facts or the subjects themselves are seen as they are presented by the party voted for.

A parallel between the Watergate crisis and the Dreyfus affair, two situations where public opinion played a crucial role, may serve to illustrate the point. It has been shown that during the Watergate crisis, Americans on the whole had the same perceptions of the facts, regardless of their partisan preferences and their judgment. In the Dreyfus affair, by contrast, it appears that even the perception of the facts differed according to the sectors of opinion: each segment of the French public perceived the facts through press organs, which reflected its partisan leanings.[47] Similarly, it has been shown that one of the salient features of recent French elections is the homogenization of party images within the electorate. It appears, for example, that in the parliamentary election of 1986, voters had approximately the same perception of party platforms. Of course, they made divergent judgments about the parties and voted accordingly, but the subjects they judged were perceived almost identically by all, whatever party they voted for.[48]

It would appear, then, that today the perception of public issues and subjects (as distinct, to repeat, from judgments made about them) is more homogeneous and less dependent on partisan preferences than was the case under party democracy. Individuals, however, may take divergent positions on a given issue. Public opinion then splits concerning the issue in question. But the resulting division of public opinion does not necessarily reproduce or coincide with electoral cleavages: the public may be divided along some lines in elections and along others on particular issues.

---

[47] See, G. E. Lang and K. Lang, *The Battle for Public Opinion: The President, the Press and the Polls during Watergate* (New York: Columbia University Press, 1983), pp. 289–91.

[48] See G. Grunberg, F. Haegel, and B. Roy, "La bataille pour la crédibilité: partis et opinion," in Grunberg and Dupoirier (eds.), *La drôle de défaite de la Gauche*, pp. 125–7.

Thus, a possibility that had disappeared under party democracy returns: the electoral and non-electoral expressions of the people on the issues of the day may not coincide.

This possible lack of coincidence stems largely from the neutralization of the channels of communication through which public opinion is formed, but it results also from the non-partisan character of the new institutions that play a crucial role in the expression of public opinion, namely polling institutions.

Opinion surveys, it must be noted, operate according to the formal structure that characterizes this new form of representative government: stage and audience, initiative and reaction. Those who draft the interview questionnaires do not know in advance which questions will elicit the most meaningful responses and bring to light the significant cleavages of the public. Thus, they take the initiative in a relatively autonomous manner. As we have seen, opinion polls are certainly not spontaneous expressions of the popular will. Rather they are constructs. But it is in the interest of polling institutions to provide their clients with results that have some predictive value and bring to light significant cleavages. Like politicians, they proceed through trial and error.

The most important factor, though, is that most polling organizations are, like the media, independent of political parties. This does not mean that they do not introduce distortions, nor even that they have no political preferences. But they are not structurally connected with the organizations that compete for votes. And they operate according to commercial, not political, principles. Whereas parties have an interest in bringing out the division that they embody as being the principal line of cleavage in all areas, polling organizations can, without discomfort to themselves, bring to light lines of division other than those exploited by candidates. Thus, opinion surveys contribute to the decoupling of the electoral and non-electoral expressions of the people's will. It must be noted too that, in contrast to party democracy, expressions of public opinion are here solicited by a different set of people. It was activists and party workers who called for citizens to demonstrate or sign petitions. Those who invite expressions of opinions are now people with training in social sciences and employed by commercial firms.

In a sense we find in audience democracy a configuration that is similar to parliamentarianism, except that opinion surveys confer a quite specific character to the non-electoral manifestation of the people. First, opinion surveys lower the costs of individual political expression. To participate in a demonstration involves high time and energy costs, and signing a petition sometimes carries risks. By contrast, anonymously answering a questionnaire imposes only a minimal cost. As opposed to parliamentarianism, where the high costs of demonstrations and petitions tend to reserve non-electoral political expression for the highly motivated, opinion surveys give a voice to the "apathetic" and uninterested citizen. Second, opinion polls facilitate the expression of political opinions because they are peaceful, whereas demonstrations often carry the risk of violence, especially when opinions are strongly polarized. As a result, the expression of the people "at the door of parliament" is more regularly present than in parliamentarianism: the people do not only make their presence known in exceptional circumstances. The extra-parliamentary voice of the people is both made more peaceful and rendered commonplace.

Trial by discussion

With the notable exception of the US Congress, Parliament is not the forum of public discussion. Each party is grouped around a leading figure,[49] and each parliamentary party votes in a disciplined manner in support of its leader. Individually, however, representatives meet and consult with interest groups and citizens' associations. In such meetings, positions are not rigidly fixed, and thus some deliberative discussion takes place.

But what is new about the third kind of representation lies elsewhere. Over the last few decades, electoral studies have emphasized the importance of electoral instability. The number of floating voters who do not cast their ballot on the basis of stable party identification is increasing. A growing segment of the electorate tends to vote according to the stakes and issues of each election. In fact, an unstable electorate has always existed, but in the past it was primarily composed of citizens who were poorly informed, had little interest in politics, and a low level of schooling. The novelty of

[49] See the section above titled "The personalization of electoral choice."

today's floating voter is that he is well-informed, interested in politics, and fairly well-educated. This new phenomenon owes much to the neutralization of the news and opinion media: voters interested in politics and who seek information are exposed to conflicting opinions, whereas in party democracy the most active and interested citizens were constantly reinforced in their opinions by their sources of information. The existence of an informed and interested electorate, that may be swayed one way or the other, creates an incentive for politicians to put policy proposals directly to the public. The consent of a majority on policy measures can be built up within the electorate itself. Discussion of specific issues is no longer confined to Parliament (as in parliamentarianism), or to consultation committees between parties (as in party democracy); it takes place within the public. Thus, the form of representative government that is emerging today is characterized by a new protagonist of public discussion, the floating voter, and a new forum, the communication media.

What is today referred to as a crisis of political representation appears in a different light if we remember that representative government was conceived in explicit opposition to government by the people, and that its central institutions have remained unchanged. It is true that those who dominate the political stage today (or are increasingly doing so) are not faithful reflections of their society. Politicians and media persons constitute an elite endowed with positively valued characteristics that distinguish them from the rest of the population. That positive valuation does not result only from a deliberate judgment by the electorate. But nor did the notables and bureaucrats who dominated parliamentarianism and party democracy respectively owe their preeminence entirely to the deliberate choice of their fellow-citizens. At least partly responsible for their ascendancy were in the one case social status, in the other the constraints of organization. Representative government remains what it has been since its foundation, namely a governance of elites distinguished from the bulk of citizens by social standing, way of life, and education. What we are witnessing today is nothing more than *the rise of a new elite and the decline of another*.

But the impression of malaise in representation owes even more to the perception that, with the rise of this new elite, history is taking an unexpected turn. When activists and bureaucrats took the place of notables, history seemed to be shrinking the gap between governing elites and ordinary citizens. Certainly, the analyses of Michels showed that mass parties were dominated by elites distinct from the rank and file, but it was reasonable to think that the distance between party bureaucrats and ordinary citizens was smaller than the one separating notables from the rest of the population. Besides, whatever the actual distance between the ways of life of leaders and ordinary voters, mass parties had succeeded in creating an identification of the latter with the former. The fact is that workers recognized themselves in the leaders of social demo-cratic parties and saw them as "like themselves." The replacement of notables by party officials was indeed a step in the direction of an identity (real or imagined) between governing elites and those they govern. It is impossible to have that impression today. The social and cultural gap between an elite and the mass of people is a difficult thing to gauge, but there is no reason to think that present political and media elites are closer to voters than the party bureau-crats were. Nor is there any sign that those elites are in a position to inspire feelings of identification on the part of voters. More than the substitution of one elite for another, it is the persistence, possibly even the aggravation, of the gap between the governed and the governing elite that has provoked a sense of crisis. Current develop-ments belie the notion that representation was destined to advance ever closer towards an identity of governing and governed.

Similarly, when people voted for a party with a platform, they enjoyed a greater ability to pronounce on future policy than when they elected a notable who personally inspired their trust. The advent of party democracy made it more possible for people to vote prospectively. Here again, the changes occurring in our time con-found the expectations that opportunities for future-oriented voting would continue to increase. When a candidate today is elected on the basis of his image, and seeks to persuade voters that he is fitter than others to confront the future, voters have less say about what he will do than when a party presented a list of measures it intended to implement. In this sense too, representative government appears to have ceased its progress towards popular self-government.

The currently prevailing impression of crisis reflects the disappointment of previous expectations about the direction of history. In that its base has expanded enormously, representative government has, since its establishment, undoubtedly become more democratic. That trend has not been reversed; history has confirmed what had been believed. However, the democratization of representation, the narrowing of the gap between representatives and represented, and the growing influence of the wishes of the governed on the decisions of those in government have turned out to be less durable than expected. While one can certainly say that democracy has broadened, one cannot say with the same certainty that it has deepened.

We need to recall, however, that in the original arrangement, the democratic element in the relationship between the governed and those who govern was neither resemblance between the two, nor the principle that the latter should implement the instructions of the former. Representative institutions aimed to subject those who govern to the verdict of those who are governed. It is the rendering of accounts that has constituted from the beginning the democratic component of representation. And representation today still entails that supreme moment when the electorate passes judgment on the past actions of those in government.

This does not amount, however, to saying that representative government has remained the same throughout its history or that the changes have been merely superficial. Party democracy was indeed profoundly different from parliamentarianism. Representation, a system devised by English aristocrats, American landowners, and French lawyers, was transformed, a hundred years later, into a mechanism that alleviated industrial conflict by integrating the working class. The founding fathers certainly had no such outcome in view. The arrangement that was devised at the end of the eighteenth century proved astonishingly flexible. It displayed a capacity, probably unsuspected at the outset, for assuming different forms to suit different circumstances. Neither the differences in form nor the durability of the structure capture *the* truth of representation. Just as representative government simultaneously presents democratic and non-democratic aspects, the latter being no more true or essential than the former, so it is capable, over time, of assuming different shapes while remaining the same.

234

	Parliamentarianism	Party democracy	Audience democracy
Election of representatives	– choice of a person of trust – expression of local links – notable	– loyalty to a single party – expression of membership of a class – activist / party bureaucrat	– choice of a person of trust – response to electoral terms of offer – media expert
Partial autonomy of representatives	– elected member voting as conscience dictates	– party leaders free to determine priorities within the platform	– election on the basis of images
Freedom of public opinion	– public opinion and electoral expression do not coincide – the voice of the people "at the gates of Parliament"	– public opinion and electoral expression coincide – opposition	– public opinion and electoral expression do not coincide – opinion polls
Trial by discussion	– Parliament	– debate within the party – inter-party negotiations – neo-corporatism	– negotiations between government and interest groups – debate in the media / floating voter

Figure 1: Principles and variations in representative government

Conclusion

Representative government, as we remarked at the beginning of this study, is a perplexing phenomenon, even though its routine presence in our everyday world makes us think we know it well. Conceived in explicit opposition to democracy, today it is seen as one of its forms. The "people" is certainly a much larger entity in our own day than it was in the eighteenth century, the advent of universal suffrage having substantially enlarged the citizen body. But on the other hand, there has been no significant change in the institutions regulating the selection of representatives and the influence of the popular will on their decisions once in office. And it is at least uncertain whether the gap between the governing elites and the ordinary citizens has narrowed or whether the control of voters over their representatives has increased. Nevertheless, we have no hesitation in categorizing today's representative systems as democracies. The founding fathers, by contrast, stressed the "enormous difference" between representative government and rule by what was then the people. We are thus left with the paradox that, without having in any obvious way evolved, the relationship between representatives and those they represent is today perceived as democratic, whereas it was originally seen as undemocratic.

Now, at the end of our journey, it would appear that this difference between the original and modern conceptions is due at least in part to the nature of representative institutions themselves. Representative government includes both democratic and undemocratic features. The duality lies in its very nature, not just in the eye of the beholder. The idea that representative systems place government in the hands of the people is no mere myth, contrary to the claims of those who, from Marx to Schumpeter, set out to demystify "democracy." Representative government has undeniably a democratic dimension. No less undeniable, however, is its oligarchic dimension. The solution to the puzzle of representative government lies in the fact that it is a balanced system. The principles of representative government form a machinery that combines democratic and undemocratic parts.

First, the absence of imperative mandates, legally binding pledges, and discretionary recall, gives representatives a degree of independence from their electors. That independence separates representation from popular rule, however indirect. Inversely, the freedom to express political opinions prevents representatives, once elected, from absolutely substituting for those they represent and becoming the only actors on the political scene. The people are at any time able to remind representatives of their presence; the chambers of government are not insulated from their clamor. Freedom of public opinion thus provides a democratic counterweight to the undemocratic independence of representatives.

Second, elected representatives are not bound by promises made to voters. If people vote for a candidate because they favor the policy he proposes, their will is no more than a wish. In this respect, the election of modern representatives is not a far cry from the election of deputies to the Estates General under the Ancien Régime. On the other hand, since representatives are subject to reelection, they know that they will be held to account, and that, at that time, words will no longer suffice. They know that their positions will be on the line when, come election day, the electorate delivers its verdict on their past actions. Prudence dictates, therefore, that they act now in preparation for that day of popular judgment. The prospective will of voters is no more a wish, but when they are not satisfied by the incumbents' performance, their verdict is a command. At each election, voters make up their minds on the basis both of what they would like for the future and what they think of the past. Here, then, the democratic and undemocratic elements are inextricably blended into a single act.

The designation of representatives by election, with universal suffrage and without qualifications for representatives, combines the democratic and undemocratic elements even more closely. If citizens are regarded as potential candidates for public office, election appears to be an inegalitarian method, since, unlike lot, it does not provide every individual seeking such office with an equal chance. Election is even an aristocratic or oligarchic procedure in that it reserves public office for eminent individuals whom their fellow citizens deem superior to others. Furthermore, the elective procedure impedes the democratic desire that those in government should be ordinary persons, close to those they govern in character, way of life, and concerns. However, if citizens are no longer regarded as potential objects of electoral choice, but as those who choose, election appears in a different light. It then shows its democratic face, all citizens having an equal power to designate and dismiss their rulers. Election inevitably selects elites, but it is for ordinary citizens to define what constitutes an elite and who belongs to it. In the elective designation of those who govern, then, the democratic and undemocratic dimensions are not even associated with analytically distinct elements (though always mixed in practice), such as the prospective and retrospective motivations of voting. Election merely presents two different faces, depending on the observer's viewpoint.

In a mixed constitution where the mixture is perfect, wrote the Philosopher, one should be able to see both democracy and oligarchy – and neither. Genealogical scrutiny discerns in representative government the mixed constitution of modern times.

Index